The Amazing Internet Challenge

How Leading Projects Use Library Skills to Organize the Web

Amy Tracy Wells

Susan Calcari

Travis Koplow

American Library Association
Chicago and London
1999

8/00

40954245

Text design by Dianne M. Rooney

Composition by the dotted i in Caxton and Univers using QuarkXPress 4.04
Printed on 50-pound white offset, a pH-neutral stock, and bound in 10-point coated cover stock by Data Reproductions

The paper used in this publication meets the minimum requirements of American National Standard for Information Sciences—Permanence of Paper for Printed Library Materials, ANSI Z39.48-1992.♾

Library of Congress Cataloging-in-Publication Data

Wells, Amy Tracy.
    The amazing Internet challenge : how leading projects use library
  skills to organize the Web / Amy Tracy Wells, Susan Calcari, Travis
  Koplow.
        p.   cm.
    Includes index.
    ISBN 0-8389-0766-0
    1. Digital libraries—Administration.   2. Computer network
  resources. I. Calcari, Susan. II. Koplow, Travis. III. Title.
  ZA4080.W45   1999
  025.04—dc21   99-25110

Printed in the United States of America

03 02 01 00 99   5 4 3 2 1

Contents

Introduction

Some years ago, the *New Yorker* ran a comic with the caption, "On the Internet, no one knows you're a dog." Though just a pithy bit of humor, the statement captures the wonderful, positive side of the anonymity possible on the Internet, and at the same time underscores one of the primary challenges of this medium. Information seekers are confounded by the volume of resources on the Net and by the fact that "anyone" can publish; here every dog can have his day. As the population of Internet users continues to expand in both numbers and breadth, the need for authoritative, trusted sites grows at an even greater rate. Increasingly, Internet users are saying, "I want to know who is behind the content I'm using on the Web. I want to know the author, the publisher, and what their credentials are. I want to know where to go to find trusted information."

Librarians, content specialists, and information professionals around the world are responding to this call, working to make it easier to find quality resources on the Internet. Individually and collectively, they are creatively adapting proven principles and practices to a new environment. New tools are being used to apply existing skills, and new skills are being developed to take advantage of the opportunities the technology provides. Centuries of experience in collecting, organizing, and disseminating information serve as the foundation for building new ways to access valued content online.

The twelve projects in this book were chosen for their international reputation as leaders in the delivery of selective, quality resources. The virtual libraries described here cover a spectrum of information services. Some focus on specialized subject areas; others are highly interdisciplinary. Eight are based in the United States and four in the United Kingdom. They use a variety of taxonomies and cataloging methods. Each serves a distinct audience and hence has a unique perspective. Yet despite their differences, with their blend of traditional and new approaches to information management, all of the projects serve as strategic examples of the possibilities inherent in online information. This book has been designed to give the reader insight into the day-to-day workflows and the long-term plans of twelve major virtual libraries and will appeal to reference librarians, catalogers, systems librarians, and administrators.

Regardless of their particular missions or audiences, all virtual libraries share common concerns and challenges. The first task to be undertaken by providers of quality resource collections is to define what is meant by "quality information" and "trusted sources" within the scope of their own project. Selection criteria must be developed that can be applied to an online environment, and that will lead to a collection that is valuable to their users. Many of the criteria will be the same as those used in the print world, such as author, content, audience, and scope. However, there are new criteria to be considered, such as design and accessibility.

Once a site has been selected, cataloged, and is part of an online collection, additional questions surface regarding the ephemeral state of Internet resources. Will the site remain in existence over time? Will the publisher need to update the content continuously to keep the site valuable to the user? How often should one check the links and/or the content?

Another challenge facing virtual libraries is the question of how best to use the technology to present and deliver information to the end user. For many information professionals, this process has required learning new skills and increasing collaboration with technical specialists. Together they need to ask questions such as: How should the collection be presented through the user interface? How should it be accessed? How many access methods should we provide? What are the best underlying technologies and formats for our purposes? How sophisticated will the technology required by the end user need to be? Should we use the most advanced technology or the most basic to be sure we don't leave anyone behind?

Project developers try to make many of these decisions based on the primary audience they serve. In most cases, that primary audience is defined by the funding source behind the virtual library. For example, the higher education community is often the primary audience for projects funded by government research agencies. There may be a secondary audience, of all lifelong learners or all Internet users, but, in general, the developers need to first serve the audience defined by those who are paying the bills.

The issue of funding is, in fact, one of the foremost challenges for virtual libraries. Projects are asking each other questions such as: Is there a way to secure continuous stable funding? Is there a way to institutionalize our efforts? Is there a way to make these directories self-sustaining? Until now, there has been a strong commitment to keeping the access to virtual libraries free. This commitment originates with the traditional culture and philosophy of both the Internet and physical libraries. However, we all know that the services aren't really free; they are just free to the end user.

Without exception, the virtual libraries profiled here are committed to serving those end users as effectively as possible. For all of the projects, this has meant addressing the issues outlined above—quality control, the ephemeral nature of the Internet, access, and funding—among others. We have, accordingly, organized the chapters around these shared issues. Each chapter follows the same basic outline:

(1) Responsible persons

(2) Mission statement

(3) Funding source(s) as well as project budgets

(4) Target audience and secondary audience

(5) A description of the collection

(6) Selection criteria and evaluation process of resources

(7) Mechanics of production including software and hardware

(8) Taxonomy or classification used and any modifications

(9) Strengths of the project

(10) Weaknesses of the project

(11) Time frames for the project

(12) Future goals of the project

(13) A vision statement concerning the future of resource location and description

Of course, each project has responded to these shared concerns in its own way. The expanded outline offered below both elaborates on most of the general topics covered in each chapter and provides selected highlights of the book, underscoring particularly unique and outstanding approaches individual projects have taken to the challenges of working in an online environment.

(1) Responsible persons including location and affiliation(s)

Though the projects in this book vary from corporate ventures to university supported or affiliated services to collaborative enterprises funded through foundations or other means, they share the commitment of the individual people involved. In fact, many of the projects included here were initially developed by individuals, as in the case of the *Librarians' Index to the Internet* (LII), which began as a one-person effort. Despite the power of individual commitment, however, all of these projects demonstrate the strength of a collaborative approach to resource discovery and cooperative cataloging. *Agriculture*

Network Information Center (AgNIC), a National Agriculture Library initiative in conjunction with four universities throughout the United States, takes this approach one step further and provides a distributed reference service in which patrons' queries are routed to the appropriate subject specialists wherever they are located.

(2) Mission statement, target audiences, and a description of the collection

All of the contributors to this book have common goals: to locate and make accessible high-quality resources, from documents to metasites to software programs. Nonetheless, their primary and secondary audiences diverge greatly, and their collections vary accordingly. Some, like *Blue Web'n,* focus on the K–12 community. The *Internet Public Library* (IPL), on the other hand, has a very broad public library audience and along with K–12 materials collects literary criticism, reference materials, materials for librarians, and more. In contrast, a project such as *Mathematics Archives* (Math Archives) is principally devoted to a very focused collection with the majority of its resources designed for the mathematics higher education community.

Interestingly, as an evaluation study conducted by *Edinburgh Engineering Virtual Library* (EEVL) demonstrates, users do not always relate the holdings of a given virtual library to the resources actually available on the Internet as a whole. Blue Web'n, for instance, mentions that their collection is thin in areas such as physical education, not because of deficiencies in their collection process, but because the field itself is not as suited to the Internet as some others. Users do not always recognize that any library's collection is tied to what is actually published, whether in print or electronic form.

(3) Size of the collection

While all of these libraries emphasize highly selected content and do not collect resources regardless of utility, the size of the projects' collections ranges from some eight hundred resources to over twenty thousand records as is the case with IPL.

(4) Funding source(s)

Of course, developing and maintaining these collections are no easy task, and it's made more difficult by the fact that the projects here are largely or completely reliant on soft funding. That is, all have funding from various entities, from corporations to government agencies to individuals to awards from library associations such as the award that *INFOMINE* received through the Library Association of the University of California. Each must devote a portion of staff time to the ongoing issue of seeking sponsorships, grants, and other awards.

(5) Selection criteria and evaluation process of resources

As *BUBL Information Service* (BUBL) notes, even without limited resources for collection development and cataloging, determining what a resource is for cataloging purposes can be extremely difficult. Is it an article or the entire journal? A Web site or some subset? And along with this determination, the process of evaluating Internet resources, while indebted in large part to traditional skills of librarianship, also requires new selection criteria. The *Scout Report Signpost* (Signpost) chapter describes in detail the need for determining a resource's authority, currency, audience, purpose, scope, and accuracy, as well as accessibility and design. The *Social Science Information Gateway* (SOSIG) details their resource evaluation matrix and describes their interactive tutorial, the Internet Detective, which teaches evaluation skills to users.

(6) Mechanics of production including software and hardware

Though pursuing funding and selecting and evaluating resources are all time-consuming endeavors, each project strives to maintain its quality while increasing its efficiency. Software and hardware decisions can greatly assist or hamper this process. Math Archives makes their collection available via anonymous FTP, Gopher, Web browser, and e-mail in a technically sophisticated way that permits access through the Web. In addition, the projects use a number of different types of software and hardware solutions, from databases to individual files to Macs to Sun Sparcs. Some are even working on integrating information currently available in their online catalogs.

In this nonphysical world, getting the information to users is only part of the battle. Keeping the information current is an ongoing struggle for all of the projects. Like a missing book or journal, bad links plague virtual libraries. As BUBL explains, while programs can check eight thousand links in under a half-hour, follow-up takes much longer. The specific policies and software solutions that projects use to deal with this problem are discussed throughout the book.

(7) Taxonomy or classification used and any modifications

There are many methods for organizing Internet resources, from using an established classification scheme to organizing around a thesaurus to developing a classification scheme in-house. As the *Argus Clearinghouse* explains, there is no clear consensus either in the literature or in production systems. Using results from an evaluative study, which are detailed in their chapter, Argus has been redesigning its internally developed classification scheme. This qualitative effort underscores a very important point: in a virtual library, some decisions do not have to be static. Although there are costs to redesigning a classification scheme, they are less than those one would encounter in the physical world. However, while audience-driven, locally developed classification schemes hold great appeal, as *Organising Medical Networked Information* (OMNI) points out, nonstandard schemes have an additional cost: it can be harder to develop collaborative relationships with other virtual libraries.

Another aspect to classification is the use of subject headings or index terms to describe the resources themselves. LII provides interesting specifics on their use of Library of Congress Subject Headings as well as their rationale and approach to developing alternative subject headings.

(8) Project's strengths and project's weaknesses

A weakness common to all of the projects is their lack of long-term planning. This is not to say that each isn't involved in strategic planning, because each is. That strategic planning has been partially responsible for the real success of all of these projects, as each enjoys respect within its peer group, and, more importantly, by its end users.

(9) Future goals of the project and a vision statement concerning the future of resource location and description

Virtual libraries all have a vested interest in increasing efficiency without sacrificing quality. The future goals and vision statements detailed by the various projects are, to a large degree, motivated by this desire. One effort, described by Infomine, is the use of data mining, or automating the discovery process by feeding human-selected URLs to an intelligent agent. Another effort is underway to increase interoperability among virtual libraries. Projects in both the United States and United Kingdom are working to develop such collaborative networks. Signpost describes the development of the Isaac Network while EEVL, SOSIG, and OMNI detail the Resource Organisation And Discovery in Subject-based Services (ROADS) and Resource Discovery Network (RDN). Both the Isaac Network and RDN allow for the development and maintenance of local collections that are searchable via a singular interface.

This book was written in this collaborative spirit so that we might learn from one another. Whether developing a system from scratch or working to establish cooperative networks, anyone involved with organizing information on the Internet will find knowledge and inspiration in the experiences of these projects.

Acknowledgments

The editors would like to thank the National Science Foundation (http://www.nsf.gov) and Don Mitchell for their ongoing and generous support (NCR-9712163) and our colleagues on the Internet Scout Project without whom none of this would have been possible.

The authors of the Agriculture Network Information Center (AgNIC) chapter would like to thank Pamela Q. J. André, National Agricultural Library (NAL) director, and Keith Russell, NAL deputy director, for their suggestions and kind support. We would also like to thank Brian Norris, NAL public affairs specialist, for his time, suggestions, and speedy responses.

Many people helped make the Argus Clearinghouse project possible: Louis Rosenfeld, Peter Morville, Samantha Bailey, and Greg Peters at Argus Associates; Professors Regula Herzog and Teresa Garcia at the Institute for Social Research; Joseph Janes of the Internet Public Library; and Associate Dean C. Olivia Frost at the School of Information. This work was partially supported by a scholarship from Fonds FCAR (le Fonds pour la Formation de Chercheurs et l'Aide à la Recherche).

The author of the Blue Web'n chapter is grateful for Pacific Bell's ongoing contributions to education in California, for the many ideas from the faculty at San Diego State University's Department of Educational Technology, and for support and feedback from her husband, Jeff Sale.

The BUBL Information Service (BUBL) is funded by the Joint Information Systems Committee of the Higher Education Funding Councils (JISC) of England, Scotland, and Wales, and the Department of Education for Northern Ireland.

Edinburgh Engineering Virtual Library (EEVL) acknowledges its funding from JISC (http://www.jisc.ac.uk/) as part of the eLib Programme (http://ukoln.bath.ac.uk/services/elib/), the hard work of the EEVL staff and the support of the EEVL team (http://www.eevl.ac.uk/team.html), and the institutional support of library (http://www.hw.ac.uk/libWWW/libinfo/staff.html) and Learning Technology Centre (http://www.icbl.hw.ac.uk/lts/) colleagues at Heriot-Watt University.

The INFOMINE team would like to thank its many participants and cooperators over the last five years, specifically John Tanno, Jack Cooper, Margo Young, Charlene Baldwin, Curt Varner, Alan Ritch, Travis Koplow, Tom Payne, Marek Chrobak, and Jim Thompson. The library of the University of California at Riverside and the Fund for the Improvement of Post-Secondary Education of the U.S. Department of Education (http://www.ed.gov/offices/OPE/FIPSE/) have been generous in their support.

The author of the Internet Public Library (IPL) chapter would like to thank the vast number of IPL students and staff who have contributed to and created the various IPL collections. Without their hard work and dedication, none of this would have been possible.

Mathematics Archives wishes to thank the following for their support: National Science Foundation (http://www.nsf.gov/) for awarding ILI Leadership Grants No. DUE-9351398 (http://www.nsf.gov/cgi-bin/showaward?award=9351398) and DUE-9550943 (http://www.nsf.gov/cgi-bin/showaward?award=9550943), the State of Tennessee Science Alliance (http://www.ra.utk.edu/scialli/), and the departments of mathematics at Calvin College (Michigan) (http://www.calvin.edu/academic/math/) and the University of Tennessee, Knoxville (http://www.math.utk.edu/).

The Organising Medical Networked Information (OMNI) chapter author would like to acknowledge the assistance of Betsy Anagnostelis in producing this chapter and the support of the OMNI team (John Kirriemuir, Lisa Gray, Frances Singfield, and Bob Parkinson) generally.

With respect to the Scout Report Signpost (Signpost) chapter, we would like to thank the National Science Foundation (http://www.nsf.gov/), our colleagues at the Internet Scout Project, and our spouses, Ruth Reinl and Dale Belman, for their continuing support.

The author of the Social Science Information Gateway (SOSIG) chapter extends many thanks to the entire SOSIG team for providing creative comments and inspiration for this chapter.

Agriculture Network Information Center (AgNIC)

Melanie A. Gardner
Richard E. Thompson
William B. Feidt

AgNIC (Agriculture Network Information Center) (http://www. agnic.org/) is a discipline-specific distributed network on the Internet. Under the leadership of the National Agricultural Library (NAL) (http:// www.nal.usda.gov/), AgNIC was established by an alliance of agricultural organizations that included Cornell University (http://usda. mannlib.cornell.edu/), Iowa State University (http://www.lib.iastate. edu/agnic/), the University of Arizona (http://ag.arizona.edu/OALS/ agnic/), and the University of Nebraska-Lincoln (http://www.unl.edu/ agnicpls/agnic.html). AgNIC provides access to sources of information and services on food and agriculture, forestry, and relevant subsets of the physical and social sciences. This model for a subject-based network uses the power of the Internet to deliver information, including online reference in selected subject areas. AgNIC demonstrates how librarians and information specialists can and should use library skills to evaluate, select, and provide access to Web resources. This chapter provides an overview of the AgNIC model, including funding, description of the collections, strengths and weaknesses, and future goals.

1.0 Introduction

Despite newly emerging electronic information technologies, no one institution can provide information on all aspects of agriculture, the environment, and rural development. A key component of the National Agricultural Library's (NAL) (http://www.nal.usda.gov/)

strategic planning over the last several years has included an examination of issues associated with NAL's ability to manage, store, and provide access to electronic, agriculture-related information. NAL has long recognized that collaboration and resource sharing among institutions with common interests in agriculture are essential to the library's mission of ensuring and enhancing access to agricultural information.

As a world information leader, NAL joined with several land-grant universities to provide quality agricultural information resources on the Internet. The result is the Agriculture Network Information Center (AgNIC) (http://www.agnic.org/). (See figure 1.) Simply stated, AgNIC is designed to fill the needs of those seeking agricultural and related information on the Internet.

Since the Clinton administration announced its intentions to develop a National Information Infrastructure (NII) "to deliver to all Americans the information they need, when they need and where they want it, and at an affordable price," there have been numerous local and state initiatives to connect Americans to the Internet.[1] With access attained by many, Internet users are now faced with millions of World Wide Web sites offering information on tens of thousands of topics.

In an April 1998 letter to NAL Director Pamela Q. J. André, Thomas Kalil, senior director of the White House National Economic Council for Science and Technology Issues, indicated that he sees AgNIC as an "exciting new project" and expressed his delight that AgNIC is gathering momentum and expanding its membership. He emphasized the important role that such networks can make to enhance communications and access to information and to overcome the obstacles of distance and distributed resources. Kalil also expressed his belief that the collaborative effort of AgNIC is eminently achievable when enough organizations get involved.

Initial digital-information and library projects have demonstrated that the success of such projects depends on the right mix of user-relevant content, user-friendly applications, and user education.[2] It is not enough simply to make research datasets and information resources available to the user. Such information must be combined with interactive interfaces to provide users with guidance on using the resources effectively. Most users do not have time to surf the Internet for hours looking for answers to specific questions. Many others find the mass of information on the Web overwhelming, unorganized, and of unknown quality. Users want to go directly to Web sites that offer the most important resources on a given subject area. Users want organized, reliable, easy-to-use information and access to immediate assistance.[3]

Paul Evan Peters, founder and executive director of the Coalition for Networked Information (CNI), whose visionary leadership fostered the development of scholarly publishing on the Internet, supported

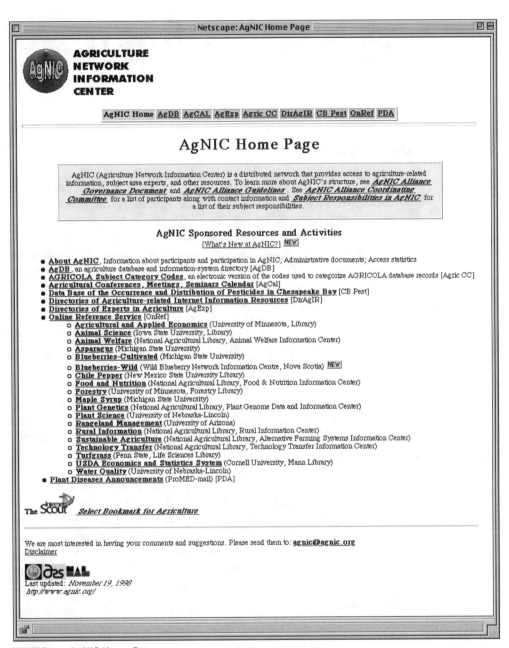

FIGURE 1. AgNIC Home Page

the library community's effort to provide services and products over the Internet. Peters, who died in 1996, was also an early supporter of the AgNIC concept and a keynote speaker at a December 1994 planning meeting of the AgNIC steering committee that led to the establishment of AgNIC in August 1995. He emphasized the importance of the relationships that were being formed among the AgNIC participants and stressed that those relationships would yield more value than any specific products or services being made available on the Internet.

2.0 Responsible Persons

AgNIC is a partnership among many institutions and organizations. The AgNIC server and the main AgNIC Web pages are maintained by the National Agricultural Library (NAL) of the Agricultural Research Service, U.S. Department of Agriculture. NAL is located in Beltsville, Maryland. Each participating institution or organization maintains its own server and Web page. Specifically, there is no one organization or institution responsible for AgNIC. There are technical and coordinating staff based at NAL and an AgNIC Alliance Coordinating Committee made up of members of participating institutions. Technical and coordinating contacts are Melanie A. Gardner, AgNIC coordinator, NAL; William B. Feidt, AgNIC Web coordinator, NAL; and Richard E. Thompson, team leader, Distributed Data Systems, NAL.

Presently, AgNIC partners include NAL, Cornell University, Iowa State University, the University of Arizona, the University of Nebraska-Lincoln, the American Society of Horticultural Science, the Canadian Agriculture Library, Clemson University, the Food and Agriculture Organization (FAO) of the United Nations, Michigan State University, New Mexico State University, North Carolina State University, Nova Scotia Agricultural College, Pennsylvania State University, Ohio State University, Purdue University, Texas A&M University, the University of California, Riverside, the University of Georgia, the University of Minnesota, and Washington State University. Associate members of the coordinating committee include USDA's Economic Research Service, Agricultural Research Service, Cooperative State Research, Education and Extension Service, and National Agricultural Statistical Service.

3.0 Mission Statement

AgNIC's mission is to facilitate electronic access to agricultural information and resources for use by the public (academia, researchers, experiment stations, extension service, and private citizens) and private (producers, agribusiness, suppliers, and customers) components of the agricultural community.

Its goals are to:

- identify major collections of information related to agriculture, subject experts, and other related resources;
- facilitate access to and retrieval of these resources;
- encourage organizations to collaborate in creating and using AgNIC while retaining ownership and responsibility for the information they provide through AgNIC;
- leverage the character of the Internet to use the expertise available and to ensure that workload and responsibility are distributed across participating sites;
- provide a test case for learning about, experimenting with, and gaining experience in Network Information Center (NIC) operations;
- facilitate collaboration within a broad agricultural community.

4.0 Funding Sources

Throughout the initial phases of development, limited funding for AgNIC was available. This challenge has not dampened the collective enthusiasm of the participants in working toward the ultimate goal of providing access to electronic agricultural information. However, low funding has resulted in the slow development of AgNIC. Participating institutions have had to rely on internal baseline funding to cover staffing and travel costs associated with AgNIC planning, implementation, and expansion.

In 1993, in support of AgNIC development, NAL provided initial funding in a cooperative agreement with Iowa State University (ISU) (http://www.iastate.edu/). This expanded a prior agreement to include research into providing access to agricultural resources online through an Agriculture Network Information Center (AgNIC). To demonstrate their commitment, ISU contributed funds in excess of the existing agreement.

In July 1995, NAL received a one-year grant from the General Services Administration (http://www.gsa.gov/) to establish an AgNIC prototype. These funds, supplemented by additional funding from NAL, provided seed money. Each participating institution contributed in-kind staff time in support of the project.

General start-up funding was less than $300,000, excluding in-kind costs covered by participants. These funds covered AgNIC central operations, which involved hardware, software, and some staff; the University of Arizona's rangeland management subject development and journal digitization (http://ag.arizona.edu/OALS/agnic/);

and Iowa State University's subject development. Since the initial start-up, all partners have contributed to AgNIC development by re-allocating resources and pursuing grants for independent but related projects.

5.0 Target Audience and Secondary Audience

Initial target audiences for AgNIC included researchers, educators, and the public at large. These users led the growing demand for access to accurate and comprehensive information in agriculture. AgNIC is one of the first collaborative efforts involving multiple part-ners to respond to this demand by providing in-depth electronic access to quality information in specific disciplines on the Internet. AgNIC's unique effort and the approach used—providing and man-aging access to information for all Americans through an alliance—serve as a model for other organizations and other subject disciplines.

AgNIC's target audience is the same as that envisioned by the developers of the National Information Infrastructure (NII)—to de-liver to "*all Americans* the information and resources they need when they want it and where they want it, and at an affordable price."[4]

6.0 Description of Collections

Each alliance participant is encouraged to provide value-added re-sources to AgNIC. As it undertook AgNIC, NAL initiated a number of projects designed to both organize Web-based resources and create entirely new Web-based information. Each project attempted to lev-erage the power of the Internet to improve both process and content. Descriptions of three seminal NAL efforts follow.

6.1 AgDB

AgDB (http://www.agnic.org/agdb/) is a searchable directory of qual-ity agriculture-related databases, datasets, and information systems. It currently describes and links to more than 850 information re-sources (mainly Web based). Resource descriptions, often referred to as "metadata records," guide users directly to relevant resources rang-ing from technical to practical.

6.1.1 Selection Criteria

Criteria considered in evaluating resources for inclusion in AgDB in-clude relevance, maturity, accuracy, coherence, focus, currency, maintenance, clarity of presentation/documentation, arrangement, format, and perspective or bias (http://www.agnic.org/docs/agdbsepo.html).

Systems not suitable for inclusion in AgDB include secondary information systems, Web pages not directly relating to an appropriate primary information resource, Web pages that primarily serve as links to other sites, ephemeral systems, overly broad or shallow systems, single research articles, and single reports of current research.

It is worth noting that some materials that were quite linear in their print iterations become more hypertextual in their Web incarnations and thus more suitable for inclusion in AgDB.

6.1.2 Mechanics of Production

AgDB consists of a database of records, each describing a separate resource. When a new item is created, staff complete a standard template record describing the resource. This process is similar to library cataloging. Both an alphabetical index list and the new items list are updated manually to reflect the new entry. At least once a day, the search index is automatically regenerated. Periodically, all AgDB links are verified using Linklint (http://www.goldwarp.com/bowlin/linklint/), a batch-mode link checker. In addition, staff review the records and their linked-to content to ensure reasonable accuracy of the brief descriptions. Pages are HTML-validated when created and periodically thereafter using Weblint (http://www.cre.canon.co.uk/~neilb/weblint/).

Subject-oriented mailing lists and news groups are fertile sources for the discovery of new AgDB resources. Often, creators announce their products in such forums. In addition, staff periodically revisit sites already hosting systems detailed in AgDB in search of new initiatives. Staff also scrutinize other systematic efforts to evaluate Web sites such as the Internet Scout's Scout Report (http://scout.cs.wisc.edu/scout/report/index.html). Despite all structured efforts, however, much of the discovery of new resources is serendipitous; some of the best discoveries have been made while "doing something else."

6.1.3 Classification

Each AgDB resource is assigned one or more subject codes that allow users to search AgDB. The codes appear in the AgDB descriptive record and are linked to a scope note (description).

6.2 AgCal

AgCal (http://www.agnic.org/mtg/), the Agricultural Conferences, Meetings, Seminars Calendar, provides a repository for information and links to information concerning agricultural conferences, with emphasis on those of scientific significance. Staff strive to include major agriculture meetings of apparent scientific importance.

AgCal consists of a series of indexes offering links to Web pages containing information about over fourteen hundred scientific meetings. As a rule, it points to pages created and maintained by meeting organizers, but in some cases, AgCal staff will create a simple Web page, and mount it locally, that is based on information posted by the organizer to a subject-oriented mailing list or USENET news group.

As a further aid, AgCal provides index pages containing categorical discipline subsets (animal, food, forestry; natural resources, plant, and soil) of the full calendar. These discipline-specific pages are easily accessed through the menu structure and permit the more focused user to avoid scanning the entire calendar list. There is also a classified list of other agricultural calendars.

6.2.1 Selection Criteria

To be listed in AgCal, meetings must have a significant amount of information on the Web. AgNIC and AgCal contributors look for announcements (including dates, location, rationale, focus, intended audience, and administrative details), calls for papers and posters, and schedules of speakers and papers. Conferences that have established an official Web site will sometimes be listed, although the site may contain only minimal information. This is done with the expectation that more detailed information will follow.

AgCal takes a broad view of what constitutes agriculture, following the core subject level Collection Development Policy of the National Agricultural Library, and thereby including such diverse disciplines as agriculture (general); animal science; plant science; agricultural chemistry; agricultural engineering; soils, fertilizers, and soil conservation; forestry and utilization and technology of raw forest products; rural sociology and rural life; agricultural economics; and food and nutrition. Occasionally, a seemingly peripheral meeting will be included because a significant segment of its scientific scope involves a core subject area.

AgCal attempts to list only meetings of scientific significance. No attempt is made, however, to evaluate the quality of science conducted. Rather, AgCal takes a form-based approach. Meetings that do such things as solicit papers, abstracts, and posters from participants; conduct scientific programs; publish proceedings; foster collaboration among the research community; discuss scientific progress; and identify future research needs are candidates for inclusion. Such functions as fairs, exhibitions, sales, and organizational business meetings without an apparent scientific component are normally excluded.

6.2.2 Mechanics of Production

AgCal consists of a series of year-based Web pages. For example, the file 1998.html contains entries for meetings that occurred in 1998. The main year files are updated manually. Subject subpages are automatically generated using UNIX shell script programs that key on subject codes embedded as remarks within each entry. Pages are HTML-validated at the time of creation and periodically thereafter using Weblint (http://www.cre.canon.co.uk/~neilb/weblint/).

To identify meetings to be included in AgCal, AgNIC employs a multifaceted approach. In addition to monitoring subject-related mailing lists and news groups, staff also periodically monitor calendars maintained by others. When a conference with an associated e-mail address but without an apparent Web presence is identified, staff send an e-mail message soliciting further information. Of course, staff also do Web searches using Web search engines, although this process is perhaps the least efficient.

For a link-dense system such as AgCal, link checking is an important activity. AgNIC staff use the shareware software Linklint (http://www.goldwarp.com/bowlin/linklint/). In scheduling link checking, staff give preference to current and future years. Prior years are checked when possible. Staff check links on current and future year pages at least once a month. Even an automated approach to the process is made arduous by the vagaries of the Internet. Many problems identified turn out to be transitory and related to Domain Name System (DNS) misconfiguration, hardware outages, and Web server problems that are eventually corrected. For this reason, staff pay closer attention to reports of "moved" pages and pages no longer present on a server. Abandoned items are deleted from the active portion of AgCal but are retained separately for historical and statistical value.

6.2.3 Classification

The Other Meeting Calendars page (http://www.agnic.org/mtg/omc.html) is classified using a subset of the subject codes. The same codes form the basis for the algorithmic extraction of entries for the subject subset pages of AgCal.

6.3 Online Reference Service

Online Reference Service (http://www.agnic.org/orsp/) completed its pilot phase in May 1997 and has continued as an ongoing component of AgNIC. Participating were Iowa State University, the University of Arizona, the University of Nebraska, Cornell University, and NAL. Each of these centers of excellence maintained a Web site on a specific subject area, demonstrating the effectiveness of creating a Web site of Internet resources and providing online reference services in that area. The areas of specialization included animal science (Iowa), plant science (Nebraska), food and nutrition (NAL), rural information (NAL), rangeland management (Arizona), and reports and data sets from USDA economic agencies (Cornell).

A significant feature of the Online Reference Service is the ability of users to ask questions online if they cannot find answers after browsing the site. A librarian or an information specialist will provide the information desired or offer guidance on finding that information.

This component is a groundbreaking model for providing online reference services in that it is a distributed system in which no single institution answers all the questions and each is responsible for their own reference workflow. Participating institutions receive the online questions pertaining to their area of expertise. Participants may expand their services by adding sections on Frequently Asked Questions (FAQs) and Frequently Used Resources (FURs) in the area of their subjects. In addition, each participant organizes the site for easy use, linking to resources on the Internet in such a way that the users should easily find what they need by browsing the site. When selecting links, staff review the potential site, evaluating reliability, quality, and timeliness.

7.0 Project's Strengths

Several factors provided a sound foundation for the potential success of AgNIC. These included

- a shared vision of collaboration to meet the information needs of a diverse community of users with a common interest in and desire for enhanced access to agriculture-related information, subject area specialists, and other resources;
- experience gained through cooperative projects between NAL and the land-grant university libraries, especially projects related to the application of new information technology to library and information services;
- extensive and invaluable collections of agriculture-related information that could be drawn upon to provide significant and substantive high-quality content;
- highly qualified staffs of information specialists to provide expert reference assistance in subject areas;
- existing land-grant university and NAL infrastructure and Internet connectivity, as well as extensive Internet experience (even prior to the emergence of the Web);
- dedication to a philosophy of identifying, creating, and providing access to value-added, demand-driven resources that were not available over the Internet.

In its role as a national library, NAL provides leadership in developing systems for accessing information in agriculture and related sciences. As one of four national libraries, NAL is mandated to provide access to agriculture-related information. It serves as coordinator and primary resource for a nationwide network of land-grant and USDA field research libraries. Two of NAL's projects that preceded AgNIC added to the knowledge and experience that has made AgNIC successful. As early as 1987, NAL and forty-five land-grant libraries began participating in a cooperative effort, the National Agricultural Text Digitizing Project (NATDP), using optical scanning, text recognition, and CD-ROM technologies to capture and deliver printed agricultural materials in machine-readable form. The land-grant libraries also cooperated in programs to improve access to the nation's agricultural knowledge through the application of technology, including Internet communications. During the text-digitizing project, NAL began a separate cooperative project in 1989 with North Carolina State University to gain experience in the transmission and receipt of digitized images over the Internet. Each project provided experience useful to the AgNIC pilot.

From the beginning, AgNIC involved multiple partnerships from diverse groups in both the public and private sectors. A variety of institutions have helped develop this subject-based, virtual, digital library for agriculture and natural resources. The concept for AgNIC, first envisioned during a series of meetings held at NAL and in Washington, D.C., in 1993 and 1994, was refined by key collaborators including USDA's Cooperative State Research, Education, and Extension Service (CSREES); National Science Foundation (NSF); USDA Office of Information Resource Management (OIRM); USDA's Economic Research Service (ERS); the American Society for Horticultural Science (ASHS); the Center for Networked Information Discovery and Retrieval (CNIDR); and four land-grant universities: Cornell, Iowa State, Purdue, and Michigan State.

NAL created several value-added prototypes for AgNIC. One prototype demonstrates that librarians can make important and significant contributions to the scientific community by collaborating with scientists to provide access to research that benefits all users. An example of this is the Web-based version of the Database of the Occurrence and Distribution of Pesticides in the Chesapeake Bay (http://www.agnic.org/cbp/), which was created by NAL in collaboration with a research scientist from the USDA Agricultural Research Service (http://www.ars.usda.gov/). (See figure 2.)

NAL is committed to providing access to quality agricultural information. Its ability to provide leadership in this area and the expertise of its staff and the subject concentrations of its information centers allow it to fulfill this commitment. NAL staff emphasize developing research collections, providing reference services, producing information products, providing outreach services (such as workshops on information sources and information-gathering techniques), and networking

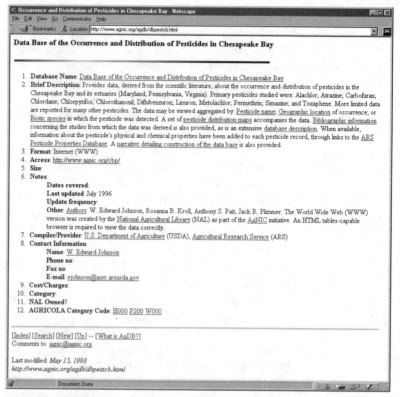

FIGURE 2.   AgNIC Records: Database of the Occurrence and Distribution of Pesticides in Chesapeake Bay

activities. Two of the information centers (the Rural Information Center [http://www.nal.usda.gov/ric/] and the Food and Nutrition Information Center [http://www.nal.usda.gov/fnic/]) were selected to be the NAL components of the AgNIC Reference Project pilot. Each center has highly regarded and heavily used Web sites through which they provide access to quality information resources, as well as online reference assistance in their respective subject areas.

Each AgNIC participant uses staff expertise in developing its site. And even though each of the participating institutions has had its own unique experience in developing part of AgNIC, most have followed a similar approach. The development at the University of Arizona is an example. Here an interdisciplinary team met regularly for nearly two years to design and implement the University of Arizona's contribution to AgNIC in the area of rangeland management. Made up of members from the University of Arizona's library and three divisions of the College of Agriculture, this team created the framework for a responsive, adaptive electronic reference tool that benefits users not only from Arizona, but in the entire western United States and other similar regions throughout the world. Content development for the site is guided by input received from members of county-based extension offices, commodity associations, and community groups to ensure the viability of the site for teaching, research, and outreach needs. Representatives of these groups are formal advisors to the Arizona component of AgNIC, and many have expressed interest in helping to develop AgNIC further. The Arizona component of AgNIC is also supported by agencies involved in land-use issues such as the USDA's National Resource Conservation Service (http://www.nrcs.usda.gov/) and the U.S. Forest Service (http://www.fs.fed.us/). In addition, the Arizona team continues to work with the Society for Range Management (http://srm.org/) on digitization of journals and other relevant documents for input on the site.

Since the AgNIC WWW site was first established in October 1995, AgNIC has experienced a steady increase in use each month throughout each of the three years it has been operational. The average daily accesses or hits grew from a starting rate of four hundred in October 1995 to over six thousand in August 1998. Average daily MB of files accessed during the same period grew from a starting point of 1.4 MB to 47.9 MB (http://www.agnic.org/adm/stats.html).

8.0 Project Weaknesses

Once the original partners had defined the AgNIC concept and agreed to develop a prototype system, the first difficulty was obtaining the funding needed for hardware, software, and staff. Section 4.0 ("Funding Sources") outlines how those resources were acquired by reallocating existing budgets and staff and by seeking new funds from internal and external sources. Delays in identifying such resources slowed the development of AgNIC. The funding and support situation is much better now.

In addition, it took the AgNIC founding members longer than expected to develop a governance structure, guidelines for participation, and other protocols for operating AgNIC and involving new organizations in the AgNIC alliance. This delay was influenced by several factors, including early changes in the membership, a shortage of staff to do the necessary work, an overreliance on volunteers to do certain tasks, and logistical difficulties in getting key participants together to focus on the issues. This difficulty has been resolved, and important documents about the operation of the AgNIC alliance are now available on the AgNIC Web site (http://www.agnic.org/docs/).

A third difficulty has been a lack of clear agreement on standards to be used for such activities as the development of descriptive records (metadata records). This issue is currently being addressed by member institutions and progress is being made. For example, late in 1997 an NAL task force examined standards currently used or being proposed for descriptive records (metadata records). The standards include USMARC (http://lcweb.loc.gov/marc/), Dublin Core Metadata (DC) (http://purl.oclc.org/dc/), Encoding Archive Description (EAD) (http://lcweb.loc.gov/ead/), Government Information Locator Service (GILS) (http://www.gils.net/), and Content Standard for Digital Geospatial Metadata (CSDGM) (http://fgdc.er.usgs.gov/metadata/contstan. html). After careful consideration at NAL, recommendations of the NAL task force will move on to the AgNIC Coordinating Committee for further discussion. Briefly, the task force concluded that the Dublin Core is substantial, widely accepted, and appropriate to create a record that would both effectively describe resources in the AgDB database and map, consistently and acceptably, to USMARC and GILS descriptive records.

9.0 Time Frame

After initial meetings during 1994 and into 1995, AgNIC went online early in the fall of 1995. The first two "live" components were AgDB and AgCal, offering general agricultural databases and a calendar of events. The Online Reference Project pilot was conducted from August 1996 through May 1997, bringing online five partners and six subject areas: animal science, plant science, rangeland management, agricultural statistics, food and nutrition, and rural information. Beginning in June 1997, the online reference component became an established, ongoing service of AgNIC. That same month, an invitation to land-grant libraries went out, inviting new participation in AgNIC. In April 1998, a newly expanded coordinating committee of twenty-one members met to finalize the governance structure, develop action items, and elect an executive board. In June 1998, a second letter of invitation was sent to all land-grant libraries, deans of agriculture, and library schools. Also in late June 1998, the newly elected executive board met to discuss priorities, marketing, assignments of task forces, and other urgent issues.

10.0 Future Goals of the Project

In 1994, Paul Peters expressed his belief that because of the discipline-oriented approach of AgNIC, developmental planning would require going beyond the questions of the impact of networks and digital libraries on communications, publications, and information product strategies and services. Peters asserted that AgNIC planners should consider fundamental questions related to the impact of networks and digital libraries on the agricultural sciences and on the practice of agriculture. Peters expressed his belief that the AgNIC project could make a significant contribution to the networked information research, development, and practice community in this area.

In preparing for a grant proposal in March 1998, seven AgNIC participants examined and planned for AgNIC's future. Their vision was, that with adequate funding levels, AgNIC will move forward by

- developing new sites based on assessments of user needs and further developing content on the original AgNIC Web sites;
- designing, testing, and implementing a dynamic, Web-based information retrieval system to provide user-friendly access to AgNIC's distributed resources through a single entry point;
- formalizing the AgNIC alliance by developing a management structure that will ensure effective operations of the alliance in coordinating overall AgNIC operations;
- developing a coordinated national plan, prioritized by user needs, to determine subject areas of future AgNIC sites;
- establishing criteria for assessing the reliability of information resources.

11.0 Vision Statement

According to Hobbes' Internet Timeline (http://info.isoc.org/guest/zakon/Internet/History/HIT.html), the number of Web servers has grown from one hundred-thirty in June 1993 to over two million in April 1998. The creators of the Google search engine, Sergey Brin and Lawrence Page, anticipate the existence of over one billion Web documents by the year 2000 (http://google.stanford.edu/), a tenfold increase over high-end estimates of what exists today. In the face of such volume and growth, Web organization is imperative. Without it, the grain will be perpetually lost in a field of chaff.

Today, there are two mechanisms to assist in Web organization: search engines and directories. Search engine problems are well known and frequently discussed. Despite their limitations, they offer an invaluable window to the Web. In fact, current Web index research projects, notably Google (http://google.stanford.edu/), hold the promise of remarkable performance improvements. Even improved, however, they will likely remain tools of the information elite. On the other hand, present-day directories typically try to cover too broad a domain with too few resources. Although somewhat useful as a point of entry, they often include the trivial while omitting real treasures. The complete automation of Web organization evokes the image of Tantalus—the fruit of knowledge, forever out of reach.

AgNIC is predicated on the belief that agricultural information on the Web can be best organized and presented by those expert in systematization of knowledge, leveraging the intrinsic strengths of the Internet and using the highest quality automated resource discovery tools available. Hallmarks for success in this effort will include domain segmentation; division of responsibility; dynamic staff retraining and task redefinition; resource reallocation; opportune adoption of proven technologies; willingness to learn from the successes and failures of both ourselves and others; ability to react, prototype, and implement quickly; effective collaboration; and above all else, commitment to a vision of democratic Web-based knowledge. NAL and the AgNIC partners believe that this model for distributed resource sharing for electronic information access and distribution helps redefine the role of libraries, librarians, and their partners.

Notes

1. U.S. Department of Commerce, *Survey of Rural Information Infrastructure Technology* (Washington, D.C.: The Department, 1995).

2. K. Hunter, "Publishing for a Digital Library—What Did TULIP Teach Us?" *Journal of Academic Librarianship* 22, no. 5 (Nov./Dec. 1996): 25–29.

3. C. R. McClure, "Network Literacy: A Role for Libraries?" *Information Technology and Libraries* 13, no. 2 (June 1994): 115–25.

4. U.S. Department of Commerce, p. viii.

2

Argus Clearinghouse (Argus)

Anna Noakes

This chapter describes the Argus Clearinghouse (http://www.clearinghouse.net/), an acclaimed Web-based directory of topical Internet guides. The Argus Clearinghouse provides a central access point for value-added topical guides that identify, describe, and evaluate Internet-based information resources. The chapter emphasizes the Clearinghouse's project to create a new browsing scheme and interface. The desired outcome of the redesign project was to improve the usability of the collection by creating a hierarchical browsing structure based on an in-house taxonomy developed for this purpose. Input from Clearinghouse users was essential for informing the redesign process and evaluating the new version of the Clearinghouse. We discuss some of the main results of the study. Finally, we suggest future directions for the Clearinghouse and for the discovery and organization of Internet resources.

1.0 Introduction

In recent years, the exponential growth of the Internet has resulted in massive quantities of digital resources that are increasingly unwieldy to navigate. Most Internet users experience at least occasional difficulty or frustration when looking for information online. The decentralized, anarchic nature of the Internet tends to militate against the kinds of top-down organizational structures that could make it much easier for the average person to use. Without any kind of organizing structure, finding the desired information can depend on luck as much as a searcher's persistence and skill. In spite of substantial work to develop better search and retrieval tools, locating online resources remains a time-consuming and tedious process for most users.

Internet directories offer users access to an organized subset of Internet resources that has been selected and arranged according to topic. In many cases, the classification schemes used to specify and structure these topics form the backbone of the browsing interfaces by which users access the desired resources. Although a variety of formal classification schemes for print materials exists, the creators of many Internet directories have chosen to organize resources using their own special-purpose classification schemes. One such directory is the Argus Clearinghouse (Clearinghouse) (http://www.clearinghouse.net/), an acclaimed research-oriented directory of topical Internet guides. (See figure 1.)

2.0 Mission Statement

The Clearinghouse is dedicated to providing a central access point for value-added topical guides that identify, describe, and evaluate Internet-based information resources. Its mission is to facilitate intellectual access to information resources on the Internet. The underlying philosophy of the Clearinghouse is a contention that automated means alone are insufficient for identifying and evaluating information resources, given the complexities and ambiguities of language. Therefore, human intellectual labor is required to assess, index, and classify Internet resources to make them more accessible to users. The skills and training of librarians and information professionals are especially valuable in achieving this end.

3.0 Responsible Persons

Numerous people have contributed to the project in a variety of roles. This section briefly describes the persons responsible in the early days of the Clearinghouse, followed by the most central figures in the redesign phase that resulted in the new Clearinghouse.

3.1 Origins of the Argus Clearinghouse

In the spring of 1993, Louis Rosenfeld, now the president of Argus Associates (http://argus-inc.com/), began instructing graduate stu-

FIGURE 1.   The Argus Clearinghouse Home Page

dents in the creation of topical guides to Internet resources. Rosenfeld published his first collection of about twenty guides on the University of Michigan Graduate Library's Gopher server as an example of innovative student work. After getting approximately seven thousand hits in the first month that the collection was online, Rosenfeld decided to formalize the project as the Clearinghouse of Subject-Oriented Internet Resource Guides and began to solicit additional guides by posting inquiries to relevant Internet news groups. This early version of the Clearinghouse became the first information-seeking tool of its kind.

By 1995, Rosenfeld had begun a full-time commitment with Argus Associates, a business that he had cofounded with Joseph Janes in 1991. Argus Associates, now an information architecture consultancy specializing in "organization, labeling, navigation, and indexing for . . . intranets and Web sites" (http://www.argus-inc.com/design/index.html), began as an Internet training business for librarians and educators. Rosenfeld continued to develop the Clearinghouse on the library's server until it was transferred to the Argus server in early 1996 and renamed the Argus Clearinghouse. By that time, the Clearinghouse was not only hosting student guides but pointing to external guides as well, which now form the vast majority of the Clearinghouse collection. As the Web superseded Gopher, Argus began to develop its first graphical interface for the Clearinghouse to enable browsing the guides via broad topical categories. Since the Clearinghouse has migrated to its graphical interface, it has expanded to include pointers to approximately two thousand guides and its usage has soared to as many as 1.25 million hits a month.

3.2 The Next-Generation Argus Clearinghouse

The Clearinghouse is maintained and developed by Argus Associates (http://argus-inc.com/). The focus of Argus Associates' activities has evolved over the years from Internet training to its present concentration on information architecture for organizations with large-scale, complex information needs. True to its origins, Argus continues to apply principles of library and information science to the design of environments that enable its clients to find and manage information more successfully. Argus continues to develop and maintain the Clearinghouse as a public service.

Early in 1996, I approached Louis Rosenfeld, president of Argus Associates, about redesigning the expanded Clearinghouse to improve its usability. Rosenfeld agreed to the project, and I began work on the Clearinghouse late that spring. During the redesign process, I worked closely with Rosenfeld and Vice President Peter Morville. Together, we reviewed my redesign proposals and reached consensus on the major indexing and classification decisions that were necessary to create special-purpose taxonomy for the Clearinghouse. Greg Peters was the programming consultant on the project, responsible for the implementation of all nonvisible aspects of the system, including all the necessary reprogramming and the provision of keyword index lists for subsequent revision. In the later stages, Samantha Bailey, senior consultant and managing editor of the

Clearinghouse, consulted with me as she oversaw and finalized implementation of the new taxonomy.

4.0 Funding Source

The Argus Clearinghouse began as a showcase for student initiatives and continues today as a professionally maintained resource offered to the public at no cost to its users. The Clearinghouse has always operated on a shoestring budget. Argus Associates is the funding source for the Clearinghouse, providing the necessary maintenance and operating budget of approximately seven thousand dollars per year. Revenues from advertising banners account for less than one thousand dollars per year. Everyone involved in the redesign project had additional full- or part-time commitments. The entire redesign project was carried out in twelve months and at a cost of less than ten thousand dollars.

5.0 Target Audience

The Clearinghouse has positioned itself as the Internet's premier research library, with a primary target audience of researchers from both the academic and the private sectors. Clearinghouse staff conducted an online survey in August 1996 to learn more about its users. The resulting audience and usage analysis showed that over 60 percent of Clearinghouse users are involved in research-intensive occupations such as professors, teachers, researchers, librarians, engineers, journalists, and students. Of these occupations, the largest portions were professor/teacher, at 19 percent; student, 16 percent; and researcher, 14 percent. Business was the organizational type of nearly 43 percent of the respondents, followed by college/university at 24 percent and nonprofit at 10 percent. Libraries, schools, government, and home made up another 23 percent.

The data indicated that 80 percent of the respondents use the Clearinghouse for some form of research: 55 percent for professional research and 20 percent for personal research. Twenty percent of survey respondents indicated that they use the Clearinghouse for more recreational purposes, such as casual browsing. In terms of usage rates, 10 percent of repeat users access the Clearinghouse daily, 60 percent use it weekly, and 31 percent use it monthly or occasionally. In addition, users were asked how the Clearinghouse compared with other Internet search services, and how it might be improved. Their thoughtful responses helped to inform our redesign project.

6.0 Collection Description

The Clearinghouse collection consists of approximately two thousand Internet guides. These guides are Internet resources that have been developed to provide convenient, centralized access to numerous on-line sites devoted to a particular subject or area of interest. The guides included in the Clearinghouse presently cover the following broad topical categories: Arts and Humanities; Business and Employment; Communication; Computers and Information Technology; Education; Engineering; Environment; Government and Law; Health and Medicine; Places and Peoples; Recreation; Science and Mathematics; and Social Sciences and Social Issues.

The Clearinghouse database also includes metadata submitted by authors about their guides and the ratings guide prepared by Argus staff. The metadata are outlined in the following section.

7.0 Selection and Evaluation Process

The selection and evaluation of guides for inclusion in the Clearinghouse are an entirely manual process. The Clearinghouse generally does not seek out guides but rather evaluates guides submitted by their authors/compilers. Automated "spam" submissions are prohibited. Authors are strongly discouraged from submitting the same guide more than once. These guidelines help keep the volume of guides being reviewed to manageable levels. Nevertheless, the Clearinghouse rejects up to 95 percent of the guides submitted. The small acceptance rate is intended to ensure that Clearinghouse users have access to a high-quality (rather than a comprehensive) collection of select Internet guides.

7.1 Selecting Guides

What was considered a guide in the early days of the Clearinghouse was fairly straightforward: it was simply a site on the Internet that pointed to other digital resources on a given topic. These guides were effectively nodes that their authors used to gather together those resources that they had found interesting or useful during their own Internet searching. The creation of topical guides meant that Internet users with similar information needs had the option of consulting these guides first, thereby reaping the benefit of someone's prior intellectual efforts. Over time, the Clearinghouse refined its definition of a guide (http://www.clearinghouse.net/submit.html) to comprise the following characteristics:

- Guides must be available in electronic format and accessible via the Internet.
- Guides must link to other Internet resources that focus on a specific topic (or more than one if topics are related to each other).
- The primary goal of each guide should be to help users access topical Internet information available from many Internet sites besides the compiler's own site.
- Guides must be free of charge for end users.

In addition to meeting these basic guidelines, guide authors are required to provide basic metadata for the resources. The metadata provide a description standard that assures some degree of consistency among guides. In addition, the metadata document has responsibility for the guide and its currency and, in some cases, may suggest the authority of the guide. Specifically, the metadata consist of

- compiler's full name,
- compiler's title and institution/company,
- compiler's e-mail address,
- brief biography of compiler,
- guide title,
- guide URL,
- date of last update,
- suggested keywords (up to three).

7.2 Evaluating Guides

Unlike many Internet directories, the Clearinghouse employs professionals trained in information and library science as guide evaluators. Each guide that meets the basic selection standards listed above is then evaluated by these professionals according to five criteria: (1) level of resource description, (2) level of resource evaluation, (3) guide design, (4) guide organizational schemes, and (5) guide metainformation. Guides receive a rating of one to five checks for each of these criteria. These ratings are then averaged to produce an overall score or rating for the guide. The evaluation criteria are described in more detail below (see http://www.clearinghouse.net/rating.html).

7.2.1 Level of Resource Description

The level of resource description refers to the presence of descriptive information that provides the user with an objective sense of what to expect from the resources to which the guide refers. This information should include the following, as appropriate:

- description of the topical content (ranging from keywords to abstracts);
- description of the traffic levels, level of moderation, and features;
- statement of intended audience;
- update frequencies for resources;
- access instructions;
- technical performance levels.

7.2.2 Level of Resource Evaluation

Evaluative information provides users with a subjective sense of the quality of the Internet resources to which the guide refers, including such issues as

- quality of the content of resources;
- usability assessment (e.g., document layout, readability, organization, appropriate use of graphics);
- authority of resource authors (e.g., reliability, credibility).

7.2.3 Guide Design

In assessing the design qualities of a guide, Clearinghouse evaluators look for a balance of pleasing aesthetics and usability indicators such as

- images and graphics that are attractive, quick to load, and that improve comprehension and/or navigation of the resource;
- layout issues, including appropriate use of sections and headers, font faces and sizes, color, white space;
- navigational aids where appropriate.

7.2.4 Guide Organizational Schemes

Guides can be organized in one or more ways, including by author, subject, chronology, region, intended audience, or digital format. Evaluators look for organizational schemes that are useful and appropriate, and add additional points for guides that offer access to their resources via a choice of organizational schemes.

7.2.5 Guide Metainformation

Metainformation refers to the information the guide provides to describe itself to users. This may include information about the authors, their professional or institutional affiliations, and the particular background from which they derive their knowledge of the subject of the guide. Additional metainformation may include the purpose of the guide, how and why it was created, what it contains, and what it leaves out. Finally, metainformation may include contact information for Clearinghouse staff for feedback and suggestions and the frequency with which the guide is updated.

Although the primary purpose of these evaluation activities is to provide a guide rating, the Clearinghouse staff also opts to recognize exceptional guides as exemplars of superior design and organization. To this end, one exceptional guide per month is chosen to receive the Digital Librarian's Award, which is highlighted on the Argus Clearinghouse Web site.

8.0 Mechanics of Production

The Clearinghouse works on a UNIX-based server running Apache 1.2.1 Web server software (http://www.apache.org/). The operational part of the site consists of a collection of Perl scripts operating on a directory of flat ASCII files. Each of these files consists of a series of attribute/value pairs. Separate directories are maintained for the data necessary to construct the hierarchical browsing structure. The search engine that the Clearinghouse uses is SWISH 1.1 (http://sunsite.berkeley.edu/SWISH-E/).

9.0 Development of Taxonomy

At this point in time, there is no clear consensus in the information science community about the superiority of either existing, formal classification schemes or the special-purpose classification schemes created in-house by businesses, institutions, and individuals who organize Internet resources in the form of directories. Informal discussion in relevant online forums appears to favor the use of formal classification of Internet resources. Research on the effectiveness of standard classification schemes as an organizational tool in Internet directories is underway but still preliminary. However, most of the most popular Internet directories today do not choose to employ a standard classification scheme. Rather, they have developed content-driven schemes in-house and in accordance with the perceived needs of their users.

9.1 The Original Taxonomy

The original Web-based Clearinghouse was designed around a very flat, loosely organized taxonomy. Guide authors would submit their choice of up to three natural language keywords that they felt best characterized the subject matter of their guides. These keywords would then be input into the Clearinghouse database essentially as submitted. Evaluators then judged the keywords as belonging to one or more broad topical categories: Arts and Entertainment; Business and Employment; Education; Engineering and Technology; Environment; Government and Law; Health and Medicine; Humanities; News and Publishing; Regional Information; Science; and Social Sciences and Social Issues.

These topical categories were used to provide a starting point for users wishing to browse the collection. Once the user had selected one of these broad topics, she or he was presented with an alphabetic list of keyword strings associated with each guide classified as belonging to the category. Although Clearinghouse users became comfortable and familiar with visual scanning of the alpha lists, there were clearly problems with the method.

First there were the obvious problems of natural language input. There was no control over synonyms, acronyms, abbreviations, homographs, variant forms and spellings, capitalization, hyphenation, plural and singular forms, and typographical errors. Any and all of these anomalies contributed to problems of collocating guides devoted to similar topics. Another major difficulty involved the way the keywords were alphabetized. For each guide, the assigned keywords were indexed as a single string. That is, the entire list of keywords for any given guide was alphabetized according to whichever keyword happened to be listed first in the string. Needless to say, this aspect of the browsing structure also tended to reduce collocation of similar guides. In addition, there were problems with the topical categories of the browsing structure. In particular, the guides were distributed unevenly across categories. Some of the categories listed only a small number of guides, while others were highly populated and required much more effort to scan and scroll through the alpha list of keyword strings. Finally, the flat structure meant that, as the number of guides in the collection increased, the keyword lists for each category became increasingly bloated and unwieldy for users. The original version of the Clearinghouse was simply not designed to scale up gracefully.

9.2 Toward a New Taxonomy

By 1996, it was becoming apparent to Rosenfeld that the Clearinghouse was outstripping its capacity under the current configuration and would have to be redesigned. I met with Rosenfeld in March 1996 to discuss working together to overhaul the indexing and classification scheme of the Clearinghouse. The task was twofold: (1) to review

problems and inconsistencies with the indexing and make the necessary corrections; and (2) to review the classification scheme and
devise a new scheme that would facilitate browsing by creating an
intuitive and navigable hierarchy. Both of these tasks were intended to
improve user access to the collection.

The first task, and a great deal of the work, was to address indexing inconsistencies in the existing version of the Clearinghouse.
This meant reviewing the cumulative index list of keywords for the
approximately sixteen hundred guides that comprised the collection
at the time. In an iterative process of review and revision, I identified
three levels of priority for keyword corrections:

- Correct errors and variations in spelling, capitalization, and
  hyphenation.

- Normalize display of acronyms and abbreviations; standardize
  singular and plural forms.

- Select preferred keyword terms and conflate variants.

The first level of priority included revisions that could be carried
out quickly and easily and that would bring the greatest improvement in the functioning of the Clearinghouse. The second level included less urgent but also important revisions. The third level included
revisions that implied some degree of ongoing vocabulary control and,
by extension, the establishment of a policy for dealing with classification in the future.

Since the guides are largely self-classified by the guide authors,
we did not attempt to impose a standard classification scheme from
the print world, such as Dewey Decimal Classification or the Library
of Congress Subject Classification. We felt it was important for authors
to be able to describe the content of the guides in their own words.
We also believed, based on our own experience and background as
librarians, that untrained guide authors would find a fully developed,
complex taxonomy difficult and discouraging to use. We were certain that, as novice catalogers, they would inadvertently produce inconsistencies that might require extensive correction after the fact.
Finally, we determined that formal classification schemes simply
evolve too slowly to deal effectively with the kind of subject matter
that tends to develop rapidly, such as computer jargon, breaking technologies, and cultural trends. Since topics such as these are typically
sought after in electronic form by Internet-savvy users, it follows that
an effective subject classification scheme for Internet resources must
be able to offer its users currency, flexibility, and topical relevance.
This, in large part, may explain the reliance on special-purpose classification schemes for so many Internet directories.

9.3 Classification from the Bottom Up

As mentioned earlier, we placed a priority on having guide authors select their own keywords when submitting a guide. However, to maintain consistency and collocation of guides, we realized that we would have to impose some degree of light vocabulary control when a guide was submitted to the Clearinghouse. To this end, we created a new classification scheme that effectively represents the content of the Clearinghouse, as determined by keywords already present in the database. Guide keywords were separated so that they were no longer processed as a single string. These individual keywords were then to be grouped into relevant subcategories, which could themselves be grouped into a number of supercategories, thus producing a hierarchical structure suitable for browsing in a hypertext environment. Last, I prepared brief scope notes for each of the subcategories and supercategories to further inform users about the definition of a given category and assist their decision-making processes while browsing.

This process represents a bottom-up, keyword-driven approach to building a classification scheme. In contrast to the more typical top-down approach, which applies broad categories to a universe of knowledge and then subdivides these categories, our method ensured that the taxonomy would be as spare as possible while precisely reflecting the Clearinghouse collection of resources. Furthermore, since there were no preexisting constraints on the structure of the classification scheme, it is free to evolve as the topical content of the Clearinghouse evolves. In this way, we could ensure the currency, flexibility, and topical relevance of our taxonomy while keeping vocabulary control and database maintenance to a minimum.

10.0 Project Time Frame

The Clearinghouse has existed in some form since 1993, first as a Gopher site, eventually in print, and now as a Web-based service. The current version emerged from a redesign phase that required approximately twelve months to complete, beginning with the initial planning stages in early 1996 to the conclusion of a small evaluation study in the spring of 1997. Work on the project proceeded in a number of stages. I began my analysis of the existing state of the Clearinghouse in early May 1996, and prepared several reports over the summer detailing needed revisions and corrections to the indexing and classification. By late summer, the most significant indexing revisions were completed and I was able to prepare a proposal for a new hierarchical browsing scheme. I further revised and refined the proposal until September.

By early October 1996, the staff of the Clearinghouse began to plan and schedule the programming changes required to implement the new system. In addition, the Argus staff contracted with a local graphic design firm, Q LTD, to design an interface that would represent the new browsing structure in an intuitive and visually appealing way. This development work continued through the winter of 1996–97. By April 1997, the prototype system was close enough to a final version that I could begin to schedule subjects for the evaluation phase. I conducted the study during a two-week period in April. Analysis of the resulting data began in early May, and I drafted a final report on the redesign project over the following two months.

11.0 Discussion of Evaluation Study

As we described earlier, the redesign project was informed by many considerations, both functional and aesthetic. However, the early impetus for change came from Clearinghouse users themselves, whose survey responses indicated an ongoing need for well-organized, easy-to-use finding aids for Internet resources. Although many Clearinghouse users were fully accustomed to the flat hierarchy and long keyword lists of the old Clearinghouse, we were certain that they would appreciate the enhanced browsing structure of the newly redesigned Clearinghouse even more.

The main categories of the new Clearinghouse can be seen in figure 1. Users can "drill down" from these broad categories to progressively more specific ones. So, for example, a user who selects business and employment can then choose from among the following subcategories: banking and investment; business; economics; employment; finance and credit; human resources; industry; and marketing.

A subsequent click on employment yields these keywords: careers; compensation; employment (general); jobs; labor; resumes; temporary employment; and workweek reduction.

Finally, clicking on the keyword *careers* displays all of the guides in the collection associated with the keyword "careers." Each guide is specified by its title, keyword, and rating. When the user chooses a particular guide from this list, the system displays a detailed guide page that provides key information about the guide such as its URL, author/compiler, affiliation, in-depth rating, and date indicating when the guide was last checked by Clearinghouse staff. (See figure 2.) From there, the user can proceed directly to the guide, or return to a previous level for additional browsing.

We believed that this new version would better meet the needs of Clearinghouse users based on the early input they had brought to our redesign process. However, we recognized the value of obtaining

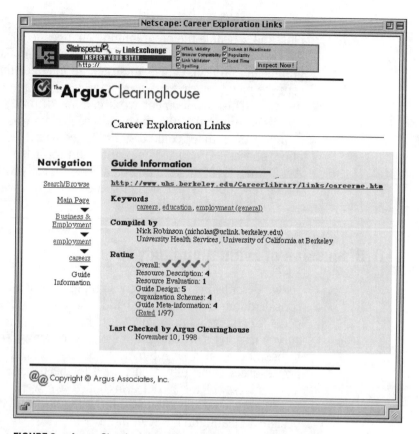

FIGURE 2. Argus Clearinghouse Record: Career Exploration Links

additional user feedback at the prototype stage to assure ourselves that the redesigned Clearinghouse would truly offer users an improvement in the site's overall usability. Accordingly, we agreed to conduct a small evaluation study to allow representative users to compare and contrast the old and new versions of the Clearinghouse.

I recruited a total of twenty-five subjects to participate in the study. These subjects were drawn primarily from masters students, alumni, and friends of the University of Michigan School of Information (http://www.si.umich.edu/), but included graduate students from other schools and departments within the university as well. These sources were chosen in part for the convenience of gathering subjects and also because this group was a fair representation of the largest demographic portion of current Clearinghouse users as indicated in the earlier audience and usage survey.

I monitored the subject on a computer workstation. Each subject was assigned two information-seeking tasks to perform, using each of the two systems respectively. These tasks were drawn from a pre-tested set of typical tasks. The tasks were fairly typical of the kind of guide-seeking done every day by Clearinghouse users. For example, subjects might be asked to "find a guide to career resources." The questions were distributed as evenly as possible between the two test systems, system A being the original version of the Clearinghouse, and system B being the redesigned version. Subjects subsequently carried out all tasks using both versions of the Clearinghouse. The system starting order was randomized to mitigate the effects of learning or starting order on the results. For similar reasons, the contents of the guides were identical for both systems.

The subject questionnaire was the primary tool during testing. I explained the test procedures to the subjects, recorded start and end times to establish a measure of the subjects' speed and efficiency, and took notes, but did not intervene throughout the test. I then questioned the subject on the system's performance. The subject then went on to perform the second task. After answering the same set of questions about the second systems, the subject was asked some comparative questions to determine if the user had a system preference and why.

The study data did not necessarily support all of the expected results. The subjects were all able to complete their tasks successfully. Furthermore, the new hierarchical browsing system did not offer significantly faster times for task completion, as I had predicted. However, subjects did demonstrate a strong overall preference for the new system, both in terms of its organization and its design.

Subjects' comments on how system A (the old Clearinghouse) might be improved were highly encouraging because they tended to validate the changes we had believed were necessary during the redesign process. For example, ten subjects, nearly half of those participating in the study, recommended separating the keyword strings and dividing them into smaller subcategories. This would prevent users from being inundated with long lists of keywords from which to make their selections. In a similar vein, five specifically suggested adding more levels to the browsing hierarchy. Five thought that breaking down the top-level categories into a larger number of more specific categories would improve the usability of the system. Two simply wanted to see the keyword lists separated so that all keywords could be properly alphabetized. One thought that implementing a set of links, internal to the page, at the top of the keywords lists would better facilitate navigation because users could jump down to specific sections of the page rather than having to scroll down manually. Finally, one thought that using precoordinated subject terms in the Clearinghouse might best enhance the usability of the system.

When asked to relate the best features of system B (the new Clearinghouse), subjects could name a wide variety of favorites. Ten subjects mentioned that they liked the system's clean design and the fact that it was not as cluttered as system A. Seven thought the system was well organized, efficient, and demonstrated good functionality. Five indicated that the consistent design and layout made the system easy to use. In a matter related to the design, four said they appreciated the way their eyes were drawn to important sections by the use of a central yellow field that highlights key information on each page in the browsing structure. Three praised the navigational guide as the best overall system feature, since they could always tell where they were in the system and could easily jump between levels.

A smaller number of subjects chose other system features as best overall. Two were enthusiastic about the way the system collocated guides on the same topic. Two liked the fact that they only had to negotiate short lists of categories or keywords and that not too much scrolling was required. Two thought the scope notes for categories and subcategories were an excellent feature. Another two liked the fact that there were no long loading graphics to wait for. One especially mentioned that the best feature of the system was its use of commonsense language for the nonspecialist. Another singled out the indirect cross-referencing of guides through hot-linked keyword terms. Finally, one thought that the guide ratings was the best overall feature.

Subjects also expressed greater satisfaction with the performance of the redesigned Clearinghouse, assigning the new system an average helpfulness rating of 4.1 on a 5 point scale, compared to the average rating of 3.2 for the old system. Out of twenty-five subjects, twenty-two preferred the organization of the new Clearinghouse. Furthermore, the same number preferred the new Clearinghouse in terms of design. Due to these results and subsequent high praise from actual Clearinghouse users, we feel justified in considering our redesign project a success: our new scheme, hypertext browsing structure, and site design are working in concert to produce an Internet directory that is attractive, intuitive, and easy-to-use.

12.0 Strengths and Weaknesses of the Project

The Internet is currently graced with many kinds of finding aids, of which search engines and directories are probably the two most common. Internet directories offer the advantage of making digital resources more accessible to users by classifying them in some way. Trained staff members who have earned graduate degrees in information and library science classify guides for the Clearinghouse, a task that requires considerable intellectual labor. In the case of the Clearinghouse, this investment in intellectual labor is compounded in several ways: there is a high volume of submissions, the selection criteria are stringent, and the evaluation of accepted guides is conducted in detail. Although the browsing structure is the primary means of accessing guides in the Clearinghouse, we also provide an easy-to-use search interface. The option to use either the browsing or searching modes offers Clearinghouse users a degree of choice in how they access the collection.

Argus Associates does not have unlimited staff hours to devote to the Clearinghouse. Indeed, maintaining the Clearinghouse requires some of the Argus staff to sacrifice time that could be spent on the primary, revenue-generating business of the organization. This is the greatest weakness of the Clearinghouse on an organizational level. As a finding aid, its greatest weakness is a lack of comprehensive coverage of the Internet, mainly due to staffing limitations and a strict policy of selectivity. However, these limitations also contribute to the greatest strength of the Clearinghouse: it contains high-quality content that has been carefully selected and thoroughly evaluated. This commitment to quality sets the Argus Clearinghouse apart from many other Internet directories. The Clearinghouse has established a niche by specializing in topical guides. It assesses their probable value to users, and then provides sufficient information to allow users to distinguish between otherwise similar guides. Users keep returning to the Clearinghouse because it gives them quick, convenient access to the information they need.

13.0 Future Goals of the Argus Clearinghouse

The Clearinghouse has come a long way since its inception as an innovative student project. It is now an established, award-winning Internet directory with a substantial collection (approximately two thousand guides), high visibility (up to 1,250,000 hits per month), and a loyal following among Internet users. The results of our preliminary study indicate myriad possible paths for continued research and development of the Clearinghouse. Priority items for future work could include determining an optimal depth for browsing structures, comparing special-purpose and formal classification schemes for use as browsing taxonomies, determining the suitability of different taxonomies for different kinds of tasks and collection content, and exploring the scalability of different browsing structures for large collections of digital resources.

In spite of its continuing popularity and numerous accolades, the future of the Clearinghouse is still in question. For the time being, Argus Associates will continue to host and maintain the Clearinghouse—even at a loss—as a public service to the Internet community. Maintenance and enhancements must necessarily be kept to a minimum. A third-generation Argus Clearinghouse is not presently planned. In the long term, the Clearinghouse will have to become economically self-sufficient. It must either attract additional sponsorship or implement some other cost recovery mechanism if it is to remain viable.

14.0 Vision Statement on Internet Resources

Since the scale of the Internet raises concerns about whether a resource-finding tool can be exhaustive, many information professionals have placed their faith in automated retrieval tools such as search engines for the future of information gathering on the Internet. Over the years, search engines have become increasingly sophisticated, offering a range of features including Boolean operators, proximity operators, stemming, string searching, date ranges, format constraints, and user-determined relevance criteria—all features intended to improve the precision of searches. Search engines that can index a large portion of the Internet have been developed, but they have a number of typical shortcomings, notably:

- lack of selection criteria for indexed resources;
- index tables that are quickly outdated;
- full-text indexing that may be inadequate to describe higher-order concepts;
- a search interface that may be difficult to learn, or may differ substantially from that of other search engines;
- result lists that can be enormous and frustrating to sift through;
- discouragingly low relevance of the returned documents.

Although they tend to offer less comprehensive coverage of Internet resources, directories can claim a number of advantages over search engines as a retrieval tool.

- Higher-order concepts and their relations to one another are manifest in the hierarchy of categories and their subordinate keyword terms.
- Browsing interfaces are generally intuitive enough that no significant learning time is required.
- The resulting retrieved document sets are usually manageable in size.
- Documents tend to be relevant to the user's intended query.

There is an ever-growing body of literature in information and library science, as well as the popular press, that expounds the importance of improving user access to Internet resources. Due to advances in computer hardware and software, it is becoming possible to have ever-larger collections of Internet resources that must be accessible by efficient and user-friendly systems. Users will continue to press for improved access to such collections. Search engines and other automated finding aids do not present an ideal solution for achieving this objective. Discerning users will continue to value the investment of intellectual labor that ensures quick, convenient, and reliable access to quality information resources.

3

Blue Web'n

Jodi Reed

Blue Web'n (http://www.kn.pacbell.com/wired/bluewebn/), created by the Pacific Bell Education First Fellows in the Department of Educational Technology of San Diego State University's College of Education (http://edweb.sdsu.edu/), indexes high-quality tools, resources, activities, and projects available on the World Wide Web for classroom and library use. The growing collection of over eight hundred sites helps teachers and librarians find exemplary models that they can adapt for their own use. The Blue Web'n library can be searched and browsed in a variety of ways, making it user-friendly. The Weekly Update electronic mailing list, with almost twenty thousand subscribers, keeps users up-to-date on new additions. This chapter describes the project's history, collection and selection process, production and maintenance, classification scheme, strengths and weaknesses, and future vision.

1.0 Background

In 1994, Pacific Bell launched the Education First Initiative (Education First) (http://www.kn.pacbell.com/edfirst/), a $100 million project aimed at providing technology resources to the nine thousand California schools and libraries in the company's service territory. The goal of Education First was to help these institutions establish the telecommunications infrastructure needed to use Internet and videoconferencing technology and to help teachers and librarians develop the necessary skills to effectively use these technologies. As part of its Education First Initiative, Pacific Bell offered free installation of up to four Integrated Services Digital Network (ISDN) lines at each school or library, plus one year of free service. Over seven thousand institutions accepted Pacific Bell's offer. For many, this offer was just what they needed to jump start their technology plan.

To help promote effective use of the Internet and videoconferencing technology, Pacific Bell contracted with teachers and librarians on sabbatical to assist with training and support. These "education advocates" (http://www.kn.pacbell.com/edfirst/advocates.html) support staff development by offering a wide variety of workshops around the state of California.

Three fellowships were funded by the Department of Educational Technology at San Diego State University's College of Education to explore effective use of Internet and videoconferencing within classrooms and libraries. In spring of 1995, Fellows Tom March, Linda Hyman, and Jodi Reed carved out goals and began the design and development of resources, tools, activities, and projects that would support teachers and librarians in their struggle to integrate telecommunications technology within their settings. As fellows, we wanted to model effective use of e-mail, the World Wide Web, and videoconferencing. We hoped to create applications compelling enough to convince educators and librarians to take that difficult first step toward the end goal of using technology with students and patrons. As we began to survey existing education and library-oriented Web sites, we realized that recognizing and sharing the work of others was a natural extension of our own development activities. One of our first and most popular applications, Blue Web'n (http://www.kn.pacbell. com/wired/bluewebn), is a directory of the most interesting, excellent, and essential Web sites for educators, librarians, and students. The Weekly Update electronic mailing list updates some twenty thousand subscribers weekly, informing them of added sites (and this number is growing by about two thousand subscribers per month).

The opening screen for Blue Web'n, shown in figure 1, orients users, offers a menu of navigation options, and allows users to subscribe to the Weekly Update electronic mailing list.

2.0 Responsible Persons

While Blue Web'n was created with input from all three fellows, Jodi Reed is the lead designer and developer. Jodi manages and updates the site with support from SDSU graduate assistant Kendra Sheldon. Initially the San Diego State University Department of Educational Technology (http://edweb.sdsu.edu/EDTEC/EDTEC_Home.html) supported

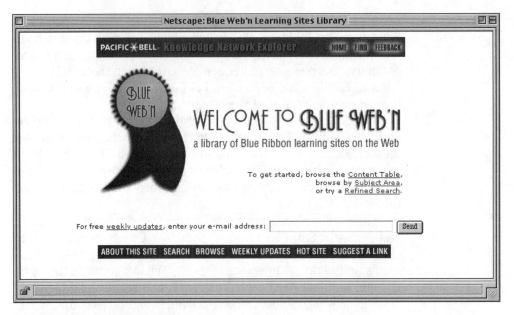

FIGURE 1. Blue Web'n Home Page

prototype development by allowing use of their Web server, but now Blue Web'n files and common-gateway interface (CGI) programs reside on a Pacific Bell server. The other two fellows predominantly work on other Education First Initiatives.

3.0 Mission

The fellows created Blue Web'n to give teachers and librarians a starting point for finding outstanding learning sites on the Web. We are especially interested in sharing tools and student-centered activities and projects that require use of the Internet. By featuring interesting models and essential resources, we hope to encourage appropriate classroom use of the Web.

4.0 Funding and Budget

Since Pacific Bell funds the work of the fellows and not just Blue Web'n, the budget for Blue Web'n is estimated based on the time spent on the project. The annual budget for funding three fellows and a graduate assistant is $250,000 to $300,000. The majority of this budget goes to salary and benefits for the fellows, but the budget also includes facilities overhead, stipends for faculty advisors, computer and videoconferencing hardware, equipment maintenance, software, and office supplies.

Initial development of Blue Web'n took approximately four months of one fellow's time, with an estimated cost of about $27,000. A major revision in 1997 took about two months with an estimated cost of about $15,000. Currently, maintenance takes about ten hours per week of fellow time and about ten hours per week of graduate assistant time, with an annual cost of about $25,000.

5.0 Audience

Blue Web'n is designed for K-12 teachers and school librarians. Most visitors to the site and subscribers to the Weekly Update are from the United States, but international educators also use Blue Web'n. Secondary audiences include teachers in higher education, college students, librarians, parents, and home-schooling families.

6.0 The Web Site Collection

As mentioned before, Blue Web'n is not intended to be a comprehensive collection. Currently, Blue Web'n has under one thousand sites. We add about five sites per week, one of which is designated as the "Hot Site" of the week. Blue Web'n can be searched using either quick or refined search options (http://www.kn.pacbell.com/wired/bluewebn/search.html), but most users prefer to browse the content table provided on the home page. (See figure 2.) The table not only shows the main categories, it also shows the number of links within the various categories. We organized the table this way to indicate the depth of the collection before a user begins to browse. As you can see from this table, our collection is heavy in some subject areas and types. Though we do attempt to fill the gaps, we also maintain a high standard for selection and are limited by what is available on the Web. Some subject areas—physical education, for example—are not as well suited as others for Web-based instruction. Educators in these subject areas are not as likely to embrace technology, because there are sometimes more appropriate media and methods for their subject area. We expect that as the Web becomes more mainstream, we will be able to fill the gaps without compromising quality standards.

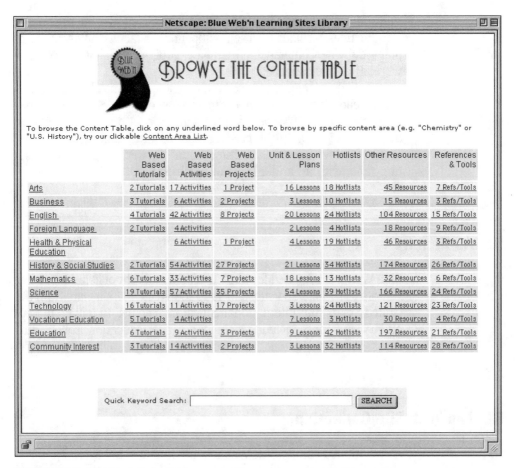

FIGURE 2. Blue Web'n Content Table

7.0 Selection Criteria and Evaluation Process

A movie critic once defended an unpopular movie review by explaining that people who see many movies appreciate different qualities than the average moviegoer. This may apply to Web-site review as well since many of the sites submitted are well done but don't fit our selection criteria.

In general, we're looking for sites that exemplify the best educational use of the Web and that will help teachers find subject area resources. We especially like activities and projects directed at the student, but we also include resources and tools for teachers. Since we want to offer starting points as well as models, we include well-organized, comprehensive hotlists (lists of links). We look for topics that match California curriculum or national standards, and we look for teacher-tested sites.

When a user searches Blue Web'n, the best sites are returned first. We use an evaluation rubric (http://www.kn.pacbell.com/wired/bluewebn/rubric.html) to help us quickly rate sites. Since we're skimming the cream of the crop, our ratings are a bit skewed toward higher scores. Lower quality sites are occasionally chosen if they show promise, fall into underrepresented categories, or were created by classroom teachers or students. We evaluate format and content for all sites and learner process when the site is an activity, project, or lesson plan.

7.1 Format

The first thing we notice about a site is its presentation. We look for sites that are easy to read, quick to load, and well organized. Navigation options should be clear, and the page needs to work with multiple browsers, platforms, and monitor sizes. We prefer simple, clean design and are not often impressed by bleeding-edge features or busy graphics.

7.2 Content

Next, we look at content. Is the information credible? Who created the site? Is the information current, well maintained, and meaningful? Is this a site worth revisiting? Is the focus narrow, or is it interdisciplinary?

7.3 Learning Process

Finally, if the site is a student activity, project, or lesson plan, we examine the learning process. We look for engaging processes that challenge the learner to think, reflect, discuss, hypothesize, compare, or classify. Processes that address multiple intelligences (linguistic, mathematical, interpersonal, spatial, musical, and physical) are also favored.

7.4 Scoring Process

To score an application, each poor rating receives zero points, each good receives one point, and each excellent receives two points in ten different categories for a total of twenty possible points. Resources, references, and tools are not rated on learner process; the score for these site types is adjusted to yield a total possible score of twenty points.

8.0 Production

The core of Blue Web'n is—believe it or not—a HyperCard (http://
www.apple.com/hypercard/) stack. While HyperCard is somewhat
dated, its scripting language is ideal for text processing and it is very
easy to use and program. In our system, one HyperCard stack holds
scoring rubrics for each site, so evaluation is automated. The second
HyperCard stack holds all of the records for the sites and a set of
HyperTalk programs, HyperCard's scripting language, that generate
HTML and text files. Perl CGI programs search the text files for matches.

While this may seem a convoluted way to structure what could
have been managed by a database, the fellows did not have access to
another database when we created Blue Web'n in 1995. Our method
also makes it relatively easy to maintain Blue Web'n, since all of the
necessary files are generated by HyperCard. The main Blue Web'n
page, as previously stated, includes a table that shows numbers of
sites within categories. (See figure 2.) Each week, the table numbers
are tallied and the HTML file created. We also have scripts that help
us notify the Web authors of new entries, scripts that generate the
Weekly Update, and even a script that helps us manage electronic
mailing list e-mail bounces. Although the files are generated on a Macintosh computer, the HTML files and Perl CGI programs are multiplatform, so while we can develop on our Macintosh systems in San
Diego, for production we use a UNIX Web server in San Ramon.

8.1 A Week in the Life of Blue Web'n

Since the Weekly Update electronic mailing list is an important component of Blue Web'n, our two-person team has a weekly maintenance cycle. Throughout the week, we gather, review, and organize
leads for potential Blue Web'n sites. We also review a broken-link report generated by a link-checking program, WebTrends (http://www.
webtrends.com/), on Pacific Bell's server, and revise records as needed.
To identify potential Blue Web'n sites, we skim user submissions,
education-oriented electronic mailing lists, conference presentations,
and print media. From our batch of potential sites, we select about
five, usually near the end of the week. We add the selected sites to
our HyperCard stack for uploading to Blue Web'n. Specifically, we
enter a title, URL, and description of the site as well as the e-mail address of the site contact. Check boxes and pull-down menus make it
easy to categorize sites by grade level, type, and content area. A
HyperTalk script assigns an abbreviated Dewey Decimal Classification number based on the first content subcategory. The Hot Site script
generates the HTML file for the Hot Site Web page. A click of the
Make HTML button generates the necessary HTML and text files,
which are then transferred to the Pacific Bell development server.

Notifying the contact people for added sites is not only an ethical practice, it's also a great way to market Blue Web'n. Contact persons are offered the opportunity to post a Blue Web'n graphical link on their site, a practice that honors their site and helps bring visitors to ours. A HyperTalk script automates this process by gathering e-mail addresses for newly added sites.

Once the sites are added and files transferred, we compose the e-mail message for the Weekly Update electronic mailing list. To do this, we copy from the Weekly Update Web page (generated by the HyperCard stack), paste into a boilerplate e-mail message, and send to the mailing list. San Diego State University hosts our Majordomo mailing list (http://www.greatcircle.com/majordomo/). The Weekly Update mailing list is sent each Friday night, when SDSU network activity is minimal, to avoid bogging down the SDSU network.

8.1.1 Mailing List Maintenance

As you can imagine, maintaining a mailing list with twenty thousand subscribers takes some effort. We not only have to handle all the subscribe and unsubscribe bounces (about seventy per week), but we also have to manage Weekly Update mailing list bounces—about two hundred e-mail addresses per week. Some of this can be automated, but some messages must be managed manually since e-mail bounces do not adhere to a standard format. In the future, we would like to use different mailing list software that automatically manages some of this mail.

8.1.2 Site Review

A longer maintenance cycle ensures the credibility of our offerings. We cycle through all Blue Web'n sites two or three times a year to make sure each site is still there and that the description and evaluation are still appropriate. We note the review date in the HyperCard stack to track and optimize our process.

8.1.3 Revision

An even longer revision process helps us keep our site user friendly and attractive. In 1997, for example, we added a frames interface for browsing subject subcategories (http://www.kn.pacbell.com/wired/bluewebn/fr_Categories.html) and we began archiving weekly Hot Sites and mailing list updates. The Pacific Bell Education Advocates frequently use Blue Web'n in their workshops and provide valuable feedback to the fellows. Their input prompted us to move the search form to a less prominent location since novice users preferred using the content table. (See figure 2.) We occasionally make small revisions as well. We recently noticed, for example, that choosing a link within our frames-based Browse by Subject page kept users within the frames. This prevented the user from seeing the URL and often led to a clunky, awkward presentation of the linked site. We quickly remedied this by changing the target of the hyperlink so that the linked site opens in the top browser window.

9.0 Classification

Different audiences browse differently. Teachers of early grades, for example, are more interested in general topics and grade level. High school teachers prefer to browse by content and subcontent area. Librarians want to search by Dewey number. With Blue Web'n, we built in several browsing options to meet the needs of all these audiences. We also want teachers quickly to find types of Web sites that they can use right away in their classes, so we created our own categorization scheme of types of applications to help differentiate resources, tools, and Web-based curriculum (activities, projects, and tutorials).

9.1 Grade Level

Grade level is important to classroom teachers and the school librarians who support them. We use U.S. grade level ranges (early learning, elementary, middle school, high school, and college) and include a category for working adult learners. When we began Blue Web'n, we lumped early learning, elementary, and middle school sites into one category, but this became inappropriate as our collection grew.

9.2 Subject Area

Blue Web'n sites are categorized by subject (or content) area and subcontent area. General categories include arts, business, English, foreign language, health and physical education, history and social studies, mathematics, science, technology, vocational education, education, and community interest. Subcategories (http://www.kn.pacbell.com/wired/bluewebn/categories.html) are shown with Dewey numbers in parentheses. (See table 1.) While most content areas and subcontent areas are based on California state curriculum frameworks, we also incorporated common topics in community college catalogs. The community interest category is based on topics popular with library patrons.

Users can browse by subject area with frames (http//www.kn.pacbell/com/wired/bluewebn/fr_Categories.html) or without frames (http://www.kn.pacbell.com/wired/bluewebn/categories.html). When the user clicks a subject name, the Perl CGI finds all relevant matches and presents them to the user.

Table 1. Content and Subcontent Areas

Arts (#700)	Business (#650)	English (#800)
• Architecture (#720) • Crafts (#750) • Literature (#800) • Music (#780) • Performing Arts (#790) • Philosophy (#100) • Visual Arts (#750) • General/Other (#700)	• Accounting (#657) • Finance (#657) • Management (#658) • Marketing (#658) • Small Business (#650) • General/Other (#650)	• Journalism (#808) • Literature (#800) • Reading (#028) • Speaking (#808) • Writing (#808) • General/Other (#800)
Foreign Language (#400)	Health & Physical Education (#610)	History & Social Studies (#900)
• American Sign Language (#490) • Classical Languages (#480) • English as a Second Language (#425) • French (#440) • German (#430) • Pacific Rim (#490) • Spanish (#460) • General/Other (#400)	• Development (#158) • Diseases (#614) • Drugs (#613) • Family Living (#640) • Health (#613) • Nutrition (#613) • Physical Education (#613) • Safety (#613) • General/Other (#610)	• Anthropology (#301) • California History (#979) • Current Events (#070) • Economics (#330) • Geography & Cultures (#900) • Government (#320) • Human Rights (#361) • Psychology (#150) • U.S. History (#973) • World History (#909) • General/Other (#900)
Mathematics (#510)	Science (#500)	Technology (#600)
• Algebra (#512) • Calculus (#512) • Geometry (#516) • Logic and Language (#515) • Measurement (#510) • Problem Solving (#511) • Statistics and Probability (#519) • General/Other (#510)	• Astronomy & Space (#520) • Chemistry (#540) • Computer Science (#004) • Earth Science (#550) • Environmental Studies (#570) • Life Science (#570) • Paleontology (#560) • Physics (#530) • General/Other (#500)	• Child Safety (#600) • Connectivity (#600) • E-Mail (#600) • Internet (#600) • Planning (#600) • Policy (#600) • Software (#600) • Web Development (#600) • General/Other (#600)
Vocational Education (#600)	Education (#370)	Community Interest (#000)
• Automotive Technology (#600) • Agriculture (#630) • Careers (#331) • Construction (#690) • Drafting/Design (#600) • Higher Education (#378) • Home Economics (#640) • General/Other (#600)	• Counseling (#370) • Curriculum (#375) • Distance Learning (#370) • Education Alternatives (#370) • Educational Technology (#370) • Grants (#371) • Reform (#371) • Special Education (#370) • School Management (#371) • Teaching and Learning (#370) • General/Other (#370)	• Current Events/News (#070) • Gardening (#635) • Genealogy (#929) • Government/Politics (#320) • Health (#613) • Leisure (#790) • Parenting/Families (#649) • Reference Desk (#027) • Regional Information (#900) • Religion (#200) • General/Other (#000)

9.3 Dewey

Though Dewey numbers were not originally included in our classification scheme, Linda Hyman, our library specialist, strongly encouraged this addition. Linda helped assign abbreviated Dewey numbers to subcontent areas. Once these associations were determined, we set up the HyperCard stack to automatically assign a Dewey number based on the first subcontent area.

9.4 Type

One of our first tasks as fellows was to survey the Internet and find out how other educators were using the Web for education and what types of sites were available. In his online article, "What's on the Web?" (http://www.ozline.com/learning/webtypes.html), Fellow Tom March described our early efforts in great detail.[1] We patterned our types after what teachers use and do in the classroom. In our classification scheme, a site either helps the user create something (tool), provides information (resource, hot list, lesson plan, or reference), or offers a learning experience (tutorial, activity, or project).

The easiest way to understand how we define Blue Web'n types is to review our categories and explore a few examples. Our Brief Definition of Types page (http://www.kn.pacbell.com/wired/bluewebn/apptypes.html) includes a table with links to help explain the types.

9.4.1 Tool

Tools help the user create something original or accomplish a task. Traditional examples include calculators, typewriters, and desktop publishing software. Online tools usually require scripting or programming and are thus more difficult to create than other types of sites. Online examples include Filamentality (http://www.kn.pacbell.com/wired/fil/) and Online Map Creation (http://www.aquarius.geomar.de/omc/).

9.4.2 Resource

The majority of Web sites we include are resources. Resources provide information but are not comprehensive. Online examples include Atlantic Monthly (http://www.theAtlantic.com/), Online NewsHour (http://www.pbs.org/newshour/), and the Whitney Museum in New York (http://www.echonyc.com/~whitney/). In 1997, we broke this category into three different categories to distinguish hotlists and lesson plans from other resources.

9.4.3 Hotlist

A hotlist is a special kind of resource with a list of links to other Web sites. We try to link to at least one credible, well-organized hotlist for each subcontent area. Good examples include Frank Potter's Science Gems (http://www-sci.lib.uci.edu/SEP/SEP.html) and American Studies Web (http://www.georgetown.edu/crossroads/asw/).

9.4.4 Lesson Plan

The Web also offers unit or lesson plan resources for teachers. These usually include learning goals or objectives along with ideas for classroom activities. Examples include Newton's Apple Lessons (http://ericir.syr.edu/Projects/Newton/) and ArtsEdge Subject Area Resources (http://artsedge.kennedy-center.org/db/cr/icr/cover.html).

9.4.5 Reference

Like resources, references also provide information. The difference is that a reference attempts to be comprehensive and usually includes searchable nodes of consistent format and content. Traditional examples include dictionaries, encyclopedias, and almanacs. Online exemplars include Merriam-Webster's WWWebster Dictionary (http://www.m-w.com/dictionary/), WebElements (http://www.shef.ac.uk/~chem/web-elements/), and Peterson Education Center (http://www.petersons.com/).

9.4.6 Online Tutorial/Lesson

Tutorials provide an active, online learning experience with highly focused goals and outcomes. Tutorials are usually created for a specific grade level and topic. Unlike lesson plans, tutorials are directed at the student. Traditionally, this kind of guided instruction is led by a teacher, prompted by a book, or mediated by a computer program. Online exemplars include Writing HTML (http://www.mcli.dist.maricopa.edu/tut/), Art Exploration (http://www.artsednet.getty.edu/ArtsEdNet/Resources/Sampler/f.html), and The Shiki Internet Haiku Salon (http://mikan.cc.matsuyama-u.ac.jp/~shiki/).

9.4.7 Activity

An online activity also provides a learning experience, but goals and outcomes are broad rather than focused. An activity usually takes a few days. Traditional examples of activities include labs, worksheets, writing assignments, or group collaborations. Online exemplars include a Black History Treasure Hunt (http://www.kn.pacbell.com/wired/BHM/bh_hunt_quiz.html), Six Paths to China: A Series of Web-based Activities (http://www.kn.pacbell.com/wired/China), CNN Interactive Learning Resources (http://www.cnnsf.com/education/education.html), and Ocean Colors (http://athena.wednet.edu/curric/oceans/ocolor/). Activities comprise the heart of classroom learning, and we include as many as possible in our collection.

9.4.8 Project

As with an online activity, goals and outcomes for a project are broad. However, the time frame for a project is longer term, lasting weeks or even months. In a project, students are engaged in a wide variety of activities, usually collaborative, and often culminating in a product, presentation, or event. Traditional examples include science fair projects and long-term group simulations. We like to select sites that effectively integrate use of the Web. Online exemplars include the ThinkQuest Contest (http://www.thinkquest.org/), the JASON Project (http://www.jasonproject.org/), and Nonprofit Prophets (http://www.kn.pacbell.com/wired/prophets/).

9.5 Using Resources in the Classroom

Resources are more abundant than Web-based activities and projects, but teachers don't usually send students to resources without an objective and some scaffolding to orient and guide learning. To help teachers turn resources into online activities, we created Filamentality (http://www.kn.pacbell.com/wired/fil/), a tool that prompts users for Web-site details and orienting information and then uses that information to build a Web page. The Web pages are automatically published on Pacific Bell's server, so even novices can author instructional Web pages with minimal effort.

10.0 Strengths and Weaknesses of Blue Web'n

10.1 Project's Strengths

10.1.1 Weekly Update Electronic Mailing List

The Weekly Update mailing list is very popular with educators. Teachers appreciate the manageable number of sites—about five each week—and the quality of the sites listed. They like having the new sites delivered to their e-mail boxes in a clear format that they can easily forward or file.

10.1.2 Credibility

The fellows and staff who select the Blue Web'n sites have experience in classroom and library settings. Blue Web'n has been in place for over three years and keeps improving. Blue Web'n sites are high quality and are periodically reviewed for accuracy.

10.1.3 Organization

The Blue Web'n site offers multiple ways to browse and search the collection. The content table (figure 2) is especially unique, offering a way to survey the classification and depth of the collection before browsing.

10.2 Project's Weaknesses

10.2.1 Search CGI

Unlike most search engines, Blue Web'n uses an *and* operator by default for the Perl CGI search. This means that all search terms must reside in the record to yield a match. This is a feature we'd like to change to reflect the major search engines' more typical use of the *or* operator. Our simple CGI program has no advanced features and only displays the first batch of matches.

10.2.2 Small Staff

Blue Web'n is just one of many projects maintained by the fellows. With two people selecting and reviewing sites in just twenty hours per week, it's difficult to keep current and cover all subject areas.

11.0 Time Frames and Future Goals

Blue Web'n began as a simple prototype in 1995 and has been refined over the three years of the Pacific Bell Education First Initiative. Though the Education First Fellowships have been renewed each year since 1995 and will be funded in 1999, the future of Blue Web'n depends on the vision and goals of Pacific Bell.

In the future, we plan to continue to update and refine the Blue Web'n collection and interface. We are considering adding grade-level options to the content table (figure 2), a feature that would make the table more useful. Some changes to the Blue Web'n infrastructure are planned, but these will be transparent to the user. We hope to upgrade our server, for example, and move the Weekly Update mailing list from SDSU to Pacific Bell.

The full Education First team is currently developing a vision for 1999 and may adjust Blue Web'n staffing to improve coverage of underrepresented categories.

12.0 Educational Resource Location in the Future

Teachers have always used a range of resources within their curriculum. Not only have teachers relied on textbooks, an efficient source of appropriate information, they have also augmented instruction with fiction, magazine articles, reference materials, computer software, and outside experts or guest speakers. Typically, teachers "repurpose" or customize resources by scaffolding them with orientation and embedding them within learning activities, a practice that helps students learn with more depth and retention. In recent years, a philosophical shift toward constructivist learning, or social environmental learning, and the easy accessibility of resources on the Web have contributed to a more student-centered, project-based approach in classroom instruction, especially at the elementary and middle school level. This shift to a collaborative mode and the Web's role in it are eloquently described by Bernie Dodge, professor at San Diego State University's College of Education and our faculty advisor for the past three years. See the electronic version of his paper, "Active Learning on the Web" (http://edweb.sdsu.edu/people/bdodge/active/ActiveLearningk-12. html) and The WebQuest Page (http://edweb.sdsu.edu/webquest/ webquest.html) for elaboration.[2]

Teachers have traditionally found education resources by word of mouth, advertising, browsing, focused research, and recommendations by respected reviewers. Now teachers have more ways to find more resources. They use electronic mailing lists, news groups, online forums, chat groups, Web directories, and search engines to locate appropriate resources for their classroom and to support their professional growth.

The most quickly evolving of these resources is search engines. For example, teachers can now use a search engine to quickly list hundreds of Web sites about frog deformity. However, of these many Web sites, which are appropriate for students and complement curriculum? Which are credible and reliable? This simple example illustrates the main challenges that arise when using search engines to find education resources on the Web.

- The number of Web sites is huge, growing, and in constant flux. No one search engine includes all sites, and keeping up with their changes is a challenge.
- The quality, credibility, level of interactivity, and intended audience (reading level, age, gender, etc.) vary greatly among sites. This is especially problematic for children, who may lack the experience, perspective, and skills necessary to evaluate the credibility of a site. Though a few search engines filter for child-friendly content, most do not, nor do they differentiate sites by quality or credibility.
- Effective searching strategies must be learned, and yet are still evolving and vary among search engines. Many people never bother to read help pages.
- Teachers have limited time for finding resources.
- Search engines sometimes display results and banner ads that are inappropriate for children.

- Many Web developers use metatags to help describe the content and key search terms for their site. Unfortunately, Web developers "spam" these tags to help their site appear at the top of search result lists, so many search engines ignore them.

The good news about search engines is that they are improving and standardizing (http://www.infotoday.com/searcher/jun/story2. htm).[3] Most now use an *or* operator by default and use + and – characters to refine searches, so many search strategies transfer among search engines. Most include a hierarchical directory for browsing, with sites classified and sometimes even evaluated by humans. Some support natural language queries and concept searching.

Many great minds are working on ways to improve search results as well. A 1997 Search Engine Report article (http://www. searchenginewatch.com/sereport/9712-metatags.html) describes emerging standards and the barriers to their implementation.[4] Basically, a successful method will need to be spam-proof, agreeable to major browser developers, and used by search engines. It would help teachers if a neutral party assigned metatags and used a controlled vocabulary or numbering system to describe subject area, intended audience, reading level, language, and learning goals (if appropriate). Teachers would probably also appreciate a push technology, agent, or subscription service that sends appropriate pointers that can be defined by users. This way, a teacher could request announcements of Web sites relevant to introductory algebra or mathematics teaching strategies.

With all this in mind, how will teachers find education resources in the future? Here are a few predictions:

- Computers will get faster, bandwidth will increase, resource quality will improve, and search engine improvements will follow. Unanticipated innovations will emerge as a result.

- Educators and librarians will use a wide variety of strategies for finding resources, just as they do now. Special-interest directories and review subscription services will continue to play an important role in resource location, as will word of mouth (e-mail, electronic mailing lists, news groups, and networking), informal browsing, advertising, and focused research using search engines.

- Special-interest directories will evolve, many narrowing their focus. Those that collaborate, innovate, organize, advertise, and evaluate will be most likely to survive.

In designing systems to support resource location, it's important to keep both users and stakeholders in mind, to innovate as technology evolves, and to collaborate when feasible.

Notes

1. Tom March, "What's on the Web?" Computer-Using Educators Newsletter (July/August 1995). (http://www.ozline.com/learning/webtypes.html)

2. Bernie Dodge, "Active Learning on the Web," paper presented to the Faculty of La Jolla Country Day School on August 20, 1996. (http://edweb.sdsu.edu/people/bdodge/active/ActiveLearningk-12.html)

3. Susan Feldman, "Web Search Services in 1998: Trends and Challenges," *Searcher* 6, no. 6 (1998): 29–41. (http://www.infotoday.com/searcher/jun/story2.htm)

4. Danny Sullivan, "The New Meta Tags Are Coming—or Are They?" Search Engine Report (Dec. 1997). (http://www.searchenginewatch.com/sereport/9712-metatags.html)

4

BUBL Information Service (BUBL)

Dennis Nicholson
Alan Dawson

The BUBL Information Service (http://bubl.ac.uk/ or connect to link.bubl.ac.uk port 210 and database name ZPub) offers two major services for the U.K. higher education community: a directory of selected Internet resources covering all subjects of academic relevance (the BUBL LINK service), and the tables of contents, abstracts, or full text of hundreds of academic journals and magazines (the BUBL Journals service). Other services offered include an extensive directory of U.K. institutions (BUBL UK) and a specialist LIS service covering events, jobs, surveys, and mailing lists (BUBL News). This chapter gives details of the history, mission, funding, usage, collections, organization, policies, procedures, and future goals of the BUBL service, plus a summary of related projects that are investigating the use of LIS tools, standards, and expertise as aids to organizing the Internet. These projects include BUBL 5:15 (browseable access to key resources in over twelve hundred predefined subjects), CATRIONA 1 (Z39.50-based distributed catalogs of Internet resources), CATRIONA II (university management of locally created electronic resources), and CAIRNS (Z39.50-based integrated searching of dynamically generated clumps of catalogs enhanced through Conspectus-based collection descriptions).

1.0 An Introduction to BUBL

BUBL (http://bubl.ac.uk/ or connect to link.bubl.ac.uk port 210 and database name ZPub) is an Internet-based information service for the U.K. higher education community. When it was first established in

1990, BUBL was aimed only at library and information science professionals, and the name stood for *BU*lletin *B*oard for *L*ibraries. Since 1993, however, it has provided a service for the wider academic and research community, largely through the BUBL Subject Tree, and so the name changed to the BUBL Information Service, or BUBL for short. (See figure 1.) BUBL has long since outgrown its initial acronym, although a specialist service to the LIS community continues to be a significant function. BUBL is now run from the Andersonian Library of the University of Strathclyde, Glasgow, Scotland (http://www.lib.strath.ac.uk/).

1.1 Background History

BUBL began life as part of Project Jupiter, which was based at Glasgow University and aimed to train librarians in the use of JANET (http://www.ja.net/), the U.K. Joint Academic NETwork. When Project Jupiter funding ended in May 1991, a group of librarians from the Universities of Strathclyde and Glasgow, coordinated by Dennis Nicholson, saved BUBL from extinction by their voluntary efforts.

The service continued on this voluntary basis until early 1994, growing in popularity and attracting small amounts of sponsorship

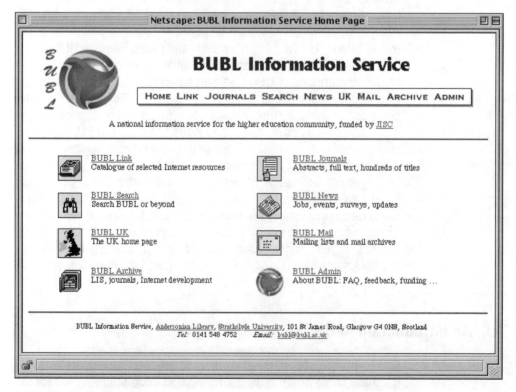

FIGURE 1.   BUBL Home Page

from commercial and professional organizations. In January 1994, one year's funding for the maintenance and development of BUBL was received from the Joint Information Systems Committee (JISC) (http://www.jisc.ac.uk/), which itself receives government funding via the U.K. higher education funding councils. This was followed by a further year's funding before JISC agreed that BUBL should be funded as a full U.K. national information service from August 1996, with funding pledged on a three-year cycle but allocated annually. At the time of this writing, BUBL funding was guaranteed until July 1999, with its future path beyond that date uncertain as JISC examines how best to develop services like BUBL LINK and related projects like EEVL (http://www.eevl.ac.uk/) (see chapter 5) and OMNI (http://omni.ac.uk/) (see chapter 10).

Between July 1991 and August 1993, BUBL was run over a JANET link between the Universities of Strathclyde and Glasgow, before being moved to Bath University in September 1993. This move brought an upgrade from USERBUL software on a VMS system to Gopher and World Wide Web server software, which allowed the service to expand significantly. From September 1993 until March 1997, the BUBL service was run over a link between Strathclyde and Bath Universities.

BUBL was the first national U.K. service to offer its users subject-based access to the Internet through the BUBL subject-tree initiative, which began in 1993 and arranged resources together by subject area. The original Gopher-based subject tree was soon supplemented by a Web-based one. However, discussions over the limitations of the subject-tree approach led to the creation of the BUBL LINK service, accessible via Z39.50 as well as the Web and searchable in the style of a library OPAC.

The decision to move BUBL from Bath to Strathclyde and the diminishing use of Gopher precipitated the decision to relaunch the service. The new BUBL service, based entirely at Strathclyde University, began on March 23, 1997. The Gopher and Web subject trees were incorporated into the BUBL LINK service, with the remaining parts of BUBL revamped and the BUBL UK service introduced.

2.0 BUBL People

A great many people have contributed to BUBL over the years, mainly as volunteers in the early days, but more recently as paid staff. At the time of this writing (July 1998), the service had two full-time staff, three part-time staff, and two vacant posts.

Dennis Nicholson has coordinated the BUBL service since May 1991 and since 1996 has had the title of BUBL director. He is head of the systems division at Strathclyde University Library, and he directs or codirects the CATRIONA and CAIRNS projects (described later). Alan Dawson is BUBL manager responsible for day-to-day running of the service. Alan joined BUBL in October 1996 and set up the new BUBL service at Strathclyde University. Andrew Williamson is information assistant with particular responsibility for the BUBL journals and BUBL news services.

Many others too numerous to mention have contributed to BUBL over the years, particularly Fiona Wilson, Joanne Gold, and Jan Simpson, who each worked for over a year as BUBL information officer.

3.0 BUBL Mission

The BUBL mission statement, approved by the BUBL steering group in May 1996, is "to provide value-added access to Internet resources and services of academic, research, and professional significance to the U.K. Higher Education community by

- direct service provision, incorporating subject-based, classified, and other organizational routes;
- creating and stimulating the creation of original electronic resources;
- mounting appropriate commercial services;
- providing organized access to other services;
- encouraging and coordinating the efforts of information specialists;
- providing associated reference, help, current awareness, and training services."[1]

To help meet these objectives, BUBL aims to offer fast, easy-to-use, and reliable access to selected high-quality resources of academic relevance, both on its own servers and worldwide.

4.0 BUBL Funding

BUBL is funded almost entirely by JISC, and currently costs £109,000 a year to run (or about $170,000). BUBL has not found it cost-effective to spend limited staff time and effort seeking commercial sponsorship, but it has received significant support from other sources, including the donation of NetPublisher (http://www.als.ameritech.com/) software from the Ameritech Corporation, educational discounts on hardware and software, free journal subscriptions (notably from

Haworth Press), and institutional support from Strathclyde University such as office space, networking connections, and access to LIS journals.

5.0 BUBL Users and Usage

When BUBL was first established, its specific aim was to function as a bulletin board on JANET for the academic library community, but the approach was soon broadened to cover the U.K. higher education community more generally, though a specialist library and information science service is still provided.

Although aimed at U.K. users, BUBL provides an international service. During 1997–98, accesses to BUBL were recorded from 141 different countries (based on Internet host names). After the United Kingdom and the United States, the heaviest usage was from Australia, Canada, Germany, Spain, Denmark, Sweden, Ireland, Italy, France, and the Netherlands, in that order. This reflects the predominance of the English language in all areas of the BUBL service.

Total accesses to BUBL during the year 1997–98 were just over six million, more than double the figure for 1996–97. This compares with an estimated three thousand per year in 1991–92.

6.0 BUBL Collections

6.1 BUBL LINK

BUBL LINK (LIbraries of Networked Knowledge) is a catalog of Internet resources of academic relevance. It holds details of around eight thousand Internet resources and services and covers all main subject areas. Resource descriptions are searchable via Z39.50 as well as the Web, and the collection can be browsed by broad subject area, by keyword, or by Dewey Decimal Classification (DDC) (http://www.oclc.org/oclc/man/9353pg/9353toc.htm). Details of how BUBL LINK operates are given below.

6.2 BUBL Journals

The BUBL journals service offers tables of contents and abstracts (where available) of around two hundred fifty current journals and other periodicals, with full text available for sixteen titles. The service acts as a current awareness tool for the library and information science (LIS) community in particular, since over 60 percent of titles relate to LIS. Other subject areas covered are agriculture, business, social work, and health. Holdings of many titles date back to around 1992 or 1993, and by mid-1998, there were over sixty-five hundred individual issues available. The content of each journal can be searched individually, and the complete collection can be searched as a whole or by broad subject area.

6.3 BUBL UK

This is an extensive directory of U.K. organizations and institutions. It has a relatively simple structure but a large number of entries, currently organized under the following headings: Regional and Local Government, Political Parties, Banks and Building Societies, Charities, Companies, Newspapers, Television and Radio, U.K. Web Directories, National Information Services, Universities and Colleges, Schools, Churches, Hospitals, Libraries, Museums, Police, and Sports Authorities. It is popular as a simple and well-maintained reference service.

Some directories, for example, government and political parties, are maintained and updated by BUBL, whereas others are simply pointers to resources held elsewhere. Most users do not care where a set of links is held, and there is significant value in maintaining a central repository of resource links. Regular link checking ensures that resource links are kept up-to-date and this is supplemented by periodical searching and checking for new institutional pages. The directory of names of all U.K. Internet sites (http://www.hensa.ac.uk/uksites/) is helpful for this purpose.

6.4 BUBL News

BUBL began life as the Bulletin Board for Libraries, and this element of the service is retained in the BUBL News service. This service holds details of job vacancies (mostly United Kingdom or United States), forthcoming conferences and workshops, details of current offers such as surplus journal disposals, and other current news items relevant to the library community.

6.5 BUBL Archive

This provides storage for thousands of old files that are rarely needed but may be of some historical value. The four main sections of the archive are journals, Internet, LIS, and other subjects. The journals archive holds abstracts or full text from over one hundred titles that are no longer held in the main BUBL journals service.

6.6 AcqLink

AcqLink (http://link.bubl.ac.uk/acqlink/), run by Catherine Nicholson, is a welcome addition to the online resources available to all those involved in library acquisitions and collection development. It supplements the well-established AcqWeb (http://www.library.vanderbilt.edu/law/acqs/acqs.html), which although excellent is naturally aimed primarily at U.S. users. Now British and European acquisitions personnel have a comparable resource directly related to their needs.

7.0 Collection Policy

The philosophy underlying BUBL LINK is that for many purposes it is better to have a relatively small and well-maintained collection than a large arbitrary selection. The broad guidelines to use when considering resources to add to BUBL LINK are

- academic relevance,
- U.K. orientation,
- up-to-date and well-maintained information,
- completeness.

Within these guidelines, certain types of resources are usually included, such as

- comprehensive sets of links to university departments or societies in a specific subject;
- sets of links to journals, mailing lists, or companies relevant to a specific subject;
- national or international societies or organizations of academic relevance;
- museums and art galleries with numerous items available online;
- online books and book collections;
- online maps and map collections;
- individual full-text online journals;
- bibliographies;
- online teaching guides or tutorial materials;
- reference data, for example, statistics, facts sheets, dictionaries, and data sets;
- collections of software or links to software for a specific subject area.

In contrast, various resources are usually excluded, such as

- individual university department home pages;
- local societies;
- company home pages;
- personal pages;
- individual mailing lists or news groups;
- individual items of software;
- journals with only contact details and tables of contents;
- events, conferences, press releases, and other transient news items.

Although such items are not normally included for their own sake, they may be included if they contain any of the desirable items, for example, if a company or local society maintains an extensive link collection or publishes a full-text online journal or magazine of wider interest. In such cases, the resource itself, rather than the company or society, is perceived to be of value and would be added to the catalog.

One of the biggest problems in applying such a collection policy to Internet resources is that of *granularity,* or deciding the level of detail to catalog. For example, one must decide whether to include a single catalog record for a learned society, or an individual record for each journal published by that society, or a separate record for every major article in every issue of every journal. In practice, the latter is not feasible with limited resources, but there are nonetheless numerous online articles or papers that may warrant individual cataloging.

7.1 Resource Discovery

BUBL is able to draw on several sources of information for locating Internet resources, such as

- mailing lists that announce new Internet resources, such as newjour (http://gort.ucsd.edu/newjour/) and netinlib (http://www.targetinform.com/netinlib/);
- colleagues and subject specialists, locally and at other institutions;
- individual user's suggestions, sent by e-mail to BUBL (bubl@bubl.ac.uk);
- printed newspapers and magazines;
- other manually compiled indexes;
- other resource discovery services, such as the Scout Report (http://scout.cs.wisc.edu/scout/report/) and the Internet Resources Newsletter (http://www.hw.ac.uk/libWWW/irn/irn.html);
- search engines.

Incoming e-mail provides a regular source of suggestions, but these usually quote only a URL and title. All resources need to be checked and cataloged before they can be added to BUBL LINK. The above sources provide a useful but somewhat eclectic set of new resources. When time permits, we take a more coherent approach to a particular subject area by carrying out subject-specific searches and following up manually compiled subject-specific indexes. This is time consuming, but it is the type of activity that users would need to undertake for themselves in the absence of a service such as BUBL LINK. Time spent by BUBL staff can mean time saved by others. The more difficult it is to locate information, the more worthwhile the task.

7.2 Resource Evaluation

Finding Internet resources usually takes less time and effort than the evaluation and classification of them. At some point, BUBL staff need to make a judgment about whether an item is suitable for inclusion in the service. Even though a resource may appear to fall within the BUBL LINK collection policy, there are several reasons why it may fail to reach the quality threshold required for inclusion. In fact, BUBL keeps a list of rejected links, so in theory they may be checked at a later date, but in practice this rarely happens as there are always other new resources awaiting evaluation. Examples of reasons for rejection include

- minimal or incomprehensible content;
- coverage restricted to one part of the United States;
- no academic content;
- much better resources on same topic are available elsewhere online;
- site under construction;
- subscription service only;
- poor layout, with several spelling errors;
- endless advertisements and information about browser options;
- author information unspecified or dubious.

Although this does not mean that all such items are of no value to anyone, they do not warrant cataloging and inclusion in a selective resource collection such as BUBL LINK.

However, evaluation criteria are not constant. Some subjects are so well covered on the Internet that a new set of general links is of no great value. If the catalog already holds details of ten sets of general business and economics links, then there is little value in adding an eleventh. However, a set of links of similar quality for a less common subject, such as radio astronomy or physiotherapy, would have a higher relative value. On the other hand, full-text online books, tutorials, or reference data of academic relevance are almost always included, whatever the subject matter.

8.0 BUBL Operations

8.1 Hardware and Software

Most BUBL pages are stored on a Viglen XX server running Windows NT 4 (http://www.microsoft.com/ntserver/) and Netscape Enterprise Web server (http://merchant.netscape.com/netstore/servers/enterprise. html). Search facilities are provided by the Verity search engine, which is distributed with the Enterprise server. The service aims to be available to users twenty-four hours per day throughout the year, although some service breaks inevitably occur. In practice, over the course of the year, the BUBL service is available over 99 percent of the time.

BUBL LINK runs on a separate Viglen Genie 2 Plus server, running Windows NT 4 and Ameritech NetPublisher software, which acts as both an HTTP and Z39.50 server. A third Viglen Genie server acts as backup for the two main servers: all BUBL content is replicated there, and it may be brought into operation on short notice in case of failure of one of the other servers.

The rest of this section focuses on operation of the BUBL LINK service.

8.2 Database Software

For any large collection of links, there are several advantages in using database software to generate menus, rather than manually editing and maintaining numerous HTML pages. Two obvious benefits are the use of templates and the provision of search facilities.

Templates allow a consistent appearance to be given to a large number of Web pages, which can be dynamically generated by the database software. This obviates the need to design and create numerous individual pages, it allows the inclusion of a standard header or footer on every page, and it allows any changes to be made only once while appearing throughout the service.

The software used for BUBL LINK, Ameritech NetPublisher, has flexible template options that allow different subsets of information to have a distinct design. This preserves consistency, yet allows for variety where required (e.g., in the AcqLink service). Most other Web database publishing software offers similar features.

The structure offered by database software allows field-specific searching, as in a traditional library catalog. This is only effective if the content is similarly complete, for example, if the author, abstract, and subject keywords are recorded in the database along with the title. This structure enables users to find, for example, documents written by Einstein, as opposed to those written by others about him, or those that happen to mention him, or pages written by people living on Einstein Avenue. Large-scale Internet search engines can be very effective for many purposes, but they are rarely able to make the distinction between different occurrences and meanings of a specific word.

8.3 Database Design and Operation

The BUBL LINK database aims to offer users far more than a mere collection of links, yet remain relatively simple in structure so that rapid data entry and updating is feasible. The database holds ten fields for every record in the catalog.

Item name:
: The title of the resource. This is not always obvious, as there may be one heading in the title bar and a different title on the Web page itself. Sometimes acronyms need expanding or further context needs adding to make the title more meaningful.

URL:
: Most items are Web pages, but Gopher, FTP, and Telnet resources may be included if still relevant and up-to-date.

Item abstract:
: This is written or edited by the BUBL cataloger and is intended to be concise, accurate, and meaningful. If extracted directly from the resource, it usually requires editing to remove value judgments and excess verbiage.

Author:
: May be an individual or an institution or both. Unattributed resources are occasionally good enough to be included, but most high-quality resources have a clear author or owner.

Author type:
: Classifies the author into a predefined category, for example, person, society, company, university, government, and so forth.

Subjects:
: One or more of around twelve hundred subject terms, described below. The intelligent completion of this field enables effective operation of the BUBL 5:15 service (http://bubl.ac.uk/link/five/). Selected major resources may be allocated numerous subject terms.

Dewey class: The Dewey Decimal Classification number (edition 21). Items are filed in menus based on this number, but cataloging need not be as detailed as that required for physical book shelving.

Resource type: One or more of around twenty-five predefined categories, such as bibliography, biography, book, dictionary, document, forum, guide, image collection, index, journal, mailing list, news, reference data, or software. This enables retrieval of specific types of resources, as opposed to those on a specific subject.

Location: The physical location of the server that holds the resource. Around 50 percent of resources in BUBL LINK are located in the United Kingdom or elsewhere in Europe, though some of these are mirror sites.

Date: The date an item was added to BUBL LINK or was last checked or updated. The main value of this field is to enable BUBL staff to review all items that are twelve months old. This field is also used to generate a list of recent additions that is published on BUBL twice each month (http://bubl.ac.uk/news/updates/) and also distributed to the lis-link and lis-subjects mailing lists (http://bubl.ac.uk/mail/) so that BUBL is able to provide an Internet resource current awareness service.

8.4 Update Procedure

To maximize flexibility and resource quality, additions to the BUBL LINK database are made in batches on a daily or weekly basis. Most resource descriptions are compiled using Microsoft Word as a powerful plain text editor, though Windows Notepad or Wordpad could be used. This means that anyone can compile a cataloging record, using a simple template format, and send it to BUBL via e-mail. For example:

<name>Beginner's Guide to Organic Synthesis

A guide to organic synthesis, including chapters on Grignard reactions, enolates, the Wittig reaction, linear synthesis, and convergent synthesis.

<author>Otto Meth-Cohn, Sunderland University

<authortype>person

<subjects>organic chemistry

<deweyclass>547

<resourcetype>guide

<location>uk

<url>http://orac.sunderland.ac.uk/~hs0bcl/org2.htm

Once a set of resource descriptions has been compiled, the spelling and subject terms are checked carefully, and they are translated in bulk to an import format understood by the NetPublisher software. This translation is carried out by a fairly simple Word Basic program specially written for the task. Addition to the database is then simply a question of filing items in the appropriate menus according to the DDC number. Once the database has been saved and reloaded, new items are automatically available to users. Web-page design and the display of search results is handled automatically by the database, so no HTML editing is required beyond initial template design.

8.5 Link Checking and Record Maintenance

Many regular Internet users find the most frustrating aspect of information gathering is the broken link problem. All large directories and search engines suffer from this. In the time lag between items being added to their database and users searching it, the Internet changes. Files are deleted, file names changed, sites are reorganized, people change jobs, software is updated, and new policies are introduced. The net result is a proliferation of broken links.

Tackling the broken link problem is not trivial. Software can help, but needs supplementing with manual labor. The policy with the BUBL LINK catalog is to run link-checking software at least once per month and to manually check each link at least once per year. This all takes time and effort, but the big benefit for users is the guarantee of less than 1 percent of links broken at any time (usually less than 0.5%). Even checking links with software takes time. The excellent Linkbot program (http://www.tetranet.com/products/linkbot-main. htm) is able to check eight thousand links in less than an hour, but the follow-up takes much longer. There are numerous possible reasons for a link to be broken at any given time, so resources cannot be deleted automatically; you can't knock down a house just because no one answers the doorbell. Further investigation is required, since sometimes a redirection is provided and the URL can easily be updated; sometimes more detective work is required; sometimes the title or author has changed; or sometimes deletion is warranted.

Internet information is volatile by nature, and any resource directory needs a strategy for dealing with this. In practice link checking is so time-consuming that at BUBL the effort is concentrated on following up "file not found" errors (error code 404) and permanent redirections. Link failures due to time-out or host-name errors are usually temporary and only require action if failure persists for two or three months.

9.0 Taxonomy

Database software provides searching facilities and ensures that a resource directory is far more than just a collection of links. But users want to be able to browse too, which means the directory requires some clear, browseable structure. The database software may or may not make such structure easy to provide, but it still requires some manual filing, just as in a physical library. BUBL LINK uses the well-established DDC number to provide a browseable structure, with a series of hierarchical menus based on DDC class numbers. As most users are not particularly familiar with DDC, this is supplemented by a simple subject keyword index so that it is easy to find the relevant menu without knowing its location in the hierarchy.

9.1 Subject Classification

Apart from broken links, perhaps the biggest problem faced by Internet researchers is that of terminology. Language is ambiguous, imprecise, context dependent, culturally dependent, and full of synonyms and subtlety. This richness has made it very difficult to develop software that understands natural language, and it also poses problems for Internet search software that relies mainly on simple word matching. Anyone searching for information on the Latin language will find thousands of resources about Latin America. This problem can be partially solved by specifying more complex searches, such as "Latin NOT America," but most users fail to do this, and in any case there are more fundamental problems. Many topics and concepts are not easily captured by a single word or phrase, especially in the social sciences or library and information science. Terminology is a big problem for any automated search system.

The approach that has evolved for dealing with this problem at BUBL has been to develop and apply a large but controlled set of subject keywords to supplement the resource abstracts. Originally we used an existing standard, Library of Congress Subject Headings (LCSH), but this had to be modified significantly to make it appropriate for Internet use. In some areas it proved far too detailed, in others not detailed enough. Currently, BUBL uses a set of around twelve hundred subject terms to describe Internet resources. As these terms are applied by BUBL staff after consideration of the content, users are able to retrieve only items that are *about the specified topic,* as opposed to items that *happen to mention it.* This important distinction is very difficult to achieve with a software-based system, though of course software is able to handle a larger number of resources. The benefits of this approach are visible to users via the BUBL 5:15 service.

9.2 BUBL 5:15

BUBL 5:15 offers a new and unusual approach to Internet resource discovery, yet it is basically a new interface to the BUBL LINK service. The reason for the name is that users are guaranteed at least five relevant matches for any subject, and in most cases will get no more than fifteen (the upper limit is not rigidly applied, and a few subjects may produce up to thirty-five hits). BUBL 5:15 is not intended as a substitute for Internet searching, but as a fast, simple, and reliable alternative method for finding information on around twelve hundred different predefined subjects via a point-and-click interface. (See figure 2.)

The twelve hundred subject terms are divided into the nine top-level headings identified by JISC (BUBL's funding body): creative

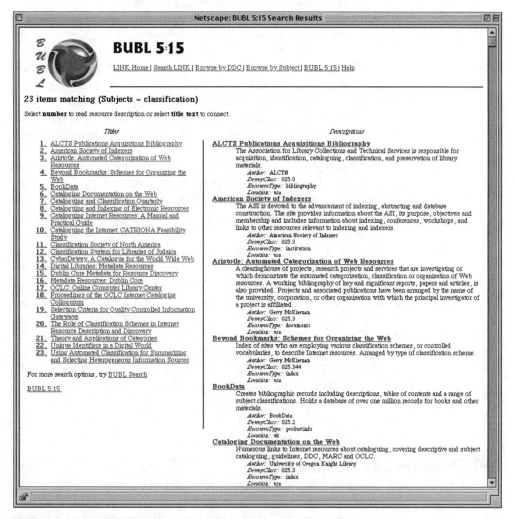

FIGURE 2.   BUBL 5:15: Classification Search Results

Arts; Engineering and Technology; Health Studies; Humanities; Language, Literature and Culture; Life Sciences; Mathematics and Computing; Physical Sciences; and Social Sciences. BUBL has added two further main headings: library and information science (BUBL's main subject specialization) and area studies (resources about all 193 independent countries), as well as a full A–Z list of all subjects. Some subject terms are allocated to more than one category.

The use of a tightly controlled vocabulary for BUBL 5:15 is highly significant as it removes the difficulties and uncertainties of searching. Users do not need to know or guess the precise term to type as all subject terms are visible on screen via a set of twelve pull-down menus. In this respect, the philosophy of BUBL 5:15 is similar to the techniques of faceted classification and view-based searching, which are currently being studied for application to large resources such as a library catalog and the EMBASE biomedical reference database (http://www.hud.ac.uk/schools/cedar/hibrowse.html).

BUBL 5:15 is particularly useful for library staff, information professionals, and Internet trainers who need to cover a wide range of subjects, as well as to students and infrequent Internet users. Librarians have found BUBL 5:15 valuable when dealing with face-to-face user inquiries as it guarantees that they will find relevant resources for a large number of subjects, removing the uncertainty of general Internet searching and the frustration of finding broken links.

The controlled approach offered by BUBL 5:15 also allows users to be directed toward important resources relevant to a specific topic, a traditional activity for librarians. It also makes resource discovery easier for users themselves by providing a more helpful interface than a search box.

BUBL 5:15 has been described as a browse engine (http://www.ilrt.bris.ac.uk/roads/news/issue6/bubl/), but the underlying implementation is by database searching. Whenever a user selects a subject term from one of the twelve menus, this term is sent to the BUBL LINK database as a request to search the *subjects* field only for that term. The effectiveness of the service is therefore dependent on the subject classification carried out by BUBL staff. Display of results is handled by a specially designed database template, which uses HTML tables to display both the list of titles and resource descriptions on the same page.

10.0 Strengths and Weaknesses

The main strengths of BUBL are the quality and breadth of its services, as described above, and its links with the library and information science community. For example, BUBL runs lis-link, the U.K.'s major library and information science mailing list, which carries discussion and information on all aspects of library operation. It is also used by BUBL to send out news relating to the service, notably the weekly BUBL Updates and the fortnightly BUBL LINK Updates. Details of lis-link and other mailing lists managed by BUBL are available via the BUBL mail service (http://bubl.ac.uk/mail/).

Other strengths of BUBL include its

- use of well-established standards, such as Z39.50, DDC, and LCSH;
- popularity and links from thousands of pages worldwide;
- daily updates;
- good record maintenance and updating, with regular link checking;
- extensive quantity of data, especially with BUBL journals;
- professional approach, for example, in cataloging and HTML usage;
- involvement in R&D, for example, CATRIONA II and Research Collections Online (RCO) projects;
- support from host institution (Strathclyde University).

BUBL has been highly praised for its extensive and timely publication of meaningful usage statistics, which include details of the most popular services, files, and journals, as well as a monthly summary of accesses. These figures are published online each month in the BUBL Admin pages (http://bubl.ac.uk/admin/usage/).

There were over six million accesses to the BUBL Web service in 1997–98 (6,070,917), an increase of over 120 percent from 1996–97. BUBL regularly features in the "Top 50 UK Web Sites" (http://www.top50.co.uk/). Over twelve thousand separate pages on the BUBL service were accessed during August 1997–July 1998, with BUBL Journals and BUBL LINK being by far the most popular areas.

Around 60 percent of accesses to BUBL can be attributed to a specific country, based on the ISO country code in the domain name of the system making the connection. Accesses were recorded from 149 different countries in 1997–98. The top six were the United Kingdom, the United States, Australia, Canada, Germany, and France.

Another method of determining our success is from our users.

> My experience since you launched BUBL 5:15 has continued to be positive, and I regularly introduce it to students and colleagues as a quick and easy way to find a selection of quality resources. (Alison McNab, Loughborough University)

> I'm impressed with the depth of such fine areas of your information service, such as drama, palaeontology, and oceanography. These confirm not only the comprehensiveness that is BUBL but also its determination to service all areas of knowledge with equitable attention. The effort and energy invested in BUBL is readily

apparent and appreciable. I'm sparse with accolades but will readily recognize excellence wherever it arises. Keep up the great work.
(Robert J. Tiess, The New Athenaeum)

The main weakness of BUBL is perhaps its vulnerability to staff
turnover, an inevitable consequence of short-term funding. This also
makes innovation difficult in certain areas, for example, in providing
additional value-added services such as mirrors or subject-specific
search services. BUBL sometimes suffers from being a small organization in a fast-moving, ever-changing environment.

11.0 Future Goals of the BUBL Service

BUBL's funding body, JISC, is currently considering how best to organize and fund subject-based information gateways over the next
few years, so the future of BUBL and of projects such as EEVL and
OMNI (see chapters 5 and 10) will develop in this context. Discussions to date have been based on the idea of a federation of information gateways integrated at some level to provide a single service to
users. The question of whether this will offer a common user interface, subject-specific interfaces, or both, is one of the threads of the
discussions. BUBL has been invited to contribute to these discussions
and has suggested a number of possible roles in any such federation
of information gateways, including

- special responsibility for developing a common user interface and
  for offering cross-gateway search facilities based on Z39.50;
- a reference service role providing subject-based access to key
  resources across all subjects (possibly by developing the BUBL
  5:15 methodology);
- specialized subject gateway services in LIS, computing, and
  physical science.

In the meantime, with the shape of future developments in this
area still unclear, BUBL's strategy is to build on existing strengths
and to focus effort on areas of the service most likely to be of future
value. In summary, BUBL is aiming to

- continue to provide a general service for the higher education
  community and a specialist service for the library and information science community;
- continue to cover all main subject areas in BUBL LINK, but concentrate in more depth on those subject areas not currently well
  covered by other JISC-funded services or projects;

- continue to concentrate on providing fast, simple, and easy-to-use services that do not require user registration or payment;
- seek to collaborate with other JISC services with a view to offering a more integrated catalog of Internet resources based on a number of distributed services, with access via the Web and Z39.50.

This strategy is designed to keep options open during a period of uncertainty while continuing to strengthen and develop the various services valued by users. At the same time, the service aims to develop knowledge and experience in the application of LIS skills, tools, and standards to organizing access for Internet resources, and to contribute to discussion and discovery in these areas by being involved in research and development initiatives of the kinds described below.

12.0 Associated Projects and Future Developments

Because of its history, BUBL's position on Internet resource location and description has, over the years, tended to be heavily influenced by the library and information science perspective, with its strong tradition of concern for user needs, and this continues to be true of its current approach to such issues.

Thus, while monitoring the potential importance of developments in the community at large, such as the use of metadata and the development of Resource Description Framework (RDF) (http://www.w3.org/RDF/), the efforts of BUBL, and its vision of the future, are focused on the concerns of librarians and information specialists and the users they serve, and on the use of LIS skills, tools, and standards to solve resource location and description problems. This general approach is illustrated in a number of recent or current initiatives in which BUBL staff have been involved, initiatives that have either exemplified or helped form a vision of the future in this area.

12.1 CATRIONA 1

The original CATRIONA project (now known as CATRIONA 1) investigated and demonstrated the feasibility of a distributed catalog of Internet resources based on library standards Z39.50 and MARC, and integrated with library OPACs. CATaloguing and Retrieval of Information Over Networks Applications (CATRIONA) was based at Strathclyde and Napier University Libraries in Scotland and ran from mid-1994 to early 1995. It envisaged that, in the long run, resource discovery on the Internet would be based on local cataloging and control of locally created resources (considered essential if the problems of broken URLs were to be reliably solved), and would be based on distributed searching of groups of Z39.50—compliant catalogs that would include, but not be limited to, library OPACs—groups of catalogs that would be created by users searching catalogs of such catalogs. Although it had no immediate follow-up, CATRIONA influenced a range of other future developments and initiatives, both within BUBL and within the Scottish library community.

- BUBL began to catalog resources in a MARC-compatible format and made the catalog accessible via both the Web and Z39.50 (the BUBL LINK service).

- BUBL began working with the Scottish Confederation of University and Research Libraries (SCURL) to mount the Conspectus-based Research Collections Online service (RCO) (http://bubl.ac.uk/org/scurl/), recognizing its possible value as a means by which users might identify groups of Z39.50 catalogs to search (in Scotland only). RCO allows groups of OPACs with research-level collections in Scottish libraries to be identified by a subject search. It is accessible by the Web and Z39.50 and is about to become the hub of the CAIRNS Z39.50 "dynamic clumping service" (see below).

- Napier University Library (http://www.napier.ac.uk/), the other half of the CATRIONA project, implemented Z39.50 access to SLAINTE (http://www.slainte.napier.ac.uk/), a service run on behalf of the Scottish Library Association.

- Z39.50-based approaches to integrating access to Scottish OPACs became a key issue within SCURL, a development that eventually led to funding of the CAIRNS project (see below).

- CATRIONA II, also a joint Strathclyde and Napier project, envisioned both a library role in the description and location of electronic resources created in Scottish universities and the use of Z39.50-based distributed servers as a mechanism for making such resources retrievable across Scotland and beyond.

12.2 CATRIONA II

CATRIONA II (http://catriona2.lib.strath.ac.uk/catriona/) is a project investigating university approaches to the management of locally created quality teaching and research resources, examining a range of issues, including: associated policy, strategy, and organizational infrastructure; the role of the library; and service design, resource description, and interuniversity integration.

Among other things, the project is examining whether universities will choose to manage services to deliver locally created electronic resources beyond the local campus, and whether the library will have a role in such services. The indications are that, in many instances, the answer to both questions will be yes, outcomes that, if put into practice, may well influence some aspects of resource location and description, at least in the United Kingdom, and may also have a bearing on the future activities of services such as BUBL.

CATRIONA II surveys at six Scottish Universities have shown that

- Academic staff are creating quality electronic teaching and research resources at a high level, with 90 percent of respondents reporting that they had such material.
- Much of this material is inaccessible to others. Only 31 percent reported having network-accessible material, and much of this material is difficult to find and in difficult to access formats.
- Eighty-three percent of academic staff feel that access to such material in U.K. universities is either important, very important, or essential to their work.

Clearly, a lot of valuable and in-demand material exists on U.K. campuses, and it is important that this material be made more accessible, whether or not universities themselves choose to play an active role in this. At present, a number of outcomes are possible, and some or all of them may have a bearing on the future of BUBL:

1. Universities may choose to manage services themselves, in which case services like BUBL may

    a. disappear entirely as cataloging of Internet resources in the United Kingdom becomes the province of universities and resources in other countries are handled by services in those countries;

    b. continue in a new role, offering value-added services such as BUBL 5:15 or a Z39.50 distributed search service;

    c. become a mechanism through which the universities might sell access to their resources;

    d. become integrated within the services offered by universities and run by groups of universities, with funding direct from service management rather than through top-sliced funding.

2. Universities may choose not to manage services themselves, in which case services like BUBL may become the mechanism whereby resources created locally at U.K. universities are cataloged and made accessible.

In either event, it is envisioned that responsibility for resource location and description will become more local. Either U.K. services like BUBL will be increasingly responsible for providing and maintaining access to U.K. resources and offering integrated access to resources worldwide through gateways offering distributed searching of foreign services, or the responsibility may devolve even further to the universities themselves, an outcome that the CATRIONA I project saw as the only practical way of controlling the problem of broken links (if both the resource URL and the resource description are controlled by the local library, then in theory, broken links should not occur).

The mechanisms whereby such resources are made available to the wider world are obviously important, and Z39.50 is viewed as a key standard in CATRIONA II. The project is examining two methods of managing resource location and description and one method of interuniversity integration:

1. the centralized model, being investigated at Napier University, where all locally created resources are cataloged by the library in the library OPAC, a Z39.50-compliant server;

2. the devolved model, being investigated at Strathclyde University, where resources are cataloged on departmental servers using embedded metadata (probably the Dublin Core [http://purl.oclc. org/metadata/dublin_core/] or IMS metadata [http://www. imsproject.org/metadata/], which is a superset of DC). The project is investigating the use of Harvest software (http://www.tardis. ed.ac.uk/harvest/) to collect embedded metadata from distributed sites on campus, with a view to incorporating it within a database mounted on a central Z39.50-compliant server (the CATRIONA II demonstrator server).

In both models, interuniversity integration, the mechanism whereby locally cataloged resources are made accessible beyond the local campus, is centered on the Z39.50-based approach being investigated within the CAIRNS project.

12.3 CAIRNS

CAIRNS (http://cairns.lib.gla.ac.uk/) stands for Co-operative Academic Information Retrieval Network for Scotland. The project aims to integrate the twenty-five Z39.50-compliant catalogs or information services of CAIRNS sites across Scotland into a functional and user-adaptive test-bed service. This will offer efficient and effective search and retrieval capabilities across a clump of services comprising all of the individual CAIRNS bibliographic databases and also across various smaller subclumps (groups of servers), and will provide

- a comprehensive union catalog for Scottish higher education without the cost and effort of setting up and maintaining a central database;

- a set of smaller specific subsets of this catalog appropriate to particular purposes (e.g., a particular subject interest);

- a means of integrating access to different types of resources (e.g., simultaneous searches for paper and electronic resources);

- a means of integrating access to these with access to other clumps elsewhere;
- a means of supporting and improving cost-effectiveness through cooperation and resource sharing (particularly between members of the Scottish Confederation of University and Research Libraries [SCURL] who make up the majority of the CAIRNS sites).

The project will take advantage of SCURL's Web/Z39.50 conspectus-based Research Collections Online (RCO) service as the basis of a subject-based, dynamic clumping service. (BUBL received funding from the National Library of Scotland to purchase, set up, and manage a server to hold the RCO data on behalf of the Scottish Confederation of University and Research Libraries.)

This will provide users with dynamically generated, subject-based subclumps of SCURL catalogs to search via Z39.50. An extension of this would enable users to be presented with subject-based subclumps dynamically generated via searches of catalogs of electronic resources: BUBL LINK, SLAINTE, CATRIONA II demonstrator and Strathclyde University Library's Z39.50-compliant Web server.

13.0 Conclusions

The mechanisms by which Internet resources will be published, organized, and accessed in the future are unclear. One of the ultimate goals is to combine the quality and precision of resource description offered by services such as BUBL with the huge scale of information handled by current Internet search tools. The extensive use of metadata by resource providers offers the promise that this goal may be reachable by enabling software to carry out the filtering, evaluation, and organization of resources that is currently a time-consuming human activity. Increased use of Z39.50 offers another means of distributed searching and resource discovery.

These approaches will only be successful on a large scale if the necessary software is in widespread use, whether incorporated into desktop browsers or used at an intermediate stage to offer enhanced user services. Information specialists will still be required to direct the operation of this software, to customize it to specific groups of users, and to design interfaces that assist users to drive the software effectively. The nature of Internet resource directories and gateways will continue to evolve, but they will still be need to be guided by the hands of librarians and information professionals.

Note

1. "The BUBL Information Service Annual Report to ISSC, 1995–1996" (August 1996). (http://bubl.ac.uk/admin/reports/report96.htm#22)

5

Edinburgh Engineering Virtual Library (EEVL)

Michael Breaks
Agnès Guyon

Edinburgh Engineering Virtual Library (EEVL) (http://www.eevl.
ac.uk/) is a gateway to quality engineering Internet sites and is
based at Heriot-Watt University Library, Edinburgh (http://www.hw.
ac.uk/libWWW/welcome.html), with technical support for the project
provided by the university's Institute for Computer-Based Learning
(ICBL) (http://www.icbl.hw.ac.uk/). The project is run in collaboration with five other U.K. universities: University of Edinburgh, Napier
University, Imperial College of Science, Technology and Medicine,
University of Cambridge, and The Nottingham Trent University. EEVL
aims to enable U.K. engineering academics, researchers, and students
to make better use of available Internet resources by improving access
to these resources. We achieve this by a process of identifying, filtering, describing, classifying, and indexing quality sites before they are
added to a database that is freely available over the World Wide Web.
EEVL also provides value-added engineering information services,
and these are also described in detail. This chapter also provides an
evaluation of EEVL's strengths and weaknesses, before offering pointers to the future of EEVL and of resource location and description.

1.0 Responsible Persons

EEVL (http://www.eevl.ac.uk/) has four funded staff: a project officer and a database officer, both of whom are full time, a technical officer (80 percent time), and a project assistant (50 percent time). The
project officer is responsible for the day-to-day operation of the ser-

vice, for user training and awareness, and for the development of the information side of EEVL. The database officer, aided by the project assistant, maintains the consistency of the various EEVL databases. The technical officer is responsible for maintaining the EEVL cluster of servers, and developing and implementing technical enhancements to EEVL. In addition, two nonfunded project managers (information and technical) manage the work of the funded staff, and the overall project is directed by a nonfunded project director, who works with a project board of "external" members. The EEVL development team, which also includes the nonfunded engineering subject specialists from the five project partners, guides the development of the project. The development team has met bimonthly since the beginning of the project and has guided the writing of the EEVL manual, the database template design, the home page design, the development of the EEVL classification scheme, and the promotion and training activities. All members of the development team are also actively involved in identifying and describing sites for EEVL and at times have taken responsibility for particular subjects or resource types. EEVL also makes active use of science and engineering librarians in higher education institutions in the promotion of EEVL. The project staff are

Project Director:	Michael Breaks, University Librarian, Heriot-Watt University, Edinburgh
Project Manager (Information):	Roddy MacLeod, Senior Faculty Librarian, Heriot-Watt University Library, Edinburgh
Project Manager (Technical):	Patrick McAndrew, Manager, Institute for Computer-Based Learning, Heriot-Watt University, Edinburgh
Project Officer:	Linda Kerr, Heriot-Watt University, Edinburgh
Technical Officer:	Geir Granum, Heriot-Watt University, Edinburgh
Database Officer:	Agnès Guyon, Heriot-Watt University, Edinburgh
Database Assistant:	Nicola Harrison, Heriot-Watt University, Edinburgh.

2.0 Mission Statement

The central aim of the EEVL project is to enable U.K. engineering academics, researchers, and students to make better use of available Internet resources by improving access to these resources. This is achieved by a process of identifying, filtering, describing, classifying, and indexing quality sites before they are added to a database that is freely available over the World Wide Web. EEVL concentrates on the major areas of engineering, including chemical engineering; civil engineering; electrical, electronic, and computer engineering; materials engineering; mechanical and manufacturing engineering; petroleum and offshore engineering; bioengineering; and general engineering. EEVL also aims to provide a wider range of engineering information services and these are also described in detail in this chapter.

3.0 Funding Source

EEVL is funded by the Joint Information Systems Committee (JISC) (http://www.jisc.ac.uk/) as part of the U.K.'s $25 million Electronic Libraries Programme (eLib) (http://www.ukoln.ac.uk/services/elib/), which resulted from the publication of the *Follett Report* in December 1993 (http://www.ukoln.ac.uk/services/papers/follett/report/). The *Follett Report* examined ways in which libraries in the United Kingdom could respond to increased pressures on their resources caused by the rapid expansion of student numbers and the worldwide explosion in academic knowledge and information. One of the conclusions of the report was that "the exploitation of Information Technology (IT) is essential to create the effective library service of the future" (http://www.ukoln.ac.uk/services/papers/follett/report/ch1.html), and this led to the creation and funding of the three-year eLib Programme.[1] The overall aims of the program were to facilitate fundamental change in, access to, and delivery of information in support of teaching and learning within U.K. higher education. Over sixty projects were funded under nine Action Lines: Access to Network Resources (ANR); Electronic Journals; Electronic Document Delivery; Digitization; Electronic Short Loan; Images; On-Demand Publishing; Electronic Preprints; and Training and Awareness.

EEVL is one of seven ANR projects that have been funded by the program, and all of the projects are concerned with the organized access to subject material on the Internet, and in particular with access to quality resources. The funding for EEVL began in August 1995 and has been successively extended to July 31, 1999, with the likely extension beyond that as part of a U.K. Resource Discovery Network (RDN) (see the "Resource Discovery Network" section for more information). EEVL has received approximate annual funding of $150,000 for its first two years, decreasing to $120,000 in the third year. The funding for direct expenditures covers staffing (the major cost), equipment, publicity, training, and dissemination, and, as JISC does not pay institutional overheads, the space costs are met by the university.

EEVL began with the implementation of a small pilot database of sites that was in place by February 1996. By August 1996, this pilot service was tested and evaluated on a cross section of potential users. EEVL was officially launched at an Edinburgh cybercafe with seven hundred sites on Friday September 13, 1996. Since then, EEVL has aimed to exploit the links between its name and Friday the 13th by launching new services on those dates. Usage of EEVL has steadily increased since its launch, and the site is now receiving between fifteen thousand and twenty thousand hits a week, excluding graphics. EEVL celebrated its one millionth hit last May.

4.0 EEVL's Target Audiences

The target audience for EEVL is engineering academic staff and students, both postgraduate and undergraduate, in U.K. universities and in institutions funded by the U.K. Research Councils. However, as EEVL also has the aim of helping to bring together academic and practicing engineers, the service is promoted to the latter through their professional press. In addition, librarians and other information professionals have an important role. They not only conduct searches for engineers, but also provide advice, training, and support to engineering staff and students, and they can therefore be considered intermediaries between EEVL and its primary audience.

5.0 The EEVL Service

5.1 Main Database

EEVL's main database now contains over 3,320 searchable descriptions of, and links to, Internet sites of interest to academic engineering staff and students. These sites include engineering e-journals, research projects, commercial companies, mailing lists, directories, software, recruitment sites, and engineering departments and research groups, mainly in U.K. universities. The emphasis is on U.K. resources; about 52 percent of the sites in EEVL are based in the United Kingdom. The collection is defined by a formal Collections Development Policy that covers the scope and content of sites to be included in the database. There has been much discussion of quality sites among the subject gateways and how they should be defined. To EEVL, *quality* is defined as "fitness for purpose." Therefore, rejection of a site by EEVL does not necessarily mean that it is not a quality site, but that it is not deemed to be of interest or use to EEVL users. In producing the Collections Development Policy, the fact that engineering is a practical discipline was kept in mind. The policy-makers were also mindful of the fact that information contained in such sources as trade directories—although commercial in scope and intention—can be very useful.

EEVL classifies selected Web sites in the main database by resource type as well as by subject classification. Resource types can be used as a filter when searching or as a basis for browsing, and records may be classified under more than one resource type. The resource types are based on a practical assessment of the kind of information available on the Internet, and at the time of this writing, the resource types used by EEVL are (the number of resources in each category are in brackets):

- Information server - Higher Education (481)
- Information server - Society/Institution (495)
- Information server - Commercial (1048)
- Information server - Governmental (184)
- E-journal/Newsletter (414)
- Database/Databank (102)
- Mailing/Discussion List (96)
- Resource Guide/Directory (354)
- Courseware/Training Materials (108)
- Reference (102)
- Conference/Meeting Announcements (28)
- Recruitment/Employment (61)
- Patents/Standards (41)
- Research Project/Centre (229)
- Software (where freely available) (140)
- Frequently Asked Questions (28)
- Document (250)
- Library Catalog (7)
- Video (22)
- Publishers (25)

The preponderance of commercial sites, most of which are company Web sites, shows the increasing commercialization of the Internet and reflects the importance of commercial interests to many engineers. However, each commercial resource included in EEVL must have some unique technical information, such as a newsletter or other quality item, to justify inclusion. Linking services, such as other virtual libraries, are not normally included in EEVL unless they have considerable added value or their subject matter is very specific.

The number of resources in each subject category is as follows:

- Bioengineering - 79
- Civil Engineering - 243
- Chemical Engineering - 671
- Design Engineering - 182
- Electrical, Electronic, and Computer Engineering - 775
- Engineering General - 632
- Environmental Engineering - 245
- Materials Engineering - 408
- Mechanical and Manufacturing Engineering - 1041
- Petroleum Engineering - 150

It is worth noting that the low number of sites in Bioengineering reflects the fact that this subject category was only recently selected for inclusion in EEVL.

We have developed various in-context help files, and these appear throughout EEVL. They are of three different types. First, general help files give guidance relevant to the page being used, and they are guides to using the various services. Second, query return help files appear in the main database when a query has returned zero or more than fifty results. They suggest an appropriate strategy, such as narrowing or broadening the search, using filters, or sending it to the U.K. Engineering Search Engine (http://www.eevl.ac.uk/uksearch.html). Third, further advice help files appear only in the result pages to suggest additional resources. The further advice help files for the browse result pages are subject specific, which means that a different help file was written for each of the headings and subheadings. In addition to providing extensive help support, EEVL also offers a number of value-added services to support the use of the main database, including What's New, which lists sites that have been added or modified in the past fourteen days; a monthly Top 25 sites, both in the .uk domain and worldwide; and a Top 250 of the most-visited sites worldwide.

5.2 Other EEVL Services

EEVL sees itself as more than a catalog of quality engineering Web sites; indeed the main database is responsible for less than half of EEVL's total usage. Other specialist information services, bibliographic databases, and targeted search engines contribute to the development of a comprehensive engineering gateway. Figure 1 shows the EEVL home page.

5.2.1 The U.K. Engineering Search Engine

The U.K. Engineering Search Engine (http://www.eevl.ac.uk/uksearch. html) is a targeted search engine that indexes every word on the pages of the U.K. sites included in the main database, and follows their links down to the third level on each site, up to a maximum of two hundred-fifty pages per site. There are now over forty-six thousand pages indexed in this service. The Harvest software (http://harvest. transarc.com/) performs the indexing and is run every month. This service supports much more specific searches than the main database while retaining a focus on U.K. engineering resources. It is now linked to the main database so that when a search returns no result in the main database, the user is automatically referred to the search engine, and doesn't have to rekey the original search terms. The display of results has recently been altered so they appear more like the results of searches performed on the main database.

5.2.2 The Engineering E-journal Search Engine

The Engineering E-journal Search Engine (EESE) (http://www.eevl. ac.uk/eese/) is slightly different from the U.K. Engineering Search Engine as all the URLs harvested are selected from among the electronic journals that are included in the main database. Although all these journals have already been assessed as quality resources, additional criteria apply for inclusion in EESE. The journals have to be all or mostly made of full-text articles and access has to be freely available without registration. We decided to include both U.K. and non-U.K. journals, and we index files in .pdf and postscript format as well as HTML format. At present, one hundred engineering e-journals are included. The journals come in a variety of formats, from trade journals, with a lot of product information, to refereed scholarly journals. Some of these journals are house magazines from important organizations; some are online versions of print journals; others only exist in their online form.

5.2.3 EEVL Engineering Newsgroup Archive

EEVL Engineering Newsgroup Archive (http://www.eevl.ac.uk/cgi-bin/nwi/) is a searchable forty-day archive of news articles from one hundred engineering news groups. This service is similar in concept to the Deja News service (http://www.dejanews.com/), but with a focus on engineering. Launched in June 1996, it was the first additional EEVL service and allows a targeted use of this often overlooked source of information. It is particularly useful for messages related to job opportunities, news, announcements, and topical subjects.

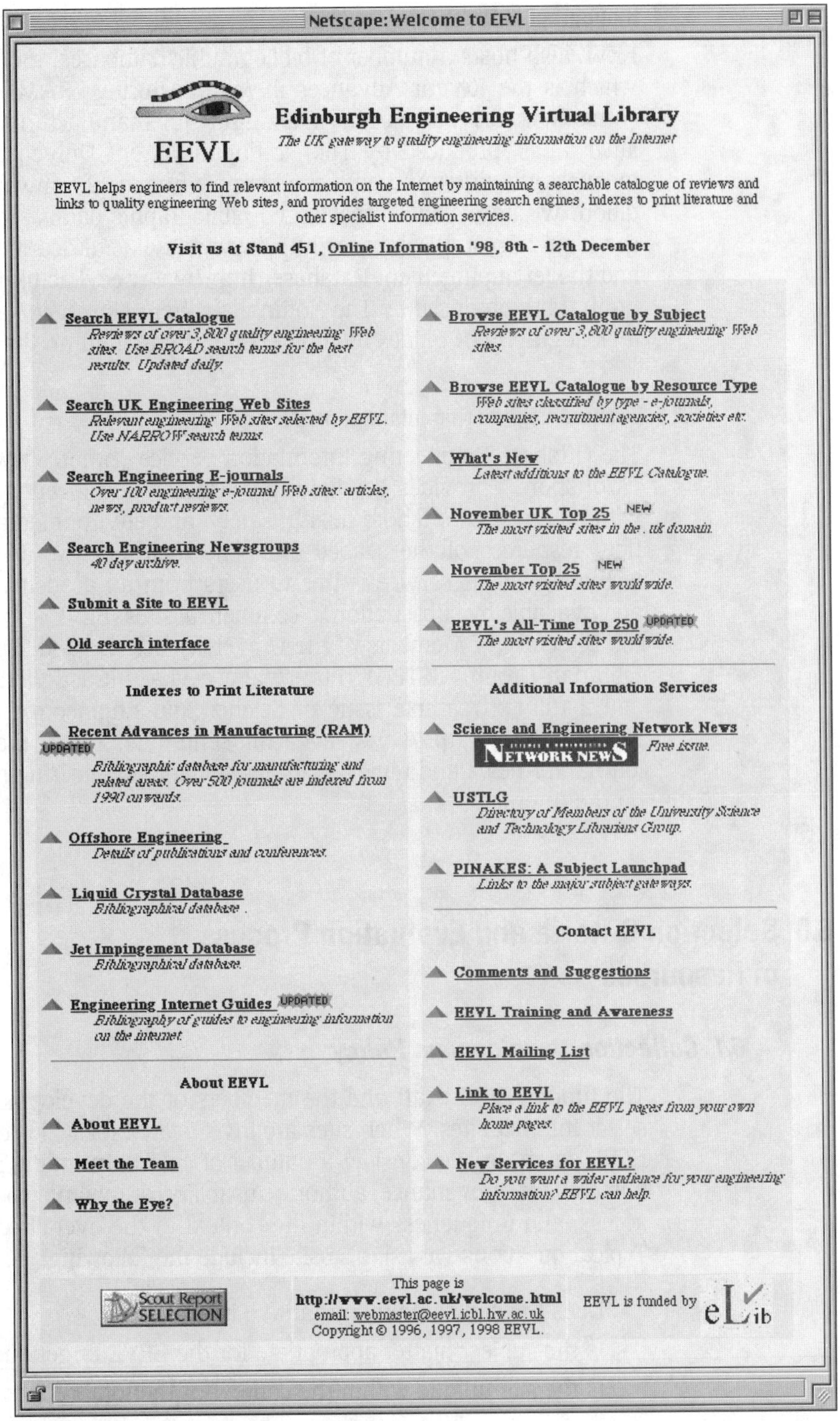

FIGURE 1. EEVL Home Page

5.2.4 Bibliographic Databases

EEVL also hosts a number of bibliographic databases, the largest of which is the Recent Advances in Manufacturing (RAM) database (http://www.eevl.ac.uk/ram/index.html) for manufacturing and related areas, produced by The Nottingham Trent University, which indexes over five hundred niche journals from 1990 onward. In addition, we host smaller specialized bibliographic databases such as the Liquid Crystal Database (http://www.eevl.ac.uk/lcd/index.html) and the Jet Impingement Database (http://www.eevl.ac.uk/jet/index.html), both produced by The Nottingham Trent University, as well as a bibliography of guides to engineering information on the Internet.

5.2.5 Offshore Engineering Information Service

The Offshore Engineering Information Service (http://www.eevl.ac.uk/offshore/) provides details of publications and meetings dealing with oil and gas; offshore health, safety, and environmental protection; resources of the seabed and renewable energy; and marine technology. This service is free to users from an academic domain and available by subscription to commercial sites. EEVL also provides the Directory of Members of the University Science and Technology Librarian Group (USTLG) (http://www.eevl.ac.uk/ustlg/index.html) and a full-text sample issue of Science and Engineering Network News (SENN) (http://www.eevl.ac.uk/senn/index.html), the premier journal for news and reviews of scientific and engineering resources on the Internet.

6.0 Selection Criteria and Evaluation Process of Resources

6.1 Collection Development Policy

The funded EEVL staff and the members of the development team select Internet sites. When sites are investigated for inclusion in the EEVL database, we consider a number of criteria including information content, provenance, authority, usability, durability, reliability of access, and uniqueness within the context of the overall collection. Typical questions we ask of a site include the following:

- Does the site contain substantive information?
- Is the subject matter appropriate for the EEVL target audience?
- Is the site unique within the context of the total collection?
- Is the information durable in nature?
- Is the information from a reputable source?

- Is the information current?
- Is there any form of quality control?
- Is access reliable?
- Is access free and unrestricted?
- Is there online help or contact details?
- Is there printed documentation?

In practice, site evaluation will include a combination of many of the above factors. Some sites will meet some criteria and not others, and a judgment about whether to include a site has to be made. The criterion that divides *include* from *exclude* is basically whether the site will be useful to engineers in higher education. The guidelines for selection also take into account the location of the site, which might affect the ease of access. The Collection Development Policy gives separate guidelines for different resource types. For example, the category Societies/Institutions includes: (1) engineering or engineering-related societies within the United Kingdom; (2) societies/institutions international in scope and of importance in their particular area (larger European societies/institutes might be included); and (3) larger, well-known, U.S. societies/institutes (e.g., ASME, ASCE). In European and U.S. cases, it is the size and importance of the society that matters, in the first instance. However, smaller societies with particularly well-developed and useful Web sites might also be included.

Not included are: (1) a server calling itself international but with a membership almost entirely made up of U.S. addresses, for example. The site may have other useful information and can be included for those reasons; and (2) smaller societies/institutions from other (non-U.K.) countries.

Resource discovery for the EEVL main database is done systematically. A set of sources is checked regularly for new sites, which are then sent to the appropriate member of the development team who reviews them for possible inclusion in the database. Sources that we check regularly include several mailing lists, as well as EEVL's newsgroup archive. The major search engines also have a What's New service. We check What's New Too (http://nu2.com/) and the U.K. Index: What's New This Week? (http://www.ukindex.co.uk/whatsnew.html) daily, and search others periodically. Other listings and virtual libraries, such as the Scout Report for Science and Engineering (http://scout.cs.wisc.edu/scout/report/sci-engr/index.html), are useful in locating new resources. The printed media are also an important source of new sites, since many magazines have regular columns reviewing Web sites. Also, the EEVL home page provides a bibliography of such magazines. The EEVL home page supplies a form allowing users to suggest a resource, which although a valuable part of the service, is not a widely used facility, with an average of about fifteen sites suggested each month.

7.0 Mechanics of Production

EEVL has used a simplified Internet Anonymous FTP Archive (IAFA) template   (http://info.webcrawler.com/mak/projects/iafa/iafa.txt) that was developed in 1995 before the Dublin Core (http://purl.oclc. org/metadata/dublin_core/) achieved its present prominence.[2] The template uses a simple attribute/value pair scheme and is comprised of twenty-two attributes, some of which are optional. Most of the administrative metadata is assigned automatically, consisting of a "handle" uniquely identifying the template, the name of the template creator, the date last modified, and the last modified by field.

Descriptive data added manually include

- Title
- Alternative title—optional
- Keywords—optional, for use only when important terms do not appear anywhere else
- Description—a free-text description or abstract of the resource
- Classification—from the in-house scheme (see the "EEVL's Strengths and Weaknesses" section)
- Resource type—selected from a pull-down menu
- Uniform Resource Locator (URL)
- ISSN/ISBN—optional

Other attributes such as relevance ranking, an EEVL Choice tick button, and the e-mail address of the site's Webmaster are presently used for administrative purposes and do not appear in the record displays. A tier system allows the record to be marked as either Active, Include, Pending, or Don't Include. To maintain a consistent database, only the funded EEVL staff can activate records, thus moving those records to the main searchable database available to the public. Other members of the EEVL team use an Include recommendation only. Pending is used when a record is either unfinished or the site itself is due to evolve, and Don't Include is used for sites that do not yet fit into the Collections Development Policy but might be revisited. An example of an EEVL record is shown in figure 2.

7.1 Technical Infrastructure

The technical infrastructure behind the EEVL service is a custombuilt Web server running on a Sun Ultra 1 with 64 MB Random Access Memory (RAM). The additional EEVL services are now held on a separate server, which was purchased early in 1998 as the growth of EEVL impacted on the performance of the single server. The EEVL system cuts several corners: unlike conventional Web servers, which

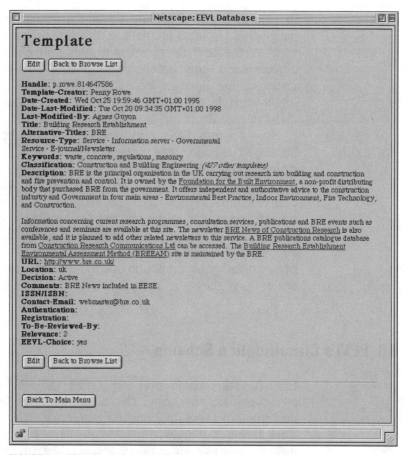

FIGURE 2.   EEVL Record: Building Research Establishment

often use a common-gateway interface (CGI) program to initiate interrogation on an underlying database, the EEVL server holds the entire database and index in memory and uses multithreading to divide up processor time for each query. The resulting system is not only considerably faster when compared to database searching using a conventional Web server, but tracking the progress of users through the system is also considerably easier. When started, the EEVL server creates an index to the database. When a user loads the search page, the program generates the form to be completed and the data are received back by the same program, which also carries out the search using the already constructed index. The response page is built and is sent back in HyperText Markup Language (HTML) to the user's client.

The structure of the EEVL server involves the dynamic production of results, which not only speeds up the search process, but also allows the results of searches to be delivered as the server generates them. In other words, the server does not need to wait to complete the search before delivering the initial results to the users. This means that resources are not sorted before they are delivered to the user, and the EEVL development team has often discussed the merits of returning a sorted list compared to the disadvantages of a slower response time. Boolean searching is allowed, with automatic AND-ing of multiple search terms; search terms may be truncated; and resource-type filters can be combined if required.

Every month, EEVL runs an automatic link checker, which was developed in-house, and gathers a list of URLs that are no longer current. These URLs have to be checked manually to assess whether the sites have disappeared, are temporarily unavailable, or have been relocated. In most cases this involves e-mailing the site's Web-master and searching the Internet for possible new locations. The records then usually have to be checked and updated, temporarily removed, or deleted. The whole process takes about two days, and from a monthly list of around one hundred URLs to check, an average of thirty sites must be updated.

8.0 EEVL's Classification Scheme

EEVL has taken the unusual step, for an ANR service, of devising its own classification scheme. This is based on the Engineering Information's (Ei) thesaurus, but the terminology has been adapted to meet the needs of organizing Internet sites. As EEVL was funded initially for only two years, the view was taken early in the project that an EEVL service, which could then be tested on the target audience, should be established as soon as possible. The EEVL development team also agreed that any classification scheme to be used should be able to cope with a significant number of Web sites that are general in subject content. Desirable features of the classification scheme were identified as flexibility, adaptability, appropriateness to the subject content, and familiarity to engineers. The development team also felt that the overhead of adhering to an established classification scheme, including the use of a thesaurus, might delay the development of a working service.

EEVL took what was essentially a pragmatic approach based on the concept that the "best is the enemy of the good." The development team was also skeptical of how much value would be added to the project by the adherence to a traditional library classification scheme that had been developed for printed information resources. The EEVL classification scheme now in use consists of ten main subject categories and forty-six subheadings. The main subject categories, with the subcategories for Civil Engineering, are

- Bioengineering
- Chemical Engineering
- Civil Engineering
     Civil Engineering (General)
     Construction and Building Engineering
     Engineering Geology
     Hydraulic and Waterworks Engineering
     Mining Engineering
     Structural Engineering
     Transportation and Planning
     Water, Sewage, and Waste Treatment
- Design Engineering
- Electrical, Electronic, and Computer Engineering
- Engineering General
- Environmental Engineering
- Materials Engineering
- Mechanical and Manufacturing Engineering
- Petroleum Engineering

This division takes into account both the size of the existing collection, ensuring a balance between the different sections, and the Ei classification scheme. As each of the subsections reaches over one hundred records, we introduce additional subsections and redistribute the records between the new subsections.

9.0 EEVL's Strengths and Weaknesses

9.1 Strengths

One of EEVL's primary strengths has been its autonomy and its ability to both make and rapidly implement decisions about its development. To this can be added EEVL's organizational structure, which has created a team ownership of EEVL and has therefore enabled the project to garner significant voluntary contributions from its partners. EEVL has also shown considerable flair in promoting its service to both the funding bodies and to its target audiences. EEVL promotional efforts have ranged from competitions for EEVL sweatshirts, EEVL calendars in the shape of a pyramid, which are widely distributed to decision makers, EEVL post-it notes, and EEVL pens, together with conventional leaflets and posters. There has also been a strategy of widely publicizing each enhancement to the service through mailing lists, news groups, Web-alerting services, and conventional press releases.

In the early stages of the project, the target audience to whom EEVL was promoted was considered to be library and information service professionals in U.K. universities. They might be encouraged to act as intermediaries between the project and their users, and this strategy conditioned the early publicity strategy. Articles and news items were therefore placed initially in the library professional press, but as the service matured, we expanded the publicity strategy to target the end users of the service through placing articles in the engineering professional press.[3] References to EEVL in both the library and engineering literature can be found at our Web site (http://www.eevl.ac.uk/press.html).

EEVL has also promoted itself by on-site demonstrations and feedback sessions for end users in U.K. universities. Engineering librarians arrange these sessions, which are attended by an average of fifteen people per session. Awareness of EEVL is high among engineering librarians, but it has proved more difficult to reach engineering staff and students by electronic or traditional print methods, so direct presentations are a very good way of raising awareness of the service. In addition, EEVL has worked with other, more general, higher education training projects such as Netskills (http://www.netskills.ac.uk/) and TALiSMAN (http://www.talisman.hw.ac.uk/), by providing the subject content to their network training seminars.

EEVL has been eager to work with similar gateway projects in other countries and has established strong links with the Engineering Electronic Library Sweden (EELS), based at the University of Lund (http://www.ub2.lu.se/eel/eelhome.html), and has supported the bid by the University of Queensland (http://www.uq.edu.au/) to obtain funding for the Australian Virtual Engineering Library (AVEL). EEVL has also developed a partnership with Engineering Information (http://www.ei.org/), the creators of the Ei Village, by providing the resources for the British Engineering Centre section of the Ei Village.

EEVL has received a number of awards, ranging from being designated a Best Library-Related Web site in a special topics issue of *Library Hi Tech* (http://www.lib.msu.edu/hi-tech/lht15.34.html), to being rated a Five-Star Cool Site by Anbar Electronic Intelligence (http://www.anbar.co.uk/coolsite/civeng/areas/professional-educational-matters.htm) and earning a Planet Science: Hot Spot in New Scientist (http://www.newscientist.com/keysites/hotspots/hotspots.html). EEVL has also received many unsolicited comments from users such as:

EEVL continually astonishes me by how good it is and the excellent new features that keep being added. Congratulations!!!!!!!!!! (Mary A. Axford, reference librarian, Georgia Institute of Technology)

EEVL is without question my topsite. Amongst its features is a brilliant search facility, leading to thousands of useful engineering web pages. (Kate Bellingham, president of Young Engineers)

. . . this is a model example of how such sites should be. (Kevin O'Donnell and Larry Winger, authors of *The Internet for Scientists*)

9.2 Weaknesses

One of the weaknesses that EEVL also shares with the other ANR projects is the inevitable short-term nature of the funding. This can lead to uncertainty among the project staff, and EEVL did lose both its full-time staff just one year into the project; one obtained a permanent post and the other joined his partner in New Zealand. However, EEVL was able to make a virtue of these losses by obtaining additional funding to employ one of the staff on a part-time experimental basis from "the other side of the world," which allowed us to gain valuable experience in the management of teleworking.[4] EEVL also is still relatively unknown among its target audience in spite of an extensive promotion and marketing program. This could be due to a lack of awareness of the potential value of the Internet among engineers, or it could be due to a reluctance among the target audience to invest time and energy in learning to use effectively a service that might only have a limited life. Further weaknesses have been highlighted by the evaluation of EEVL services detailed below.

10.0 Time Frame

EEVL was established on August 1, 1995, with the appointment of the two original staff, Malcolm Moffat (project officer) and Richard Kirby (technical officer), and by February 1996 a database of core resources was in place. By August 1996, a pilot service had been tested on a cross-section of potential users, and EEVL launched its full service on Friday September 13, 1996, following it up with an EEVL Breakfast on Friday, December 13, 1996, in a local Internet cafe. During the second year of the project, EEVL continued to add sites to the main database, and added the Engineering News Group Archive (using software developed for another project in the university), the Harvest Index to UK Engineering Sites, and the pilot RAM service, which became a full service beginning January 1998.

11.0 Future Goals of EEVL

11.1 Evaluations

EEVL has undertaken two evaluations of its service to test its visibility and usefulness to the target audience. EEVL was first evaluated between April and June 1996, when a pilot service was introduced to a number of test sites through workshops. Overall, the pilot service was well received, though the sessions did reveal a widespread ignorance of the Internet and its potential on the part of many engineers. Researchers from Queen Margaret College, Edinburgh, carried out a second and more extensive evaluation of EEVL. The evaluation, which was completed in May 1998, produced some interesting pointers to the future development of EEVL and possibly of other subject gateways.

The evaluation study made several recommendations that broadly accorded with feedback obtained during workshop sessions. It confirmed that users' perceptions of EEVL's usefulness are closely bound up with the quality of information actually available on the Internet. For example, a comment that EEVL is "not technical enough" was actually a complaint that this kind of technical information is not freely available on the Internet. The evaluation report has been a valuable addition to EEVL's development plans, and it confirmed EEVL's view that the usefulness of the service is increased by providing full-text searching of quality engineering Web sites. It also confirmed EEVL's feeling that some users have an inadequate mental map of what EEVL is and what it does. Librarians and information professionals are very clear about the role of the subject gateways, but for users EEVL is one more search tool in the myriad of search engines and subject listings available.

The evaluation report recommended more targeted online help and user training, wider promotion of the service, and steps to ensure that users have an adequate mental model of EEVL, in particular the differences between EEVL's search engines, and between EEVL and other search engines. The report showed that most users did not, in any case, make distinctions between different Internet search engines. The evaluators raised some interesting points on how best to evaluate a Web gateway given the fact that a successful interaction with a such a gateway is one that is minimal and painless. The actual interaction may only last a few seconds, and once a worthwhile site is found, the gateway is forgotten as the user moves on, even though it was the means of easily finding the resource.

The recent evaluation study indicated that some of the users' confusion with EEVL stems from the diversity of information resources that the service now provides. The user needs to employ different search engines for the main EEVL service, the Harvest and

News-group services, and the various bibliographic databases. EEVL is now looking at redesigning its home page to give a clearer picture of the overall service, and at the possibility of providing a single search facility for all of the services, but with a mechanism to divide the results by information categories.

A further general issue that emerged from the evaluation was the relevance of a single gateway to engineering, given its diversity as a discipline. There are at present over three thousand reviewed sites, which might sound substantial, and in terms of the overall value and the work involved is indeed substantial. However, when divided between the disciplines that EEVL covers, the figure can be seen as, on average, only a few hundred sites per discipline. If these sites are then further spread between subdisciplines, subject areas, and specialist topics, it is no wonder that some specialties are to date underrepresented. This raises the issue of whether relevant sites are available on the Internet in some subjects and also the general issue of the scalability of subject gateways.

11.2 New EEVL Services

The popularity of existing additional services, in particular the U.K. Engineering Search Engine and EESE, has motivated EEVL to consider other specialized search engines, using the Harvest technology. This thinking has been reinforced by an analysis of the log files, which showed that searches on the U.K. search engines and EESE had fewer zero hits than those on the main database. This result might be caused by a number of reasons, but the users' familiarity with major search engines, where search terms have to be as precise as possible, might lead them to fail to make the best use of the main database. In particular, many users seem not to realize, when they use the main database, that they are searching within EEVL metadata records rather than actual Web sites.

Another factor to consider is the extent to which engineering Web sites have developed. With the development of the Web, sites have grown in size and complexity so that quality material may be found several levels from the home page. These complex sites, such as university department sites or research projects, often cover many specialties, and it is increasingly difficult to describe all of them in the records, even with the use of keywords. Specialized search engines would therefore be useful in locating material from complex sites or when very precise search terms need to be used. The Harvest software may be used to create a number of subject-based indexes by indexing all the sites under specific subject classifications. The recent evaluation of EEVL services singled out commercial sites as being of great interest for some users and an annoyance for others. A product index could therefore prove very useful, along with a search interface that makes the inclusion, or exclusion, of common sites more intuitive.

In the area of e-journals, and building on the success of EESE, EEVL plans to add a forum where publishers of e-journals can announce new issues. Similarly, we feel an announcement service for courses in engineering in the United Kingdom would be useful. A longer-term plan we are considering is the development of user-customizable services, such as an alerting service, informing users of new Internet resources according to their particular subject interests. In the long term, we will also consider including a thesaurus.

11.3 Resource Discovery Network (RDN)

The wider thinking within JISC on the future of the subject gateways has developed since the establishment of the ANR projects in 1995, and it is likely that an integrated and managed U.K. Resource Discovery Network (RDN) will be established in 1999. The RDN will aim to include "hand-crafted" gateways to all subject areas, probably on the model of one gateway per subject grouping (e.g., engineering, physical sciences, humanities), with a central executive to undertake as many of the common gateway tasks as is practical. The aim will be to retain the identity of each subject gateway and to encourage it to develop links with its target community, but also to ensure that common services such as cross-searching are provided and that coherent marketing and training programs can develop across all of the gateways. This model could allow the gateways to continue as a centrally funded service to the U.K. higher education and research community, but might allow the development of a subscription-based service for other users. It is likely that the final blueprint for the future of the U.K. subject gateways will emerge toward the end of 1998.

12.0 A Vision Statement on the Future of Resource Location and Description

The Internet is changing and developing day by day. New search tools, intelligent agents, and customizable services have an impact on user expectations and on service providers. However, the subject gateways need to steer a middle course between being at the leading edge of network resource discovery and providing a universal service that meets the needs of the technologically challenged.

The development of consistent metadata standards is of fundamental importance; the key concept is interoperability. This is apparent in the development of many cross-searching projects such as

ROADS WHOIS++ cross-searching server, which searches across several ANR databases, or the project Isaac, developed by the Internet Scout Project.[5] However, flexibility is essential to maintain the diversity of material found on the Web and allow for idiosyncrasies. Creator-generated metadata, such as those encompassed in the Resource Discovery Framework (RDF) (http://www.w3.org/RDF/), would greatly facilitate the resource location process, but human input is necessary as this embedded metadata can also be easily manipulated or simply misused by the author.

In the longer term, the development of RDF, based on a mathematical model that enables relationships to be defined, could lead to what Tim Berners-Lee refers to as "knowledge representation" (http://www.w3.org/Talks/1998/0415-Evolvability/overview.htm).[6] The result of a query would reply to a real question, instead of returning a list of resources containing the appropriate keywords. Quality is another aspect that needs to be taken into account when considering metadata. The intervention of third-party services, such as subject gateways or metadata repositories, where resources are selected or reviewed according to certain criteria, remains necessary.

12.1 Distributed National Electronic Resource (DNER)

Within the United Kingdom, much of the strategic thinking in this area is centered around the development of a Distributed National Electronic Resource (DNER), which will establish a managed collection of electronic resources supporting a wide range of constituencies: academic researchers, postgraduate and undergraduate teaching and learning, and distance and open learning. It is intended that the DNER will consist of a wide range of information resources and will not be restricted to such traditional resources as scholarly journals, monographs, and textbooks. It will extend to manuscripts, maps, music scores, sound recordings, diagrams, photographs, and slides for use in disciplines ranging from medicine to computational linguistics. A major objective will be to build a critical mass of information in individual disciplines to help effect the cultural shift to electronic information, which is at the heart of JISC's mission. The DNER will not only aim to include material that is already in digital form, but also will identify print collections that could be digitized to support U.K. higher education and research. The aim is to build the DNER in collaboration with organizations outside higher education such as museums; art galleries; learned societies; commercial publishers; online hosts; public, special, and national libraries; and national government publishing agencies.

The DNER, which would include the subject gateways, will be supported by a technical and service infrastructure that will address standards for access to, use of, and long-term preservation of content; the development of metadata; and licensing and copyright issues. Institutions will be charged for access to the information, but fundamental to the DNER will be the principle that the resources should be free at the point of use to staff and students in higher education. Besides the development of content, it is also important to develop an information architecture to ensure that users can have seamless access to the processes of discovery, location, requesting, and delivery. This work is being led by the MODELS (http://www.ukoln.ac.uk/dlis/models/) project at the U.K. Office for Library and Information Networking (U.K.OLN) and builds on the eLib Programme.

Notes

1. Sir Brian Follett et al., *The Follett Report* (Bristol: External Relations Department, 1993).

2. P. Deutsch et al., "Publishing Information on the Internet with Anonymous FTP" (Internet draft; working draft now expired), in The IAFA Working Group [Referenced July 1998].

3. Roderick MacLeod and Linda Kerr, "EEVL: An Internet Gateway for Engineers," *Library Hi Tech* 15, no. 3–4 (1997): 110–18; Roderick Macleod and Linda Kerr, "EEVL: Past, Present and Future," *Electronic Library* 15, no.4 (1997): 279–86; Roderick MacLeod, Linda Kerr, and Agnès Guyon, "The EEVL Approach to Providing a Subject Based Information Gateway for Engineers," *Program* 32, no. 3 (1998): 205–23; and M. Moffat, "An EEVL Solution to Engineering Information on the Internet," *Aslib Proceedings* 48, no. 6 (1996): 147–50.

4. Malcolm Moffat, "No Worries from Down Under," *Library Association Record Library Technology Supplement* 2, no. 2 (1997): 38, 40.

5. Michael Roszkowski and Christopher Lukas, "A Distributed Architecture for Resource Discovery Using Metadata," *D-Lib Magazine* 6 (June 1998).

6. Tim Berners-Lee, "Evolvability" (Keynote talk at WWW7, the annual meeting of IW3C2, Brisbane, Australia, April 1998).

6

INFOMINE

Steve Mitchell
Margaret Mooney

ADDITIONAL CONTRIBUTORS:

Pat Flowers, Wendie Helms, Julie Mason,

Mark Radleigh, Lynne Reasoner, Carlos Rodriguez,

Lorelei Tanji, Mike VanCamp, Fred Yuengling

INFOMINE (http://infomine.ucop.edu/; http://infomine.ucr.edu/) is a virtual library of value because of its collection of over fourteen thousand annotated and Library of Congress Subject Heading-indexed records with links to selected, university-level Internet resources in most major academic disciplines. (See figure 1.) Information in INFOMINE is well organized and easy to find with multiple access points for browsing and searching. Begun in January of 1994, INFOMINE was among the first of library-originated projects on the World Wide Web. Based at the library of the University of California, Riverside (UCR) (http://library.ucr.edu/), INFOMINE is a product of the cooperative efforts of front-line librarians throughout the University of California and elsewhere.

1.0 Personnel

INFOMINE was initiated and is coordinated by Steve Mitchell, science reference librarian, and Margaret Mooney, head of the Government Publications Department, both of the library of the University of California, Riverside. Recent and short-term development has been guided by Margaret and Steve who, together with Carlos Rodriguez, science reference librarian, and programmers Mark Radleigh and Mike Van Camp, have worked to implement new ideas in regard to collection policy, content, and systems development. These individuals work closely with the facilitators and contributors of each INFOMINE

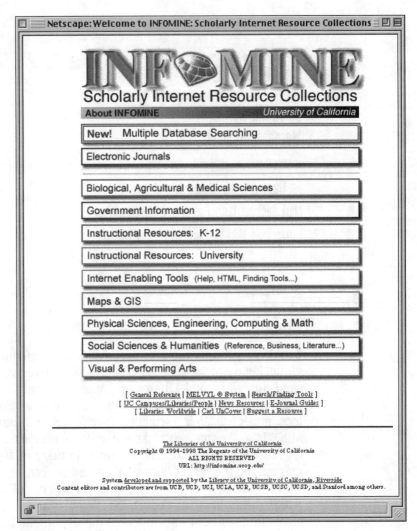

FIGURE 1. INFOMINE Home Page

subject focus area as well. This team, as of fall 1998, works jointly with a team of UCR computer science (CS) faculty (Professors Marek Chrobak, Dimitri Gunopolis, Tom Payne, and Vassilis Tsotras) and graduate students on Project INFOMINE. This team is concerned with the long-term planning, software development, outreach, and funding as well as the exploration of intelligent Internet finding tools for academia.

Each of INFOMINE's ten subject focus areas has a facilitator or cofacilitators in charge of content:

(1) Biological, Agricultural, and Medical Sciences: Steve Mitchell, UCR;

(2) Ethnic Resources: Carlos Rodriguez, UCR; and the American Indian Library Association, Asian/Pacific American Librarians Association, and Chinese-American Librarians Association;

(3) Government Information: Lynne Reasoner and Margaret Mooney, UCR;

(4) Instructional Resources - K–12: Julie Mason, UCR;

(5) Instructional Resources - University: Steve Mitchell, UCR;

(6) Internet Enabling Tools: Steve Mitchell, UCR;

(7) Map and Geographic Information Systems (GIS): Wendie Helms, UCR and Mary Larsgaard, UC Santa Barbara;

(8) Physical Sciences, Engineering, Computer Sciences, and Math: Fred Yuengling, UC Santa Cruz;

(9) Social Sciences, Humanities, General Reference, and Business: Pat Flowers, UCR;

(10) Visual and Performing Arts: Lorelei Tanji, UC Irvine.

INFOMINE is the product of more than thirty contributors, the majority of whom are front-line University of California librarians. The contributors and facilitators communicate via an e-mail reflector, telephone, and an annual meeting. The facilitators train new contributors. We frequently have interns from library/information studies graduate programs around the state working with us. The various libraries in which we work support our efforts. The UCR library supports technical development of the INFOMINE system.

2.0 Description, Mission, and Goals

2.1 Description

INFOMINE is a well reviewed and academically popular virtual library and subject guide containing librarian-selected and annotated links to valuable Internet resources in research and education. The journal *Science* explains, "Much of the Web is ephemeral; too many pages just quietly come and go. Some sort of award is therefore owed to *INFOMINE,* one of the first high-quality information resources on the Web and still going strong . . ."[1] INFOMINE's long list of honors includes a Point Top 5 percent of the Web award (http://point.lycos.com/reviews/GovernmentIndices_5392.html). We have been cited in the Argus Clearinghouse (http://www.clearinghouse.net/)—our arts facilitator received a digital librarian award from Argus; *PC Computing*'s (http://www.zdnet.com/pccomp/) Map to Navigating the Web; the Internet Scout Report (http://www.scout.cs.wisc.edu/); and the *Los Angeles Times,* among many others.[2] Most importantly though, we consider it an honor that over six thousand other resources, mostly of an educational or scholarly nature, have created links to our service. In the past year, INFOMINE has received over 600,000 hits per month.

INFOMINE is based on a hypertext database management system combined with a user-friendly front end. It was one of the first Web sites to combine the power of the Web with that of a database management system (http://lib-www.ucr.edu/pubs/italmine.html).[3] As opposed to many virtual libraries that return static, preexisting pages, INFOMINE uses common gateway interface (CGI) scripting so that each search result is unique because it yields a dynamically created HTML results document customized to users' interests.

2.2 Mission

INFOMINE began because we wanted to create a virtual library to make the many new and valuable Internet resources more easily visible and accessible to the academic community. Through our project and others like it, librarians have brought to bear our profession's considerable, time-honored expertise to help develop a conception of what is academically worthwhile on the Internet and to create structures, such as INFOMINE and other academic finding tools, that can be easily accessed by others. For hundreds of years, this is what librarians have done for print resources. We believe that few groups are as qualified as librarians to continue the identification and organization of scholarly resources of value to students and researchers in the electronic age. INFOMINE and other successful virtual libraries are evidence of the worth of this concept.

2.3 Goals

INFOMINE has a number of primary goals.

Goal 1

Provide a useful, high-quality Internet finding tool for faculty and students both within and outside the University of California. We work to identify, organize, describe, and thus add substantial value to Internet resources. In this way, we make valuable Internet resources very visible so that they can be more easily found, assessed, and integrated into academic research and educational activities.

Using information-finding tools and methods successfully has always been critical to scholarship and postsecondary teaching and learning. This is as true or truer now in the Internet age because along with the tremendous growth and popularity of the Web has come the accompanying problem of near chaos in efficiently finding relevant information. The difficulty of finding information continues to be one of the most important concerns Internet users have, according to a recent survey (http://www.gvu.gatech.edu/user_surveys/survey-1997-10/).[4] In practice, INFOMINE helps students, instructors, and researchers easily and quickly learn what is on the Internet and what is useful to their needs.

INFOMINE is a value-added Internet information tool (see the "Collection Description" section). Much of INFOMINE's utility is due to each record's associated annotation and index terms. (See figure 2.) Through these and other means, such as including hyperlinks to related pages within an annotation, we add value to the links we organize. The indexing/retrieval terms include controlled subject terminology,

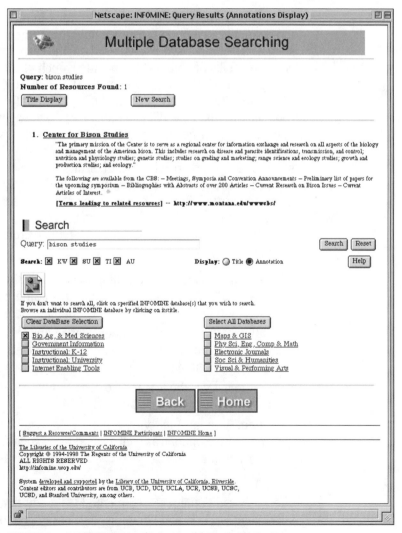

FIGURE 2.   INFOMINE Record: Center for Bison Studies

specifically Library of Congress Subject Headings (LCSHs) and modified LCSHs, that represent a long-established method in describing information in U.S. academic libraries.

Goal 2

Demonstrate the Internet's enormous value to faculty, students, and librarians. INFOMINE's ease of use, its simplicity, the quality of its content, and the enriched information (e.g., annotations, LCSHs, and modified keywords) provided for each resource have made it very worthwhile as a vehicle to demonstrate the enduring worth of useful Internet resources and, through them, the value of the Internet itself.

Goal 3

Demonstrate the value of librarians' efforts in making the Internet a more useful research and educational environment. Virtual libraries, such as INFOMINE, which are based on and carry forward the knowledge and skills of librarians, correct for much of the overkill that can be common when using a generalized search engine such as Alta-Vista (http://www.altavista.digital.com/). For in trying to give us the capability to find a needle in a haystack, these engines often succeed only in transferring the haystack to our search results sets. Search engines are very useful for general Internet searching but will not soon replace users' needs for higher-quality, expert-mediated, selective approaches as embodied in virtual libraries. General search engines and virtual libraries continue to proliferate because both in fact satisfy different finding needs on the Internet.

Librarian-built virtual libraries will remain crucial for a variety of reasons.

- In many situations, there simply is no substitute for subject experts making intelligent selections regarding content value and thereby filtering out irrelevant or inappropriate information.
- Different types of information, for example, research, instructional, or popular, can be better distinguished, categorized, and described, thus yielding more successful retrieval for users.
- Controlled vocabulary and fielded searching are often supported, providing higher precision in searching.
- Often, librarian-built virtual libraries provide many more search and browse options as well as better-designed and more intuitive user interfaces.

Very importantly, the best of virtual library-type finding tools often use traditional research methods, already familiar to academic information seekers and librarians, that have been modified as appropriate for the Internet. These provide for continuity in information-seeking patterns between the environments of print and Internet information.

Goal 4

Effectively use information and Web-related technology to amplify, augment, and thus conserve the time and expert efforts of librarians in a collaborative environment. Our database approach has allowed a relatively small group of librarians to make a major contribution in helping students and academics find useful Internet resources during the last five years. Contributing and editing content is easy and faster than most static page (i.e., nondatabase) approaches because a single change can be reflected in multiple records instantly. In addition, our decentralized approach to cooperation among many librarians at multiple campuses and universities to produce a service with uniform presentation, collection policies, and goals, all accessible via one site, has functioned as an effective organizational model. Instead of creating redundant link sites, participants have worked together to create a single, high-quality tool that allows for resources to be added and maintained, thus saving effort and resources.

Goal 5

Explore new roles and services for academic librarians and libraries in the Internet age. INFOMINE has served as a model collaborative effort and is helping to define new roles for academic librarians.

In carrying out their work, "INFOMINErs" have extended traditional skills and defined new skills in new arenas. We have developed nontraditional activities in Internet-related acquisitions (searching and finding), collection development (identifying and assessing), cataloging (indexing and adding to the collection), and ultimately, in reference tasks (http://nucleus.cshl.org/CSHLlib/BLSD/seattle/mitchell.htm).[5]

Concrete examples of innovative work in developing new skills have included, on the most general level, simply defining and coordinating the multitude of tasks involved in operating a virtual library. A more specific example is that of being among the very first to define and use a simple metadata record format, which includes usage of a standard, library-related descriptive language (i.e., LCSH) prior to Dublin Core (http://purl.oclc.org/metadata/dublin_core/). We assessed issues of cataloging the Web versus indexing it and decided to index— given the time required to catalog, the masses of significant resources we expected to appear on the Web, and the significant print cataloging backlogs common in many, if not most, academic libraries.

We developed means to index new information types. What should we call a site that's simultaneously a scouting tool, Web-site directory, and dataset archive? Should we break it up into these constituent components (e.g., facet it) or create a single record for the whole site? Or should we do both? Sensing the durability of a site is another art. For instance, though we have them, we are hesitant to collect student sites as they are often too impermanent. Should we collect yet another subject list of links? Sometimes yes, if the content is of high quality, the presentation good, and the links many. These are among many questions we have had to answer in collecting and indexing Internet resources.

Another important example of a newly coined area of expertise is the enhanced Internet reference skills found among our participants. Contributing to INFOMINE has provided a valuable continuing educational experience. INFOMINE participating reference librarians, perhaps more so than many reference librarians, have a fully developed sense of how and when to best use the Internet and how to search it effectively. Similarly, we've learned how to rapidly and effectively navigate Web sites through the various graphical and hyperlink mazes that often accompany them. We've learned the small signs that lead us to real content quickly. Needless to say, these are useful skills when a patron is standing next to us. After all, to collect it and describe it is to know it.

Finally, INFOMINE has been designed to fill a service need. Practical interface design for the Web, within a library context, is yet another set of skills we have helped define. For example, INFOMINE was one of the first Web virtual libraries featuring hyperlinked subject and keyword indexing terms to help refine searches.

Goal 6

Provide a collaborative effort model that allows us to work together across traditional campus and administrative boundaries. The library without walls is a working reality, albeit in fits and starts, in most academic libraries right now.

Internet projects such as INFOMINE have contributed to changing the concept of "place" in relation to information users, collections, and collectors. It has become less important where a document resides and more important to have reliable, well-organized access to it. We want to know the document's quality, focus, and intent; who produced it; who identified it as valuable; and who selected it for our use. But the selector does not have to sit at the desk next to us. Nor do we need to own a copy of the information in our private institutional domains; instead, we must provide the appropriate technological and organizational infrastructure to access it reliably.

INFOMINE has been a model for multicampus, collaborative collection development activities through both informal and formal cooperative arrangements. Originally, a small number of volunteer librarians saw the need and began to work on INFOMINE to provide a useful finding tool and gain experience in an innovative library

Internet project. Later, INFOMINE became affiliated with several stand-ing groups who support and contribute to the database and policy development.

(1) The UC/Stanford Internet Government Information Project, sup-ported by the UC/Stanford Electronic Government Initiatives Group (EGIIG), is a formal project for the collection of Government In-formation resources, with participants from the UC campuses and Stanford. It was the first official University of California/Stanford multicampus collaborative Internet resource collection project.

(2) Members of the Western Association of Map Librarians (WAML) from several libraries are adding resources collaboratively in the Maps and Geographic Information Systems section.

(3) The Gallery of Art Research Libraries in California (GARLIC) is a consortium of art libraries and librarians in California who focus on issues of collection development, resource sharing, and in-formation services.

(4) The American Indian Library Association, Asian/Pacific Ameri-can Librarians Association, and Chinese-American Librarians Association are partners in the development of the Ethnic Re-sources section.

Goal 7

Provide a public-domain academic finding tool that will remain free or inexpensive to use into the future. It is crucial to point out that INFOMINE is a public domain virtual library provided by a state uni-versity system in conjunction with other interested parties. We be-lieve that support for noncommercial virtual libraries such as ours will result in substantial long-term savings for academic users.

We believe that librarians can do this kind of work and moreover must exercise professional self-reliance and leadership instead of simply letting commercial, usually nonlibrary-focused operations, do this work for us, and often less well. While many commercial sites are currently free, they may later charge handsomely for their ser-vices. Librarians must not passively hand over the reins to commer-cial organizations whose primary interests naturally lie more in their return to investors than in providing solid, unbiased information.

3.0 Funding and Budget

The University of California provides one half-time INFOMINE sys-tem administrator at an annual rate of $16,400. Over thirty partic-ipating information professionals, primarily from the University of

California but also including Stanford University, the University of Southern California, and others, contribute over $120,000 per year of in-kind assistance through their time. The INFOMINE server and associated equipment costs have been less than $3,000 per year. The total annual cost for INFOMINE is estimated at $139,400 per year. At six million hits a year, this represents a cost of two cents per access.

The U.S. Department of Education, through its Fund for the Improvement of Post-Secondary Education (FIPSE) (http://www.ed.gov/offices/OPE/FIPSE/), is contributing approximately $100,000 per year over the next three years to INFOMINE. The grant will support continued development and improvement of our system. The majority of the money will fund programming and system design.

In conjunction with our FIPSE related projects, the computer science (CS) department at UCR is donating significant amounts of equipment and laboratory space. Most importantly, four CS faculty members and three graduate students are contributing their time to join with us in designing and implementing new features for INFOMINE.

We have also received smaller grants, the most important of which was ten thousand dollars awarded by our peers via the Librarian's Association of the University of California.

4.0 INFOMINE Audiences

INFOMINE's primary mission is to serve as an Internet finding tool for the university community generally and the University of California community specifically. We help educate researchers, educators, and students who might not otherwise be aware of, or have the ability or resources to capitalize on, the value of the Internet. We also focus on K–12 educators, students, and parents as a crucial community service.

5.0 Collection Description

Our collection goal has been to include items most relevant to university-level faculty and students. Generally, this has meant selecting the highest quality and most comprehensive resources.

5.1 Subject Strengths

As of July 1998, the INFOMINE collection contained over fourteen thousand records linking to Internet-accessible databases, journals, textbooks, guides to the Internet for most disciplines, conference proceedings, and many other types of resources. We have emphasized an expansive, interdisciplinary view of academic endeavor. Separate virtual collections of INFOMINE, which can be searched collectively or separately, exist for

(1) Biological, Agricultural, and Medical Resources (3,958 resources);
(2) Ethnic Resources (beginning January 1999);
(3) Government Information Resources (3,358 resources);
(4) Instructional Resources - K–12 (760 resources);
(5) Instructional Resources - University (including online classes, textbooks, and tutorials) (228 resources);
(6) Internet Enabling Tools (including tutorials, classes, and reference charts) (879 resources);
(7) Maps and Geographic Information Systems (GIS) (1,226 resources);
(8) Physical Sciences, Engineering, Computer Science, and Mathematics (1,623 resources);
(9) Social Sciences and Humanities (including General Reference, Business, and Library/Information Studies resources) (1,795 resources);
(10) Visual and Performing Arts (881 resources).

5.2 Types of Information

INFOMINE weaves numerous types of resources together into one coherent academic information tapestry. This is one of the primary values of INFOMINE. As of July 1998, INFOMINE included

- 2,401 databases (17% of INFOMINE's total content);
- 1,261 electronic periodicals (9%);
- 1,689 directories (12%);
- 2,260 Internet finding tools (16%, 2,089 including subject guides and 171 search engines);
- 1,896 reference tools (14%, ranging from calculators to dictionaries to authoritative databases);
- 1,149 educational sites (8%);
- 547 maps (4%).

5.3 A Value-Added Collection

Above and beyond subject emphases, information/publication types, and the number of resources, the INFOMINE collection, as mentioned, has a strong value-added component because of how its resources are organized and presented. Specifically, this takes the forms discussed below.

5.3.1 Level of Indexing

On average, over five LCSHs are applied per record in INFOMINE, while keywords average eight or more. The number of indexing terms that can be used to retrieve a resource is much greater than the number in many library or Internet-related databases. This has been a major factor in INFOMINE's value.

5.3.2 Subject Terminology

Subject terminology originates from a standard controlled vocabulary, the Library of Congress Subject Headings (LCSHs).

5.3.3 Level of Description

The level of description is deep, given both the type and number of indexing terms employed as well as the in-depth annotations.

5.3.4 Access Points

INFOMINE allows a multiplicity of access points. INFOMINE provides for Boolean searching of one or more fields (title, subject, keyword, author, and generic subject category—e.g., government resources); browsing through our indexes including the table of contents (titles interfiling under their subject terms), titles, subjects, keywords and author indexes; and browsing hyperlinked subject and keyword indexing terms embedded within a record.

5.3.5 Ease of Use

All of the above factors, accompanied by a simple and to-the-point presentation, make the INFOMINE collection quite easy to use.

6.0 Resource Selection and Evaluation

6.1 Expertise

Our service pivots around librarian expertise. Most, if not all, participants have extensive experience as selectors or bibliographers in their respective subject areas. The same skills and training we have used to help build physical collections in the libraries where we work have been brought to bear in building INFOMINE. We have found that print-savvy librarians understand the selection of Internet resources, which has almost always resulted in well-chosen materials without a great deal of extra training. Content quality remains the crucial factor for both print and electronic materials, and this we know well.

6.2 Overall Policy and Issues in Making Good Choices

Our rule of thumb is simply that the resources we add be of use in research or educational activities at the university level. To that end, we collect as many of the most useful, high-quality tools as possible for a university-level patronage. This reflects most traditional print libraries' efforts since we work toward comprehensive coverage in many subjects and representative coverage in most others.

There are, however, some special concerns with Internet resources relating to site stability, currency of information, and access to archival information. Questions our selectors ask include: Does a large and/or apparently stable corporate sponsor (e.g., research program, college, corporation) support the site? If part of a program or college, is the site a personal or institutional presence? Is the content of the type that will need updating, and if so, do changes occur frequently?

6.3 Collecting Tools/Methods and Collection Maintenance Issues

We use a number of sources to find resources. These generally can be classed into collecting tools that provide either relatively unfiltered information about sites (e.g., AltaVista) (http://www.altavista.com/) or, conversely, relatively filtered information (e.g., Signpost) (http://www.signpost.org/signpost/). These can be referred to as primary and secondary collecting tools, respectively.[6]

Collection maintenance is always a challenge, and we rely on feedback from users and site creators to maintain our links. We also use a simple but useful (formerly shareware) utility called WebWatch to periodically sweep subject areas. The goal is to sweep our links annually. At least as challenging as link maintenance, however, is maintaining annotation and indexing accuracy as sites grow and change.

7.0 Mechanics of Production: Our System

7.1 INFOMINE System Technical Summary

The primary INFOMINE Web server is a Dell Poweredge 2300, 400 Mhz, Pentium II with 256 MB of RAM and a 9 GB ultra2/LVD SCSI hard drive. We are running Apache server software (http://www.apache.org/) on Linux (http://www.linux.org/), a form of the UNIX operating system. We chose Linux, specifically Redhat (http://www.redhat.com/), because of its price (free) and performance capabilities. We were one of the first library applications of Linux, which has become quite popular. INFOMINE also works on SUN Sparc stations via the Solaris variant of UNIX. INFOMINE is optimized for the current versions of Netscape Communicator (http://home.netscape.com/products/index.html?cp=hom10cnpr) and Internet Explorer (http://www.microsoft.com/products/prodref/206_ov.htm) but can be accessed by all major Web browsers.

INFOMINE uses mini SQL (mSQL) (http://www.hughes.com.au/) as a shareware database management system to index, store, and retrieve records; mSQL compiles on many popular UNIX systems. While there are many more robust database management systems in existence, our design biases are to develop our system using freely available software (hence, mSQL and Linux). At some point, we would like to distribute the INFOMINE system. It is probable that we will migrate to Oracle, a commercial database.

INFOMINE uses Javascript and Lite programming languages for all user-interface functions (e.g., searching, displaying the table of contents, adding/editing resources, etc.). For INFOMINE system maintenance functions/programs, we use PERL and C++.

7.2 INFOMINE's Hypertext Database Management Approach

Creating and maintaining content in INFOMINE is based on our hypertext database management system. Participants can easily add, edit, provide access to, and generally manage several thousand records. For example, all indexes (e.g., the table of contents) are automatically generated by the database management system rather than manually constructed. This is an important time-saving feature because, instead of modifying several HTML pages to effect changes in a record, we simply make the changes on our editor form, and then the database management system automatically indexes and updates these changes.

7.3 INFOMINE System Version 3

Version 3 was introduced in January 1999 and will contain significant enhancements over version 2. Separate database files will be merged into one large file, which will better facilitate interdisciplinary searches. INFOMINE has been rewritten to be more portable and distributable. We have added an author field where previously author information was included in our keyword field. Javascript and Lite have been used throughout for speed and portability. Contributors will have many more options in adding or editing records (e.g., easier batch loading/removal). We have upgraded to the current releases of mSQL, Apache, and other constituent software. Record display choices include more options, such as a titles only display. Choice of exact string or keyword searching is present in all user-searchable fields. And we have added new graphics.

8.0 Classification and Resource Description

INFOMINE has been designed with easy and quick content adding and editing in mind. Our goal has been to strike a balance between full cataloging (e.g., MARC cataloging, which can require close to one hour per item) and an uncontrolled, minimal approach to indexing and annotating (e.g., Yahoo spends about one minute per item).[7] There is a strong need to provide more and better structure and content for access without however devoting large amounts of personnel time to perform full cataloging.

In addition, our approach has been specifically designed from the beginning so that the pool of potential participants could include many more types of librarians than just catalogers. For instance, public service librarians, who routinely search numerous and differently structured databases, are usually quite versed in basic modes of indexing and resource description (to provide accurate searching) and, with a little training, adept at doing such work themselves. Their participation has been invaluable for INFOMINE.

8.1 Subjects

INFOMINE uses LCSHs. These have a lengthy tradition and are the primary U.S. academic library-descriptive subject language. They will provide us with a bridge to our legacy systems, such as our online catalogs, and will eventually connect Internet and print resource access in INFOMINE. While problems exist with LCSH's overall effectiveness for retrieval, because of some users' lack of awareness of terms and the delays in up-to-date LCSHs for describing new phenomena, this language remains quite valuable and is "spoken" by most U.S. academic librarians and their patrons. Much of our reason for applying keywords is geared toward correcting for some of the LCSH deficiencies (see the "Subject Categories" section). The following two sections discuss our methods and techniques in applying LCSHs.

8.1.1 INFOMINE LCSH Methods

We use LCSHs within a simple metadata record format that is DC compliant. This means that creating a record is a twenty-minute process. Our time-efficient means of selecting and applying LCSHs is based on "mining," using the immense wealth of LCSH and other subject terms to be found in TEN, the current ten-year subset of the Melvyl Catalog (http://www.ucsd.edu/data/library/melvyl/), the University of California's online union catalog. Mining TEN remains very useful though we began this practice at a time when other sources for LCSH cataloging were not freely available on the Internet or required special equipment for access. Some of us also use Classification Plus (http://lcweb.loc.gov/cds/). Because TEN is the work of numerous catalogers throughout our system, we benefit from seeing which LCSH terms were actually used to describe a particular subject over time. For many INFOMINE records, we are able to locate very similar records in TEN and apply appropriate associated LCSHs. We simply cut LCSHs from the record of a similar resource in TEN and paste these into the subject fields of an INFOMINE record.

8.1.2 INFOMINE Techniques for Applying LCSH

We assign LCSHs for each of the major subject focuses of an Internet resource, generally at three levels.

- We assign LCSHs at the first level of abstraction. That is, a resource, as in figure 2, which is concerned with the study of bison (and which describes the work of the Center for Bison Studies, including its bison-related information utilities), will have its main subject concerns represented as AMERICAN BISON—BIOLOGY; AMERICAN BISON—ECOLOGY; AMERICAN BISON—MONTANA.
- We then assign LCSHs at the next higher level of abstraction. Thus, this resource receives the following LCSH as well: AMERICAN BISON.
- In addition, we also usually assign LCSHs at a broad, discipline-specific level relating to fields of study or subject disciplines. Hence, the terms WILDLIFE CONSERVATION and WILDLIFE MANAGEMENT have been applied to the example.

Note that in using LCSHs, we used to parse or break up subdivided headings. Typically, the subdivision or end phrase of a heading (e.g., *directories*) would be placed in our keyword field (discussed below). For the last couple of years though, we have used full headings with subdivisions in our subject field. This means that 80 to 90 percent of INFOMINE subjects are authorized LCSH terms while the remainder are modified LCSHs and will be changed as time allows.

Also, following a standard library tradition, we have used a small number of what could be considered locally applied subject headings. These are meant to correct for LCSH deficiencies. For example, we would have described the World Wide Web Worm under "navigators" in 1994 and 1995. There was no comparable, specific LCSH term at that time. Now, for similar tools, we can use the authorized LCSH Web search engines.

8.2 Subject Categories

Similarly, in another separate subject category field, each record receives one or more very broad subject category designations reflecting the item's most general focuses. The example in figure 2 has been assigned to the Biological, Agricultural, and Medical subject category. These subject categories, though not visible, can be searched via user-selected options that can broaden or narrow the search.

8.3 Keywords

We apply keywords, which often include commonly used and/or specialist terms, to adjust for some LCSH shortcomings as well as to simply apply more handles through which a resource can be found. Keywords may be natural-language terms, or more rarely, controlled-language LCSH terms, and/or specialist, and/or lay terms. Typically, in contrast to subject headings, we assign more rather than fewer keywords (on average, eight). In the example given in figure 2, several terms have been applied to augment the LCSH subject terminology, such as ANIMAL HUSBANDRY.

Keywords not only greatly increase retrieval in subject-type searches, they also often enable subtitle, acronym, site sponsor, and many other types of searches. We feel that our keyword content is probably as important as our LCSH content for effective information retrieval. It's important to note that our keyword field reflects an additional priority: enabling users to re-find a resource that has moved. To this end, it often includes several entries regarding site sponsor and site affiliation (which supplement the author and title fields).

Types of keywords include

(1) minor subjects (the metadata for the CENTER FOR BISON STUDIES, for example, contain the keywords ANIMAL HUSBANDRY and LIVESTOCK);

(2) synonyms and closely related terms for assigned subjects (the metadata for the CENTER FOR BISON STUDIES, for example, contain the synonyms and closely related terms AMERICAN BUFFALO, BISON, BUFFALO, WILDLIFE BIOLOGY);

(3) subtitles;

(4) titles of important publications, series, databases, journals, and so forth, included within the resource;

(5) personal or corporate author names were formerly identified in the keyword field (the metadata for the CENTER FOR BISON STUDIES, for example, contain the corporate author CENTER FOR BISON STUDIES);

(6) site sponsor or affiliation names, personal or corporate (the metadata for the CENTER FOR BISON STUDIES, for example, contain the site sponsor or affiliation names BOZEMAN and MONTANA STATE UNIVERSITY);

(7) acronyms for names or subject concepts (the metadata for the CENTER FOR BISON STUDIES, for example, contain the acronym CBS);

(8) geographic/place names or types;

(9) publication/data types such as databases (the metadata for the CENTER FOR BISON STUDIES, for example, contain the publication/data type ARTICLES, BIBLIOGRAPHIES, CONFERENCES, MEETINGS);

(10) Internet information types (the metadata for the CENTER FOR BISON STUDIES, for example, contain the Internet information type WEB);

(11) International Standardized Serial Number (ISSN);

(12) publisher.

8.4 Author

In 1999, personal and corporate authors will be moved to their own distinct field and will still be searchable during the move.

8.5 Annotations

Supplying annotations, a big part of our service, has become easier over the last three years because providers of academic resources are increasingly addressing the need for sites that contain accurate, short descriptions. Often, these descriptions can be evaluated and then cut and pasted, sometimes with slight modification, into INFOMINE's database. This field should be searchable by the end of 1999.

8.6 Titles and URLs

Titles are occasionally enriched. For example, a resource with the title CPAN can become, with a subtitle enriching it, Comprehensive Perl Archive Network.

9.0 Strengths/Challenges

9.1 Experience

In our sixth year, INFOMINE's contributors are among the most experienced in operating and running an academically focused Internet finding tool or virtual library. Resource identification and evaluation by trained professional librarians are pivotal for INFOMINE and is one of our greatest strengths. Being among the very first to define and operate a cooperative, distributed model for resource selection among multicampus and university libraries, we have amassed a great deal of experience with such a model. Moreover, the majority of us are working line librarians, most in public services, and this has helped ground our service in a practical, simple, patron-centered approach.

9.2 Information Seeking Standards/Traditions Brought Forward

In INFOMINE, the traditions (e.g., the use of LCSHs, Boolean searching, the generation of many access points for browsing) with which academic information seekers are familiar have been appropriately modified and brought forward to provide continuity in information-seeking behaviors.

9.3 Ability to Evolve

Through resourceful use of limited funds, INFOMINE has evolved and improved significantly over the last five years and first three versions. Recent grant funding will allow us to move to a new level of service, one that promises to greatly improve our system (see the "Limited Area Search Engine" section) and perhaps the way virtual libraries are routinely designed.

9.4 Overall Strengths: High Quality, Simple, Uniform, Easy-to-Use, and Effective

For a scholarly virtual library, we are very comprehensive and larger than most. The value added to our collection is great. We provide uniform access to important Internet resources in most major academic disciplines through a singular front end. We also provide rich approach descriptions. For users at all skill levels in searching, this means that important Internet resources are quickly and easily found. In addition, for contributors, building and maintaining INFOMINE have been relatively simple and cost-efficient.

9.5 Challenges

9.5.1 Corporate and Structural Constraints

Library involvement in Internet information organization and usage has been hampered to some degree by the library and academic corporate culture. With some exceptions, librarians do not generally see themselves, and are not perceived on most campuses, as leaders, explorers, or risk takers. It's not that we're at all incapable of assuming these roles, of course; it's simply that our funding and economies of time don't actively encourage us. Though this is changing, our days can be dominated delivering the well-defined and time-tested traditional services we always have.

It's really a question then of seeing the critical importance and long-term advantages achievable for the profession by doing the extra work necessary to launch ourselves into the more significant, technology-driven services and roles. Obviously, this kind of change is very difficult given that it will require that librarians take a more expansive role in information provision without the proper level of financial backing to do this initially.

Consequently, the incentive to participate in virtual libraries like INFOMINE could be stronger. While the multicampus effort has been and is significant, participation for many individuals is not as consistent as would be desired. There are a number of specific reasons for this. At many UC campuses, a great number of librarians retired in the early 1990s during a regional economic depression, and vacant positions were not always filled. Hence, fewer people and more work per person are commonplace on many campuses. Therefore, there isn't a great deal of time for librarians to do work that doesn't directly accrue to solving or providing for immediate, traditional library problems and needs; that is, increasing the visibility of the library on their own campuses and/or working with legacy systems in which a great amount of resources have been invested. Additionally, career advancement structures may reward single-campus rather than multicampus efforts and, following an older model of academic achievement, solo rather than team contributions.

We hope that much of this will eventually change, and we are trying to contribute to this change. In the new electronic environment where collaborative effort can be critical for success, the degree to which we do actually contribute to this change may actually represent INFOMINE's largest professional contribution. Overall, we believe that while integrating the Internet into our work unquestionably represents more effort and a great deal of uncertainty, it also equally presents unparalleled opportunities to provide better service and make ourselves more central to the workings of higher education than ever before.

9.5.2 Technical Problems

While we do have occasional technical problems, these problems are minor and transitory in relation to the problems mentioned above. The problems of virtual libraries in general (such as coping with large numbers of Internet resources), and the very significant challenge of finding and keeping competent technical support in one of the most competitive job markets represent other challenges.

10.0 Future Goals for INFOMINE

INFOMINE has several goals for the future. Our annotations are not currently searchable but will be shortly. We are going to implement a Limited Area Search Engine (LASE) that builds on our expert-based manual approach to content identification. The LASE, as eventually constituted, would seek and find significant academic resources (see the "Internet Visions and Virtual Library Visions" section).

We are investigating ways to move INFOMINE records into our online public access catalog (OPAC), at UCR and elsewhere in the university, and from there into other related systems. However, there are many pros and cons to this. We are also looking at integrating OPAC records into INFOMINE. A good approach might be to employ each type of tool, virtual library and catalog, so that their respective strengths would be used to best advantage by the patron (http://www.bookwire.com/LJdigital/diglibs.article$25937) (http://www.ariadne.ac.uk/issue15/main/).[8]

In following this theme, as an adjunct service, INFOMINE users will be able to search specific OPACs for Internet materials since, at this time, most OPACs at UC are of course primarily comprised of print materials.

We are talking with other large virtual libraries to see what degree of common ground we have and to what degree amalgamation would be beneficial. We currently are working with the Agriculture Network Information Center (AgNIC) (http://www.agnic.org/) (see chapter 1) of the National Agricultural Library and are responsible for collecting in the area of subtropical horticulture.

On a similar front, as mentioned, a major priority remains exploring multicampus cooperation for Internet resource discovery, description, and delivery. Our goal is to increase participation within the UC System and to expand involvement to include other interested universities and colleges around the world.

11.0 Internet Visions and Virtual Library Visions

To facilitate INFOMINE'S redesign work, we undertook a survey of current and possible future trends in parallel design communities as well as virtual libraries. This survey can be found in the article "Interface Design Considerations in Libraries" (http://lib-www.ucr.edu/pubs/stlinfoviz.html).[9] In the course of writing this chapter, it became very clear that there should be several coming revolutions in information technology and service that may directly affect virtual libraries, but in ways that are very difficult to predict. It is crucial that librarians become familiar with the relevant possibilities and the research and user communities behind them (e.g., human-computer interaction, hypermedia, educational technology/distance education, and others). Librarians must go beyond reacting to information technologies and play a large role in creating or structuring them. We need to work with the above communities to create (and demand from vendors) better products—products that intrinsically include our vast knowledge of information usage and organization.

11.1 Benefits and Problems of the Virtual Library Approach

Today, after gaining thousands of hours of experience with robotic search engines and other finding tools and after spending a similar number of reference service hours helping and instructing Internet searchers in the use of these tools, we feel as strongly as when we began that for the majority of Web users, regardless of their skill levels, INFOMINE and similar virtual libraries play a growing role as a major finding tool. It is noteworthy that many of the major search engines (e.g., Lycos [http://www.lycos.com/] and AltaVista) now employ some type of the virtual library approach in providing subject categories and browseable interfaces. Certainly this niche hasn't been replaced, as many predicted, by artificial intelligence/smart search/fuzzy-logic-augmented supersearch engines. While these technologies are improving, they are not yet highly effective and probably won't be for many years. Successful searching depends on knowing when to effectively employ which type of tool for specific searches. At the same time, user skill levels must be matched with the appropriate finding tool. For instance, you may not want to encourage users who are overly challenged by your online public access catalog and/or who are looking for resources related to broad concepts to use AltaVista or HotBot (http://www.hotbot.com/). Similarly, you wouldn't usually expect most general virtual libraries to yield good results if you are browsing or searching for an Arctic insect species, rare chemical, or arcane poem.

11.2 Economizing Efforts within and among Virtual Libraries

The obvious major problem with the virtual library approach is that it takes time and human energy to keep up with and to organize and maintain the growing numbers of useful resources. While multiple-subject virtual libraries such as INFOMINE and some of the other projects listed in this book remain quite achievable and very useful to large numbers of people, it is clear that greater economy of effort will always be the rule for us. There are both organizational and technical dimensions to achieving greater efficiency, and these efforts could take a number of forms.

For academic libraries that are developing virtual collections, the degree of effective collaboration increasingly will determine the scope, range and depth, and ultimately, service value. The larger virtual libraries need to begin working better together. Cooperative networks within universities and across university systems need to be organized. We need to better distribute the burdens of keeping current and well-maintained resources; providing in-depth subject coverage; keeping up with searching/user/system traffic/requirements; and developing systems. By working together, we will be able to provide much better and more comprehensive resources at a lower cost.

There are many levels of potential cooperation. Already, many librarians share collection duties informally through our What's New indexes and similar services. Furthermore, within reason, we need to standardize content and quality guidelines, front ends, and indexing schemes (many of us do share similar approaches to indexing and searching), and make more solid commitments to serious collection efforts and reasonably similar user interfaces. The goal could be either a single unified tool or, much more likely, a ring of semi-independent virtual libraries that would allow searches to be passed from one virtual library to another with the special features of each retained. The latter approach challenges us to develop a Z39.50-like query translator that is streamlined but that would lessen the "dumbing down" of specific resources to achieve the desired standardization.

11.3 Limited Area Search Engines (LASE)

A direction INFOMINE is taking uses LASE. This would augment, not replace, our current service. LASEs essentially consist of Web-exploring spiders and indexing programs that, while similar to the approaches of the generalized search engines, such as Alta Vista, are limited to exploring—and this is crucial—a predetermined and controlled domain of human-selected URLs. Sites closely related (or linked) to this domain of URLs could be included as well. This complementary, virtual library/limited area search-engine approach should allow virtual libraries to approximate some of the reach and full-text retrieval capability of the large search engines while retaining a selective, quality-oriented academic focus that remains based on the subject expertise of librarians. The LASE component should significantly broaden and deepen retrieval options (searching full text as well as fielded information). In turn, it should increase users' success in searching as it increases the total amount of relevant material retrieved.

Academic librarian judgment about content value and knowledge in organizing information should be strongly amplified through the LASE approach given that significant resources typically link to other significant resources. LASE would exploit these linkages. Advanced forms of the LASE automated harvester would be trained to recognize significant similar patterns of content, form, and URLs extrapolated from INFOMINE's collection. By incorporating the LASE approach as an augmentation of the core manual indexing approach, virtual libraries would have the best features of both worlds of Internet finding tools: the quality, focus, precision, and relevance of the virtual library approach and some of the greater reach and retrieval potential of the general search engine. Our hope is that this work can remain in the public domain and be of benefit to others.

11.4 Agent Technology in Virtual Library Construction

Agents are machine processes that can be set to run autonomously, performing specified activities such as finding URLs and placing them in the proper field and reporting when finished. While fully autonomous, intelligent searching agents would be extremely hard to achieve and would be unlikely to come close to the quality of direct-expert involvement, there are virtual library building processes that could benefit from lightly supervised agents. There is no reason why such agents couldn't be devised, for instance, to help in the process of virtual library database data input and content building. Programs like MARCit (http://www.marcit.com/) are simple steps in this direction. These agents could be important time savers.

11.5 Preserving Access to an Information Commons

While virtual library-related technology and design will change, one factor that will remain a constant is the need for the university community to have recourse to high-quality, effective finding tools that will remain in the public domain. It is likely that currently free commercial finding tools will begin charging for use or conversely provide search rankings that have been purchased or increase their advertising to the point of distraction. Academic and other librarians and faculty need to work together to ensure the existence of objective, mostly free, finding tools.

Notes

1. David Voss, "Webwatch," *Science* 279, no. 53 (January 2, 1998): 43.

2. Neil Randall, "Map to Navigating the Web," *PC Computing* (August 1996); and Thomas S. Mulligan, "The Cutting Edge," *Los Angeles Times,* 3 February 1997, Business section, p. 1.

3. Steve Mitchell and Margaret Mooney, "INFOMINE: A Model Web-based Academic Virtual Library," *Information Technology and Libraries* 15, no. 1 (March 1996). (http://lib-www.ucr.edu/pubs/italmine.html) [Referenced Jan. 1999]

4. Graphic, Visualization, and Usability Center, GVU's 8th WWW User Survey (Atlanta, Ga.: Georgia Institute of Technology, 1997).

5. See Steve Mitchell, "INFOMINE: The First Three Years of a Virtual Library for the Biological, Agricultural and Medical Sciences" (Proceedings of the Contributed Papers Session, Biological Sciences Division, Special Libraries Association, 88th Annual Conference, Seattle, Wash.: June 1997). (http://nucleus.cshl.org/CSHLlib/BLSD/seattle/mitchell.htm) [Referenced Jan. 1999]

6. Ibid.

7. Anne Callery, Yahoo employee, personal comm., April 1996.

8. Roy Tennant, "The Art and Science of Digital Bibliography," Library Journal—Digital, 10/15/98 (http://www.bookwire.com/LJdigital/diglibs.article $25937) has discussed various strategies that could be used to best employ each type of tool, as has Terry Hanson, "The Access Catalogue Gateway to Resources," Ariadne—The Web Version, 5/98. (http://www.ariadne.ac.uk/issue15/main/)

9. Steve Mitchell, "Interface Design Considerations in Libraries," *Science and Technology Libraries* (in press).

7

Internet Public Library (IPL)

David S. Carter

The Internet Public Library (IPL) does not consist of one collection of Internet resources, but rather of many individual collections, each of which organizes a particular type of resource, or is built around the needs of a particular audience. This chapter attempts to provide a basic description of the current state of IPL collections, including the genesis of each collection, the types of resources found within each, the selection criteria used, and the technological mechanics of production. It also examines the strengths and weaknesses of IPL's approach and ends with a unique look at how lessons learned in the past can affect our view of organizing the Web today.

1.0 Introduction to IPL Collections

The Internet Public Library (IPL) (http://www.ipl.org/) (see figure 1) began in early 1995 as a class project at the University of Michigan's School of Information and Library Studies (as it was then known). As originally conceived, the IPL was not going to have any collections. Looking back, this position is somewhat ironic, as the IPL's collections, with nearly twenty thousand items, are one of the most visible and most frequently used components of the IPL Web site. But back in its infancy, the IPL was designed around library services, not "stuff." We were going to provide reference services, youth services, educational services, and services to library professionals, but

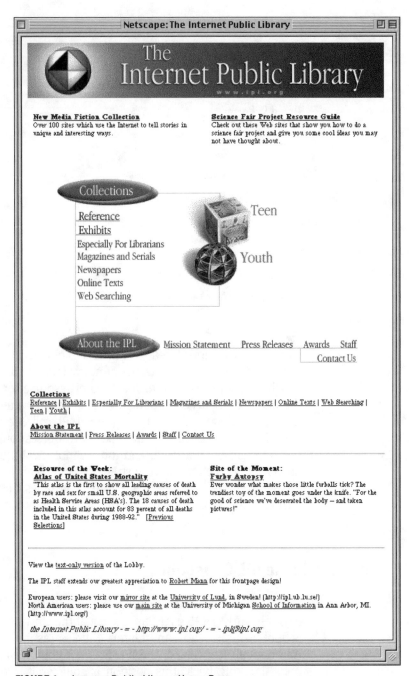

FIGURE 1.　Internet Public Library Home Page

we didn't need stuff. The Internet itself would be our collection, the search engines and spiders our catalog.

It didn't take too long before we realized how wrong a notion that was. As we attempted to translate traditional reference work to a networked environment, we realized the importance of having carefully chosen reference resources at hand when answering questions. To rely solely on Internet search engines, spiders, and sites like Yahoo in answering questions would be like going to a different room and looking through every book for an answer each time a new question was asked, instead of just grabbing the *World Almanac* (or a like source) from the nearby shelf of frequently used reference books. Even worse, because the search engines and spiders were designed to deal with everything on the Internet at a fairly basic level, there was none of the organizational or evaluative value that professional librarians bring to a library collection. It became apparent to us that a collection of Internet reference resources, selected and organized by professionals (and professionals-in-training), would be a good idea. It also made sense to us that, if we were going to go through all the trouble of putting together such a collection, we might as well share the fruits of our labor with the rest of the world by making this collection available via the IPL Web site. Thus, the IPL Ready Reference Collection was born.

When the IPL opened, the collection consisted of approximately two hundred items in the Ready Reference Collection, all hand coded into HTML pages, plus a handful of Shakespeare texts linked to a Shakespeare page. As the IPL grew, we identified other types of collections to create, either to serve a particular audience (youth, teens, and librarians), a type of resource (texts, newspapers, and serials), or a specific reference need (associations, literary criticism, and Native American authors). Today the IPL collections number nearly twenty thousand items and represent the hard work of over one hundred students and staff.

This chapter attempts to provide a basic description of the current state of IPL collections. Due to space limitations, it is by necessity a surface exploration; for those interested in much detail, plus theory and the practical means for applying IPL lessons to your particular situation, please read the collections-related chapter in the forthcoming book, *The Internet Public Library Handbook.*[1]

2.0 IPL Mission Statement

The mission statement of the IPL (reproduced below) fairly explicitly calls for the IPL to develop and maintain collections of Internet resources.

> The Internet is a mess. Since nobody runs it, that's no surprise. There are a lot of interesting, worthwhile, and valuable things out there—and a lot that are a complete waste of time.
>
> Over the last few hundred years, librarians have become skilled at finding the good stuff, organizing it, and making it easier for people to find and use. Librarians also fight for important ideas like

freedom of expression and thought, equality of access to information, and literacy.

The Internet Public Library is the first public library of the Internet. As librarians, we are committed to providing valuable services to that world. We do so for many reasons: to provide library services to the Internet community, to learn and teach what librarians have to contribute in a digital environment, to promote librarianship and the importance of libraries, and to share interesting ideas and techniques with other librarians.

Our mission directs us to:

- serve the public by finding, evaluating, selecting, organizing, describing, and creating quality information resources;
- develop and provide services for our community with an awareness of the different needs of young people;
- create a strong, coherent sense of place on the Internet, while ensuring that our library remains a useful and consistently innovative environment as well as fun and easy to use;
- work with others, especially other libraries and librarians, on projects which will help us all learn more about what does and does not work in this environment;
- uphold the values important to librarians, in particular those expressed in the Library Bill of Rights. [http://www.ala.org/work/freedom/lbr.html]

We are committed to providing free services to the Internet community, in the greatest tradition of public libraries. However, we can not sustain our library without a solid financial base. We are continually seeking enterprises that provide both services to our community and funding for our operations. We are always open to new ideas and partnerships. [http://www.ipl.org/about/newmission.html]

3.0 IPL Funding

The IPL's main funding source at present is via its host institution, the School of Information at the University of Michigan (http://www.si.umich.edu/). The school receives the funds it supplies to IPL as part of two separate educational grants from the W. K. Kellogg Foundation (http://www.wkkf.org/). Additional past funding has come from a direct grant from the Andrew W. Mellon Foundation (http://www.mellon.org/) and from funds obtained from software licensing and contract work.

The budget for the entire IPL for fiscal year 1998–99 is approximately $130,000, the majority of which goes for staff salaries and benefits.

4.0 Overview of IPL Collections

The IPL does not have one singular collection. Rather, we have several collections, all built around a specific purpose or for a certain audience. Each of these collections was created independently, though not in a vacuum: lessons and techniques learned in creating one collection were often applied to subsequent collections. So instead of trying to cover all of our collections as a whole, each collection will be described individually. The collections are divided up broadly (and rather arbitrarily) into four main groups: reference collections, reading room, libraries and librarians, and youth and teen.

4.1 Reference Collections

4.1.1 Ready Reference

Location: http://www.ipl.org/ref/RR/
Approximate size: 2,800
Open date: March 1995

Genesis: The Ready Reference Collection is the original IPL collection. It was created by the original reference team as a resource primarily intended for internal use by those of us who were answering reference questions. But we figured as long as we were going to put our hard work into creating the collection, we might as well make it available to the general public as well. Little did we realize that the Ready Reference Collection would become one of the most popular sections of the IPL.

Description and selection criteria: The IPL Ready Reference Collection is a collection of Internet resources gathered together with the needs of the Internet community in mind. It is not intended to be a comprehensive hotlist to all sites on every subject, but rather an annotated collection, chosen to help answer specific questions quickly and efficiently. Sources are selected according to ease of use, quality and quantity of information, frequency of updating, and authoritativeness (paraphrased from the Web site, http://www.ipl.org/ref/RR/).
The IPL seeks to collect Internet resources that

- are high in useful content, preferably those that provide information in their own right rather than simply providing pathways to information;
- are updated consistently (unless the nature of the resource is such that updating is unnecessary);
- are designed such that any graphics are an attractive complement to the information rather than a flashy distraction from it;

- provide text-only interfaces for nongraphical browsers;
- show evidence of having been proofread carefully (no spelling or grammatical errors or faulty tagging);
- contain only live links to documents that are as relevant as the primary document.

A resource that does not meet all the above criteria may still be added to the Ready Reference Collection if the selector feels that it is still a useful source (paraphrased from the Web site, http://www.ipl.org/ref/RR/Rabt.html).

Creators: David S. Carter, Chris Farnum, Lydia Ievins, Nettie Lagace, Sara Ryan, Paul Schaffner, Schelle Simcox, Jessie Tropman, and Nancy Vlahakis. Significant additional contributions were made by Ernie Kurtz and Steve Toub.

Access: The Ready Reference Collection can be browsed alphabetically or by a custom-developed hierarchical subject structure. A simple search feature is also available.

4.1.2 Associations on the Net (AON)

Location: http://www.ipl.org/ref/AON/
Approximate size: 1,200
Open date: April 1996

Genesis: An example of an IPL collection that is also a reference tool, the Associations on the Net (AON collection) grew out of a need identified by those answering IPL reference questions. A typical strategy employed in a traditional reference setting is to refer a patron to a professional organization or association related to the topic of their inquiry. So, to aid in the identification of associations with Web sites, a group of students in an IPL class was enlisted to create such a collection, modeled after the Ready Reference Collection.

Description and selection criteria: The AON is a collection of Internet sites providing information about a wide variety of professional and trade associations, cultural and art organizations, political parties and advocacy groups, labor unions, academic societies, and research institutions. Abstracts summarizing information about the association and its site are provided onsite (paraphrased from the Web site, http://www.ipl.org/ref/AON/).

AON seeks to collect official sites for associations and organizations, typically those that are nonprofit and membership centered. AON can serve as a useful reference tool to find information about a broad range of subjects, issues, and interests represented by associations. The associations in this collection are mostly nonprofit organizations whose mission is to

- disseminate news and research;
- create educational and professional opportunities;
- foster discussion and debate of issues;
- provide various services to members and nonmembers;
- influence policy and legislation;
- promote contacts among members in their fields of interest (paraphrased from the Web site, http://www.ipl.org/ref/AON/about.html).

Creators: Suzy Im, Elisabeth Klann, Joseph Mencigar, and Mary Metiva

Access: The AON Collection can be browsed alphabetically or by a custom-developed hierarchical subject structure. A simple search feature is also available.

4.1.3 Native American Authors (NAA)

Location: http://www.ipl.org/ref/native/
Approximate size: 750
Open date: April 1997

Genesis: The Native American Authors (NAA) Collection started with an idea: that it would be useful to have information about Native American authors all in one well-organized place. Interested students in one of the IPL classes were enlisted, obsession ensued (as is often the case in IPL projects), and a collection was born. The NAA Collection is one collection of Web sites in the IPL where the sites are not the point. Rather, the main purpose is to provide information about the authors and a bibliography of their work. The sizable collection of related Web sites is simply a wonderful bonus.

Description and selection criteria: This Web site provides a place to learn about and honor the works, lives, and achievements of Native North American authors. To be included in the project, authors must be American Indian or First Nations by blood and be accepted as such by other Native American people. Federal recognition is not necessary.

The current scope of the project includes written works by contemporary and historical Native American and First Nations authors in the geographical area of the United States and Canada. Possible future expansion of the project may include widening the geographical area covered or broadening the range of artistic expression to include other forms such as storytelling, speaking, musical expression, and artwork.

Web links to outside resources for further research are also provided. These links are selected according to the collection policy listed below.

- Web links are chosen because they provide additional useful information about Native American authors, tribes, or books in the project.
- Links about authors may include online interviews, biographical information, discussions of the author's literary works and style, and the author's own home page.
- Links about tribes are provided to help users interested in learning more about the contexts, cultures, backgrounds, and perspectives authors bring to their work. Official tribal Web sites are linked whenever available, and Web sites created by Native American people are actively sought. However, non-Native American authored sites may be included if they are found to provide useful information. Examples of linked Web sites about tribes include cultural and historical information, official tribal Web sites, tribal organizations such as tribal colleges and tribal newspapers, and Web sites encouraging study of Native American languages.
- Links about books are provided to offer as much information as possible about specific titles. They may include online book reviews, literary discussions about the book, news releases, author comments about the book and the process of writing it, online excerpts or full-text of the book if available, and other miscellaneous information such as links showing the cover art. In providing this information, links are sometimes made to Web pages on commercial sites such as online book publishers or booksellers (paraphrased from the Web site, http://www.ipl.org/ref/native/policy.html).

Creators: Nicole Campbell, Karen Jania, Lorri Mon, Michelle Sampson, and Yolisa Soul

Access: The NAA Collection can be browsed by author name, work title, or tribe.

4.1.4 Online Literary Criticism (LitCrit)

Location: http://www.ipl.org/ref/litcrit/
Approximate size: 1,300
Open date: April 1998

Genesis: Another example of an IPL collection that was created to fill a need is the Ask a Question service. Noticing a rise in the number of questions about locating author information and literary criticism online, and tired of creating Webliographies from scratch in response to each question asked, the IPL reference staff undertook the task of preemptively putting together a collection of sites about authors and their works.

Description: The Online Literary Criticism (LitCrit) Collection primarily seeks to collect evaluative or explanatory writings about works of literature. While the collection does not provide evaluation of the collected writings themselves, certain standards must be met for critical works to be included in the collection (paraphrased from the Web site, http://www.ipl.org/ref/litcrit/about.html).

At present, the LitCrit Collection contains only sites related to works of literature written in the English language. Future plans call for sites related to literatures of other languages to be added.

The LitCrit Collection is the only IPL collection that contains a significant number of sites that are not freely available to the general public. Notably, the LitCrit Collection contains items from both Project MUSE (http://muse.jhu.edu/) and the Northern Light Special Collection (http://www.northernlight.com/docs/premiumcontentalpha. htm), both of which are fee based.

Selection criteria: We prefer that works included in the collection be written by a scholar of literature of at least the graduate student level. This includes professors, doctoral students, and graduate students of literature. Works published under the aegis of some external editorial body are particularly important.

Of similar importance are professionally published reviews of literature. These may be reviews originally published on the Internet under the aegis of an authoritative editorial body or reprints of reviews originally published in print publications.

Also acceptable are works written and published under the supervision of academic professionals. Works written for an undergraduate college class and published (made available on the Internet) of the students' own accord are generally not acceptable.

The fourth category of acceptable works, those works produced by authors of unverifiable academic standing but nevertheless marked by serious critical analysis, may be considered for inclusion. References (bibliographies, footnotes, etc.), good editing, Web-site design (indicating serious and sustained effort), and listing in other academically oriented literary collections are all indications in favor of inclusion for such sites (paraphrased from the Web site, http://www. ipl.org/ref/litcrit/about.html).

Creators: Ken Irwin, Katie Stottlemyer, and David S. Carter

Access: Each site in the collection is assigned a code designating either one or more authors, one or more works by an author, or one or more literary periods. Each author's work is assigned a code designating one or more authors. Each author is assigned a code designating one or more literary periods. Users can thus access the sites in the collection via an intricate, yet free-flowing, Web of period-author-work. For example, a link from the front page of the LitCrit Collection labeled Twentieth-Century American Literature leads to a list of all of the authors in the collection from that period, plus sites that deal more generally with literature from that period. A page for each author lists sites related to that author generally and links to separate pages that list sites that deal with a specific work by that author.

4.2 Reading Room

4.2.1 Online Texts

Location: http://www.ipl.org/reading/books/
Approximate size: 7,800
Open date: December 1995

Genesis: The Online Texts Collection has its preorigins in the days immediately preceding the opening of the IPL. To add some measure of literary weight to this enterprise that we were calling a library, we constructed a collection of links to the works of Shakespeare (http://www.ipl.org/reading/shakespeare/shakespeare.html). Later that year, one of the students in the second IPL class took it upon himself to expand on this by using a simple program to troll through pages listing various other texts available online—extract author, title, and URL information—and place the sorted listings into HTML pages. The next summer, the listings were moved into a database where more descriptive cataloging and subject access were added; and the modern IPL Online Texts Collection was born.

Description and selection criteria: Any online text that resembles a traditional nononline text is eligible for inclusion. Generally, materials that were created specifically for primary distribution on the Internet have not been included, nor have materials that are likely to be ephemeral (i.e., disappear in a few weeks). Typically, an online text is an electronic version of a book; however, individual poems, essays, letters, dramas, and so forth are also considered for inclusion.

Creators: David S. Carter, Nigel Kerr, and Lars Nooden

Access: The Online Texts Collection can be browsed by author, title, and by a modified, hierarchical version of the Dewey Decimal Classification (DDC) (http://www.oclc.org/oclc/fp/index.htm). DDC 20 is used as the basis for assigning subject-based classification, with modifications made as needed. Users can perform searches by author and/or title or search the DDC subject headings. Library of Congress Subject Headings (LCSH) are now being added to the records for new items, but are not presently available to the users because a majority of the older records have not yet been assigned LCSHs.

4.2.2 Other Text Collections

Location: http://www.ipl.org/reading/books/other.html
Approximate size: 125
Open date: January 1997

Genesis: Created mainly as a tool to help keep track of where we have and haven't looked for texts to include in our own Online Texts Collection, this small database is also made available to our users.

Description and selection criteria: The Other Text Collections contains listings of significant collections, depositories, and catalogs of places where electronic texts can be found on the Internet.

Creator: David S. Carter

Access: The Other Text Collections can be browsed by name of the collection. The major collections are available directly from the main collection page.

4.2.3 Online Serials

Location: http://www.ipl.org/reading/serials/
Approximate size: 2,600
Open date: December 1995

Genesis: The Online Serials Collection was created at the same time as the initial Online Texts Collection and initially was gathered in much the same manner. After being moved to a database, the Online Newspapers Collection was spun off into its own collection (see the following page).

Description and selection criteria: The IPL Online Serials Collection lists online versions of magazines, newsletters, and professional journals, as well as such similar publications that exist only in electronic form, such as e-zines and e-journals. To be considered for inclusion, the online version of the serial must include some significant amount of articles and other information that is free to the general public, not just tables of contents and subscription information (paraphrased from the Web site, http://www.ipl.org/reading/serials/about.html).

Creators: David S. Carter and Lars Nooden

Access: The Online Serials Collection can be browsed alphabetically or by a custom-developed hierarchical subject structure. A simple search feature is also available.

4.2.4 Online Newspapers

Location: http://www.ipl.org/reading/news/
Approximate size: 2,000
Open date: December 1995

Genesis: Originally part of the Online Serials Collection, the Online Newspapers Collection was spun off when it became apparent that the type of access desired for newspapers (i.e., regional) was quite different from that of other types of electronic serials (i.e., by subject).

Description and selection criteria: The IPL Online Newspapers Collection lists online versions of print-based newspapers. In addition to traditional local and national newspapers, it also lists official and student-run newspapers from colleges, universities, and primary and secondary schools. To be considered for inclusion, the online version of the newspaper must include some significant amount of articles and other information that is free to the general public (paraphrased from the Web site, http://www.ipl.org/reading/news/about.html).

Creators: David S. Carter and Lars Nooden

Access: The Online Newspapers Collection can be browsed alphabetically or by location, including countries divided by continent or by individual state for the United States. A simple search feature is also available.

4.3 Libraries and Librarians

4.3.1 Especially for Librarians

Location: http://www.ipl.org/svcs/
Approximate size: 200
Open date: March 1995

Genesis: Originally part of the Ready Reference Collection, the section of library and librarian-related resources was spun off during a reorganization of the Ready Reference Collection, acknowledging the fact that the librarian section was serving a different user population than the general Ready Reference Collection. Since then, the Especially for Librarians Collection has been at the center of a sporadic effort by the IPL to serve the greater community of librarians on the Internet.

Description: The Especially for Librarians Collection is comprised of a directory of Internet resources of particular interest to librarians, including resources for On the Job, News, Employment, Library Advocacy, Librarianship Issues, Organizing the Web, Internet for Libraries, and Fun Facts.

Selection criteria: Any well-designed Web site with useful content that is of interest to librarians can be included.

Creators: Lydia Ievins. Nettie Lagace and Jill Roberts have made significant further contributions.

Access: The Especially for Librarians Collection can be browsed by a simple topical subject system.

4.3.2 Great Libraries on the Web

Location: http://www.ipl.org/svcs/greatlibs/
Approximate size: 160
Open date: April 1997

Genesis: This collection was created in conjunction with National Library Week in 1997. We had a booth in the exhibit hall at the ALA Midwinter Conference that year and asked librarians who stopped by to fill out a form telling us about special projects they had done on their library's Web site. We also took information via a form on the IPL site. We then compiled the information we collected and put a site together.

Selection criteria: Any special section of a library's Web site is eligible, as long as the library is proud of it!

Creator: Schelle Simcox

Access: The Great Libraries on the Web Collection can be browsed by name of library, location of library, type of library, or special feature of the Web site.

4.4 Youth and Teen

4.4.1 Youth

Location: http://www.ipl.org/youth/
Approximate size: 700
Open date: April 1997

Genesis: When the IPL first opened in March 1995, there was very little available on the Internet aimed at a youth audience. Thus when the Youth Division was originally developed, we focused on creating original resources, such as online stories and science experiments for kids. As time passed, the Internet literally exploded with material aimed at and appropriate for a youth audience. Thus we saw it as our duty to develop a collection of resources for youth to help kids and their parents find useful and entertaining sites on the Web. (See figure 2.)

Description and selection criteria: The Internet is a vast collection of materials authored and compiled by numerous individuals from a multitude of disciplines. While it is true that sites and resources of questionable value exist on the Internet, others that are thoughtfully developed, well maintained, and well organized are also available. The Internet Public Library's Youth Division librarians have composed the following selection policy for the inclusion of Internet resources and sites into its collection.

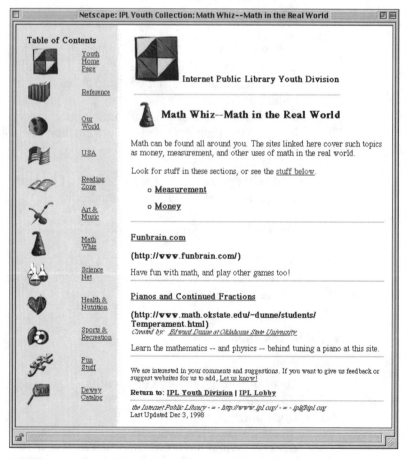

FIGURE 2.   IPL Youth Collection: Math Whiz

The collection of the Youth Division of the Internet Public Library was developed for children ages four through eleven, their parents, teachers, and anyone else interested in literature and information directed to and about children. Material used and sites recommended are chosen based on their appropriateness for the subject matter (i.e., science projects, math, stories, literature discussion, etc.) and should be written and maintained by an authoritative source. The information should be current, accurate, and presented in an objective and well-organized manner. While the resources may not be aimed specifically at children, their contents should be of interest and useful to these age groups or to their parents and teachers (paraphrased from the Web site, http://www.ipl.org/youth/SelectionPolicy.html).

Creators: Sara Brodkin, Hillary Corbett, and Schelle Simcox. Candace Goss, Stefanie Halliday, Michele de la Iglesia, Marianne Le, and Jean Milligan have made further significant contributions.

Access: The Youth Collection can be browsed by either a simplified hierarchical version of the DDC (no more than three levels deep) or by a custom-developed hierarchical subject structure.

4.4.2 Teen

Location: http://www.ipl.org/teen/
Approximate size: 500
Open date: December 1995

Genesis: While the original IPL had a youth division and plenty of materials for adults, it was missing an important element of library service, specifically teens and young adults. To rectify that situation, a group of students in the second IPL class took on the task of creating an IPL teen division. While they did not set out to create a teen collection per se, the four initial sections that they developed, entertainment, colleges/universities, social services, and sports, all ended up having elements of a protocollection. Greater detail on the creation of the teen division can be found in "Making Web Space for Young Adults: Issues and Process[,] a Case Study of the Internet Public Library Teen Division" (http://www.isoc.org/isoc/whatis/conferences/inet/96/proceedings/h4/h4_3.htm).[2] Later, these sections were taken apart and re-formed into a true IPL collection, and the modern IPL teen division was born.

Description and selection criteria: The collection of the teen division of the Internet Public Library is developed for teenagers ages thirteen though nineteen and their parents, teachers, and anyone else interested in information directed to and about teenagers and young adults. Material used and sites recommended are chosen based on their appropriateness for the subject matter and should be written and maintained by an authoritative source. The information should be current, accurate, and presented in an objective and well-organized manner. While the resources may not necessarily be aimed specifically at teens, their contents should be of interest and useful to these age groups.

Some areas of the Teen Division cover information about difficult topics with which teens are confronted in today's rapidly changing society. The teen years are a time of tremendous growth and development, and today's teens are exposed to issues and experiences that would challenge even adults with the most developed coping skills. The Internet is potentially one such source of exposure for teens, yet it also has profound potential for the information dissemination that teens desperately need.

The IPL Teen Division seeks to provide teens with access to basic information about many of the difficult issues that they face. In doing so, we recognize that we have provided links to sites that some teens and adults will consider inappropriate. We actively seek sites that are authoritative, and we avoid sensationalistic sites that lack content. At times, however, we make the decision to include sites that have potentially questionable material because the usefulness of other information at the site makes that site's benefits outweigh its disadvantages (paraphrased from the Web site, http://www.ipl.org/teen/selecpol.html).

Creators: Samantha Baily, Susan Hollar, Holly Piwowar, and Cynthia Webster. Sara Ryan has made further significant contributions.

Access: The Teen Collection can be browsed alphabetically or by a custom-developed hierarchical subject structure. A simple search feature is also available.

5.0 Production Mechanics

With a few notable exceptions, the IPL collections function as described below.

Each collection has its own set of FileMaker Pro databases, which reside on an old PowerMac 6100 that we use as a Macintosh server in the IPL offices. Typically, there are two databases for each collection: a main database, which contains the records for each item, and a subject heading database, which contains information about the headings used (name of heading, scope notes, etc.).

Variations on this scheme abound, depending on the access points, as detailed in the collection descriptions. For example, the LitCrit Collection has three databases, one for the sites, one for the authors, and one for the works. The Native American Authors Collection has four databases: author information, work information, tribe information, and site information. Since the Youth Collection has two sets of subject access points (DDC and homegrown), there are two databases of subject information. The Newspapers, Especially for Librarians, and Great Libraries Collections do not use complicated access structures, so each has only one database.

For most collections, new items and changes are made directly to the database; for the Ready Reference, AON, and Serials Collections, separate entry databases are used and are periodically imported into the main databases. Entry databases are used for these collections as there are usually many students in the IPL classes who are doing collection development for these collections, and quite frankly, it is safer not to allow everyone access to the main databases so that a minor mistake doesn't destroy everything. Periodic backups are made of all the databases.

Approximately once a week, each collection is processed. New items are checked over for accuracy and appropriateness; then a series of internal FileMaker scripts are run to output the data in tab-delimited format into the IPL's working space in the Andrew File System (AFS). (Notable exceptions to this process are the Online Texts and Especially for Librarians Collections, which are discussed below.)

Once the data is in the IPL working space, we run a series of custom-made Perl scripts to create indexes for the database output files. Generally, these indexing scripts create a subject index and a simple full-text inverted file index for the search engine to use. We then copy new data and index files over to the IPL's production space on the IPL Web server, a Sun Sparc 10 running Solaris. The Web server is a version of Apache (http://www.apache.org/).

The Especially for Librarians Collection uses a different approach; before exporting data from FileMaker, we use calculation fields to create HTML code for each item. We then use FileMaker scripts to sort the records and write out the HTML code to various files in the IPL working space. Then on the server side, Apache Server Side Includes (SSIs) inserts the chunks of HTML code within the appropriate pages in the IPL Web site; no indexing or other processing is required. Why was this collection done differently? Novelty, more than anything else; we wanted to experiment with different ways of dealing with the presentation of collections.

The Online Texts Collection is stranger yet. The collection is a joint effort between IPL and the University of Michigan's Humanities Text Initiative (HTI) (http://www.hti.umich.edu/). Before exporting, we transform the data for the item records and DDC headings into Standard Generalized Markup Language (SGML), according to a custom document type definition (DTD) developed by Nigel Kerr (at HTI) and myself. We export SGML records and transfer them over to HTI, where Open Text (http://www.opentext.com/) is used to index and serve out the information via the IPL's Web site. Again, the reason for doing things differently was curiosity; we wanted to see how well an SGML system would work for purely bibliographic information for Web sites. The jury is still out, though the fact that we have not rushed to convert all of our other collections to this process should serve as some hint about our feelings of success.

6.0 Strengths and Weaknesses

The chief strength of IPL collections lies in the human element. Each resource found in the collections has been identified, cataloged, and abstracted by a real-life librarian (or librarian-in-training). We tend to be choosy about what goes into our collections, meaning that users of the IPL find select lists of high-quality resources rather than a multitude of resources of varying quality. This value-added approach to Internet collection development is highly prized by our user community.

A main strength and weakness of the IPL collections lies in the collections' individuality. By custom tailoring a collection around a specific type of resource or for a specific audience, we can create a collection that better serves the resources and the people looking for them. Every collection that uses subject headings for browsing has its own separate hierarchy, custom built for the intricacies of the types of resources, the coverage of the subject matter, and the intended audience. At the same time, the lack of cohesion serves as a barrier, as a person looking for chemistry resources in the Ready Reference Collection may not be aware that there are related resources in the AON, Teen, Youth, Serials, and Online Texts Collections. Further, the individual subject hierarchies do not map well to each other, making it difficult to draw those connections automatically for the user.

Since the IPL relies mainly on the work of students and volunteers, we are stuck with pursuing collection development in the areas that are of interest to whoever is working with the IPL collections at a given time. So, if for one semester no one is strongly interested in health resources, the Health section of the Ready Reference Collection gets short shrift. This ad hoc method of collection development is necessitated by the IPL's low level of funding, which translates to a skeleton professional staff that, quite frankly, is inadequate to manage an enterprise of this size.

Collection maintenance is a nightmare. With twenty thousand items spread out over twelve collections and no good technological solution, we are forced to rely on spot checks and messages from our patrons to identify and correct bad links.

To this point, the largest impediment to the development of IPL collections has been their centralization. Due to the mechanics involved, it has been necessary for those working on IPL collections to be physically present on the University of Michigan campus.

Many of the problems discussed above are being addressed in our upcoming move to an integrated, distributed collection system, discussed in the next section.

7.0 Time Frame

IPL began in early 1995 as a collaborative effort by Joe Janes and in the University of Michigan's School of Information and Library Studies (as it was known then). Today, directed by David S. Carter and still housed in the University of Michigan's School of Information, it has funding through August 1999.

8.0 Future Goals

Our current plans are to move all of the IPL collections from their individual FileMaker Pro databases into some form of large-scale database (perhaps Oracle [http://www.oracle.com/]) and to use a Web front-end program (possibly ColdFusion [http://www.coldfusion.com/]) to make the collections available to IPL users. The collections will still be available as individual entities, and with the exception of added searching features, the user will probably not notice much difference at first. However, we will also be able to offer a unified IPL collection that users can both use and search simultaneously. More importantly, we will be able to distribute the work of adding to the IPL collections out across the Internet—to students at other library schools and librarian volunteers—in much the same way that the IPL's Ask a Reference Question service (http://www.ipl.org/ref/QUE/) operates.

We'll also be adding some new collections. We've been working off and on putting together an Internet New Media Collection, which would cover things like Internet soap operas, interactive hypermedia fiction, and the like. We'd also like to do a collection of online exhibits, things that are similar to the original exhibits in the IPL exhibit hall (http://www.ipl.org/exhibit/) but are hosted and produced elsewhere.

And, of course, expansion of our current collection will also be in the cards. We hope our new collection development mechanism will allow us to enlist many other volunteers.

We also need a comprehensive IPL collection development policy; such a beast is at least a year overdue. Perhaps we'll lock everybody up into a room for a winner-take-all collection development policy cage match.

9.0 Vision Statement for Internet Collections

While we could elaborate about the need for cooperative collection development and standards in an electronic environment, we thought instead that it might be illustrative to undertake a grand IPL tradition of looking forward by looking back. Bear with us as we examine the life of a book in a traditional library setting to see how truly complex the activity of processing a physical book is.

First, the book must be identified. Librarians as a whole are busy people, and we don't have time to even glance at every single book that has been published. So, over the years, we've developed numerous mechanisms for bringing books to our attention that merit consideration for inclusion in our collections. These mechanisms range from book vendors and approval plans to patron suggestions to sitting down every so often and reading a publisher's catalog.

Second, the book must be selected. Many factors go into the selection of a book, from coverage to intellectual worth to entertainment value to patron desire to audience appropriateness to cost to the sturdiness of the physical container. Again, since librarians are busy people, we don't have time to read through every book that we are considering obtaining for our collections. So we rely on things such as reviews; publisher (or author or editor) reputation; reading the table of contents, the foreword, and the book jacket; skimming through the index; looking at the typeface and layout; and examining the spine and binding.

At this point, the book typically leaves the attention of the selector for a period of time ranging from a few days to a few weeks. When the book returns, it is seemingly magically ready for use in the library. But during this time, many things happen to the book.

Third, the book must be obtained. This includes paying for the book and actually getting a copy from the publisher.

Fourth, the book must be cataloged. This involves determining descriptive cataloging, such as figuring out authors, titles, page counts, and so forth, and assigning subject terms, generally either from DDC or LCSH. Librarians have developed strict rules for cataloging (AACR2) (http://www.ala.org/market/books/technical.html) so that consistency can be maintained and we can do that most common activity of librarians: sharing. An entire industry has sprung up around the idea of cooperative cataloging, so that one librarian can catalog a book once, and then librarians around the world can just copy the already existing record rather than requiring everyone who owns a copy of the book to duplicate the effort.

Fifth, the catalog record must be entered into a catalog. This seems obvious, but it is an important part of the process and is functionally different from the intellectual work of cataloging. Without a way to file and access the bibliographic information, we might as well just toss all of our books into a pile and go through them one by one when we need to find a specific one (gee, sounds an awful lot like relying on a general search engine to find a Web site). In the not-too-distant past, for libraries cataloging meant typing the information on one or more index cards and filing these into the card catalog. Today, this usually means entering the information into a database, more often than not as a MARC record. What is usually overlooked in this process is the large amount of time, money, and effort that went into the development of these bibliographic databases and the time and money necessary to maintain and upgrade them. Most libraries don't create their own database; rather, they purchase their bibliographic database system (such as Notis, Innopac, etc.) from a library systems vendor. Thus, again we see the time saving involved in creating a system once and using it many times.

Sixth, the book must be processed. This involves doing things to the physical book itself for reasons of identification (stamping the library's name inside), security (adding magnetic theft deterrent tags), protection (binding paperbacks with hard covers), location (adding spine labels with call numbers), and circulation (adding a bar code or a pocket and sign-out card).

At this point, the book usually comes back into the realm of the librarian who selected it. However, still more must be done before the book can be used.

Seventh, the book must be shelved. Generally, libraries choose to shelve their books by subject, using a call number derived from the assigned subject heading(s), but many other arrangements (by author, by genre, by accession, etc.) have been and are still being used. The difficulty, of course, is that a book is a physical object and can only be shelved in one place, so if a book is about the physics of baseball, it can only be shelved with other physics books or with other baseball books, but not with both. (Even when libraries own more than one copy of a book, they tend to shelve all copies together.)

Eighth, the book must be circulated/used. Libraries are not only about storing information, but more importantly about sharing the information contained within. Libraries have developed rather elaborate schemes and rules for making sure that people who need the information can get to it and that everyone plays fair (circulation policies, overdue fines, etc.). Some libraries rely on an honor system, while others make use of circulation clerks and security systems to enforce the rules.

Ninth, the book must be maintained. As inanimate objects, books do not take care of themselves. Worn bindings must be rebound. Damaged or missing books must be replaced. Misplaced books must be found and returned to their proper place on the shelves.

Tenth, the book may be removed. Books are removed from collections for a number of reasons. These reasons may be voluntary, such as weeding for lack of use or timeliness, or involuntary, such as if the book is missing or damaged beyond repair and irreplaceable. Generally, a removed book cannot just be discarded (or forgotten) but must be even further processed: its record must be removed from the catalog and circulation system and it must be marked as having been removed. Some removed books are given away to patrons; others find their way to a used book sale while the least fortunate end up in a recycle bin or trash can.

Now realize that this process (or one similar) is replicated for every book in a library's collection. It's a wonder that libraries can function at all!

The one common thread that runs through the above is an almost compulsive tendency for librarians to standardize processes and devise time-saving methods so that we can reduce the time to something manageable and share the fruits of our labor. These processes and methods have been developed over decades, even centuries, and some of the librarian holy wars fought over such things as cataloging would make today's struggles over HTML syntax seem like a game of Stratego. As we translate this process into the digital realm, what you'll notice most is the complete absence of these methods and processes; the Internet as a collections resource has only been in the collective consciousness of librarians for a few scant years. In other words, we're working here without a net and have to build systems from the ground up; this is exciting but also a bit scary.

You'll also notice that some of the things we do for books don't make much sense or are radically altered when we are dealing with Web sites. Since an Internet resource need not be tied to one physical location, any number of people can use it simultaneously. We don't even have to individually store an electronic resource; we just let it reside on the host server. Suddenly, out go such things as circulation and shelving. But if we want a networked resource to be considered part of our collection, we probably still have to catalog it and store that catalog record in a system of some sort. In short, all of the steps are still there, but in many ways are altered beyond our traditional way of thinking. The main goal still remains, but the steps taken to achieve that goal look different. Our challenge as a profession is to examine those lessons we've learned over the past decades and centuries regarding the acquisition and management of physical information resources and apply them to the brave new world of distributed electronic resources where appropriate. We must also rethink and create new tools and paradigms where the old ways no longer work. This is a heady task to be sure, but one of which I'm sure we're capable.

Notes

1. David S. Carter, "Collections," in *The Internet Public Library Handbook* (New York: Neal-Schuman, 1999).

2. Samantha Bailey and Sara Ryan, "Making Web Space for Young Adults: Issues and Process[,] a Case Study of the Internet Public Library Teen Division" (paper presented at meeting of the Internet Society, Transforming Our Society Now, Montreal, June 24–28, 1996).

8

Librarians' Index
to the Internet (LII)

Holly Hinman
Carole Leita

The Librarians' Index to the Internet (LII) (http://sunsite.berkeley. edu/InternetIndex/) is a searchable and annotated subject directory of more than four thousand Internet resources that have been selected and evaluated for their usefulness to the public library user's information needs. Resources are selected and indexed by a cadre of trained volunteer librarians from California libraries. A federal Library Services and Technology Act (LSTA) grant from the California State Library supports a project coordinator and indexer training. The University of California, Berkeley Digital Library SunSITE provides computer space and technical support. The LII receives over 120,000 hits per month and is linked to by more than two thousand Web sites worldwide.

1.0 Background

The Librarians' Index to the Internet (LII) (http://sunsite.berkeley.edu/ InternetIndex/) is currently an experiment in distributed indexing of the Internet that uses a cadre of volunteer librarians from throughout California, but it started as the personal bookmark file of Carole Leita, a reference librarian at the Berkeley (California) Public Library (BPL) (http://infopeople.berkeley.edu:8000/bpl/). The Gopher bookmark file that was to become the LII began in 1990 but had no public presence until the city of Berkeley set up a Web server in mid-1993. The BPL was one of the first city departments to establish a Web site, and included in that site was Carole's Gopher bookmark file, transformed into the BPL Index to the Internet. At the time that it moved to the city of Berkeley server, the file consisted of approximately three hundred unannotated but categorized sites.

The BPL Index grew and soon became well known within California, in part because of BPL's participation in the InFoPeople (http://www.infopeople.org/) Project. The California State Library initiated the InFoPeople Project in 1993–94 to provide points of public access to the Internet in public libraries throughout California. The project supplied hardware, software, Internet connectivity, training, and technical support to public library sites selected through a competitive grant process. The four Berkeley public library branches were among the first cycle of libraries selected for grant awards. The BPL Index was highlighted at InFoPeople workshops and meetings as a tool that could help public librarians find Internet resources to answer their patrons' questions quickly and accurately. Usage of the LII expanded beyond Berkeley and, as search engines discovered the LII and general users discovered its value, beyond California.

It was through the InFoPeople Project that Roy Tennant, the University of California, Berkeley (UCB) Digital Library SunSITE (http://sunsite.berkeley.edu/) manager, learned of the BPL Index. Roy was looking for projects that would be appropriate for inclusion in the SunSITE, and thought that the BPL Index could be improved and enhanced by the move. As he said in a recent e-mail, "I could see a way I could move [it] away from the bookmark thing into a Web-accessible maintenance interface. Then of course I liked what [Carole Leita] had done and wanted to sign her on as one of my 'digital librarians.'"[1] A description of the Digital Librarians Program can be found on the SunSITE (http://sunsite.berkeley.edu/Admin/librarians.html).

The LII moved from the city of Berkeley server to the SunSITE in March 1997 and changed its name to the Librarians' Index to the Internet. UCB provided computer space and technical support, but Carole Leita continued to be solely responsible for content and organization of the LII. Experimentation in the recruitment, training, and use of volunteer indexers began in April 1997.

The California State Library recognized the value of the LII as a statewide resource and awarded a federal Library Services and Technology Act (LSTA) grant in 1997–98 for the purposes of enhancing the LII, expanding the size of the database, and increasing the number of contributors. A major effort of the 1997–98 fiscal year was recruitment and training of eighty volunteer indexers, who are librarians from all over California. While most are from public libraries, there is representation from special, school, and academic libraries as well. A list of the indexers can be found at LII (http://sunsite.berkeley.edu/InternetIndex/indexers.html).

2.0 Mission

The driving force behind the LII is the information needs of public library users. The LII seeks to provide a mechanism that will enable public librarians and public library users to have "one-stop shopping" for quality and reliable Web sites that will answer most of their reference questions. The LII enlists the distributed knowledge and experience of librarians throughout California to accomplish this task. This largely volunteer, collective effort is totally noncommercial and must, at this point in its evolution, be regarded as experimental.

The LII mission statement from the LSTA grant documents reads, "The goal of this project is to improve access to serious and significant information on the Internet by creating and maintaining an index to Internet sites selected, evaluated, and indexed by professional librarians from throughout California." This goal should be understood in both a global and a local (California) context, because the need for a tool such as the LII is both global and specific to California.

On the global level, the Internet environment is such that the individual searching for a precise bit of information is confronted by an overwhelming quantity of constantly changing Web sites, many of which are of dubious quality at best. Even the search tools that have been created to help the user find information are constantly changing. What this means for the typical public library user, who is not a college student or a corporate information worker accustomed to daily computer use, is confusion, frustration, and often failure to find the desired information. End-user surveys conducted by the InFo-People Project indicate that the unaided public library Internet user finds what he or she is looking for somewhat less than half the time (http://infopeople.berkeley.edu:8000/stats/).

Librarians seeking to assist users in finding information on the Internet are themselves often frustrated by changes in Web sites and search tools. (To help librarians with the constant change in search tools, the InFoPeople Project maintains a Search Tools Chart, which is updated as needed [http://infopeople.berkeley.edu:8000/src/chart. html]). While recognizing that it is a professional responsibility to find, evaluate, and catalog Internet information, there are few individual public librarians who have either the time, dedication, or skills to do more than put a few links on the branch home page. As Roy Tennant writes, "Digital libraries need librarians to collect, organize, and provide informed access to their collections. But where are the digital librarians who can build tomorrow's library's today? They are far and few between" (http://sunsite.berkeley.edu/Admin/librarians.html).

In the specifically California context, the LII has developed as a life raft for what many have seen as a sinking public library ship. Over the last twenty years, California public libraries have suffered from numerous economic hardships, and collectively are understaffed and underfunded when compared with public libraries in other states. As Peter Schrag writes in *Paradise Lost: California's Experience,*

America's Future: "Statewide in the twenty years since the mid-1970s, per capita public library spending declined by nearly 20 percent, staffing by an equal amount, and service hours by over 40 percent."[2] Many branch libraries have been operating with either minimal or no materials budgets for much of this decade; to these libraries, Internet access has truly been a lifesaver. A number of librarians interviewed by the InFoPeople Project consultant said that Internet access had changed the library's fortunes by repositioning the library as an information provider within the community. These librarians often staff the library by themselves and need to be able to direct the novice Internet user to a site that will provide sufficient structure that he or she can navigate independently without getting lost, and sufficient information without overwhelming or confusing users. LII has become that site for many California public librarians.

3.0 Funding

The LII had no funding for the first seven years of its existence. Carole Leita was the sole creator and contributor and did all of the work on the LII as an unpaid volunteer. The city of Berkeley provided free space on its server from November 1993 to March 1997, when the LII moved to the UCB Digital Library SunSITE. The SunSITE provides a basic level of support to all of its digital librarians. That support involves space on the SunSITE, which is a Sun SPARC-center 2000E, and technical assistance as needed. In the case of the LII, technical assistance has included a number of enhancements including the application of the Simple Web Indexing System for Humans - Enhanced (SWISH-E) (http://sunsite.berkeley.edu/SWISH-E/) search engine and programming to accommodate the distributed volunteer indexers.

In 1997, the California State Library funded a grant proposal from the Peninsula Library System (http://www.pls.lib.ca.us/pls/pls.html) for support of the Librarians' Index to the Internet. Federal Library Services and Technology Act funding in the amount of $37,290 was awarded for the fiscal year that began on October 1, 1997. This funding supported a coordinator for up to thirty hours per month, plus additional time to recruit and train eighty volunteer indexers. It also supported some modest fees to UC Berkeley for technical support and enhancements, as well as travel expenses for the volunteer indexers to attend training workshops. Carole Leita continues to contribute thirty hours per month of her own, unpaid time to the project. Organizationally, although the LII is a separate grant, the LII is under the administrative oversight of the InFoPeople Project consultant, who provides overall policy direction and general support.

A second year of LSTA funding in the amount of $74,470 will provide for continuation of thirty hours of paid coordinator time, software upgrades, the addition of an intern to provide routine database maintenance and identify subject gaps, and the addition of forty more indexers. The estimated value of the contributed or in-kind time of the volunteer indexers and coordinator is $111,200.

An integral part of the plan for the 1998–99 fiscal year is the development of a plan for the long-term continuation of the LII. The LII cannot be supported indefinitely on federal grant funding, nor can it rely on the continued volunteer efforts of an individual, no matter how dedicated. It is sufficiently valuable to the California library community and greater library profession that it should have an institutionalized and secure future. Several private-sector companies have expressed interest in acquiring or partnering with the LII, but part of the appeal of the LII to the public library community is its noncommercial nature. Concerns about commercialization also weigh against such strategies as selling advertising or obtaining corporate sponsorships. All options will be explored however and a written plan will be presented to the California State Library. Ideally, the LII will become part of the future structure of libraries in California, possibly through new state legislation that envisions a network called the Library of California.

4.0 Audience

As has been noted, the primary audience for the LII consists of California public librarians and public library users. The secondary audience consists of public librarians outside of California, librarians from other types of libraries, and the general public.

There are several measures that demonstrate that the LII is indeed reaching its target audience. According to August 1998 statistics from the Digital Library SunSITE (http://sunsite.berkeley.edu/cgi-bin/stats.pl?Name=InternetIndex/), the LII is being accessed close to 30,000 times in a seven-day period, or approximately 120,000 times per month. It is the most heavily used file on the SunSITE by a factor of two to one. According to Roy Tennant, most of the usage is from libraries within the United States. However, some two thousand Web sites throughout the world link to the LII, according to an August 1998 search on AltaVista for links to sunsite.berkeley.edu/InternetIndex. The domain breakdown for those links is 29 percent from the .edu domain, 27 percent from .us, 17 percent from .com, 10 percent from .org, 6 percent from .net, 5 percent from .ca, 3 percent from .gov, 2 percent from .au, and 1 percent from .uk.

In addition to this quantitative information about the LII audience, there is a variety of qualitative information. The LII coordinator receives frequent unsolicited user comments and requests to link to the site. Librarians say that the LII is invaluable for training staff. Many libraries use the LII as a structured front end or gateway to the Internet because of the selectivity, quality, organization, and annotations of the entries. The LII is especially helpful for students and novice users, as indicated in the following two testimonials:

> I use the Index at least once a day, five days a week. I used it very successfully yesterday—an 18 year old had promised his 8 year old brother they would get pictures of dinosaurs off the Internet. They used Yahoo and found no pictures. After a half-hour or so, they requested help. I immediately took them to the Librarians Index. I told them these had been evaluated as useful sites, and it says immediately IF there are pictures or not. The first site listed under the subject "dinosaurs" led us to wonderful pictures of the 3 dinosaurs he had chosen, and we printed them out in color for the 8 year old. They were very happy, and so were we! (Jill Stockinger, branch head, Perris Branch Library, Riverside County Library System, under the administration of LSSI)

> If a patron has used a search engine and has not been able to find relevant sites, I recommend that they use the Index because then they will be able to find relevant sites. One patron was searching for information about alternative therapies for cancer. A search engine brought up sites that would sell her various products, but no site that had the information she wanted. I showed her how to use your site and she was pleasantly surprised to see how easy it was to use. (Brenna Ring, librarian I, San Diego County Library—El Cajon Branch)

Linda Woods Hyman, who as a librarian with the Pacific Bell Education First Project is herself involved in developing another Internet index, Blue Web'n (http://www.kn.pacbell.com/wired/bluewebn/) (discussed in chapter 3), uses and recommends the LII and says of it:

> The site is critical for two reasons. The first is that it is an excellent resource. It is easy to use, well maintained, and contains the "right stuff" for the audiences that I target (public and school librarians and teachers). The second reason is that I know from experience most librarians do not have the time, ability, or the inclination to develop a resource such as this. It is important for librarians to have access to sites such as the Librarians' Index to the Internet so that they do not waste their time searching for good sites. They can [go] straight to the resources there and use them, or refer users to them. There is no need to reinvent the wheel, it is already up and rolling.

5.0 Collection

The LII is a searchable and annotated subject directory of more than four thousand Internet resources that have been selected and evaluated for their usefulness to the public library user's information needs. Approximately 15 percent of the resources are directories, 10 percent are databases, and 75 percent are specific resources. The LII is organized into approximately forty major categories that are further divided into subcategories. Figure 1 shows the top-level categories and subcategories that are displayed on the LII home page. The number of categories and subcategories has tended to remain stable, but the categories themselves have evolved over time and continue to undergo refinement and redefinition. Subject coverage is broad, reflecting the varied interests of public library users. Staffing and technical limitations preclude the ability to report the relative subject strengths, and when the search software was applied to the LII, the ability to browse by broad subject category was lost. It might be said that the collec-

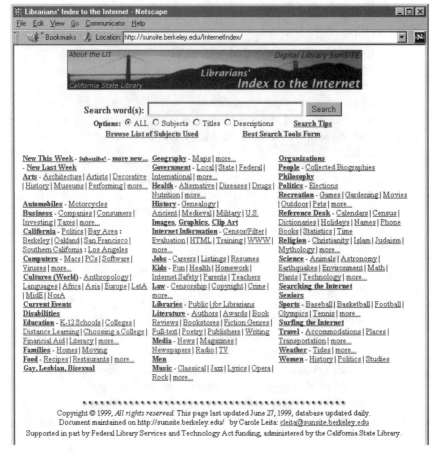

FIGURE 1.   Librarians' Index to the Internet Home Page

tion has a California focus in that it includes specific California sites of a nature that have not been included for other states.

The collection initially focused rather narrowly on sites that were electronically analogous to resources that might be found in the Ready Reference Collection. As the LII has grown, that focus has broadened, and the collection now has more in common with a good general public library, with value-added annotations. The indexer who selects a particular resource writes the annotation for that resource. The annotation is subsequently checked for accuracy and edited by the LII coordinator. Within specific subject areas that are in high demand in public libraries, efforts are made to identify and describe the best resources for that subject. Users cite this kind of selectivity as being of particular importance to them in areas such as medicine, consumer health, business information, government resources, legal topics, and homework assistance.

Clicking on a top-level category retrieves those resources that have been assigned that general, top-level heading; it does not necessarily retrieve resources that have been assigned subject headings that fall into one of the subcategories for the top-level heading. Thus, for example, clicking on Literature retrieves a page of resources that have been assigned that subject heading; not included in the list would be resources that are assigned the subject heading of Poetry, which is a subcategory under Literature. Search capability for the LII database is provided by SWISH-E. A search box is found near the top of the home page and at the bottom of any second-level page. The default search mode is to search all fields, but searches can be limited to subject headings, titles, or annotations. The ability to search annotations is particularly valuable, and often compensates for subject heading limitations. A Boolean *and* is assumed between multiple search terms. *Or* can be used to broaden searches, and *not* to exclude terms. An asterisk can be used as a wild card for truncation at the end of a word.

Whether a list of resources is retrieved by clicking on a subject heading or subheading or by means of a search, the resources are displayed by the following categories: Best of, Directories, Databases, and Specific Resources.

Future growth in the size of the LII is difficult to project because the indexers are volunteers, but if only half of the one hundred twenty trained indexers contribute one resource per week, that will add almost three thousand new resources per year.

6.0 Selection and Evaluation

The resources that are included in the LII are selected and evaluated by the coordinator and trained volunteer indexers. The indexers are professional librarians from libraries throughout California, recruited through workshops, meetings, California-based electronic mailing lists such as CALIX, and personal contact. Many are affiliated with the InFoPeople Project.

A major thrust of the LSTA-funded aspect of the LII has been directed to indexer training, motivation, and supervision. Volunteer indexers are trained in groups of twenty in daylong, hands-on indexer workshops held at central locations in northern and southern California. The training covers keeping up with new resources, evaluating Internet resources, writing annotations, indexing (assigning subject headings and categories), filling out the input form online, and maintaining the LII. Most of the materials used in the training are available on the Web (http://sunsite.berkeley.edu/InternetIndex/workshop/). After the workshop, new indexers choose a password, receive authorization clearance and the URL for the database maintenance page, and are on their way. Each indexer makes a commitment to add one new resource a week and to maintain a section of the LII database. Maintenance of the database involves checking the existing entries to make sure that annotations are still accurate and correcting inaccuracies.

The primary selection criterion for the LII is the usefulness of a resource to public library patrons (http://sunsite.berkeley.edu/InternetIndex/manual/criteria.html). Since public library user information needs are so broad in scope, the indexer is further advised to "think about the relative value of the resource in comparison to the range of information resources, on and off the Web."[3] Additional general considerations are listed on Selection Criteria for Adding Resources to the LII (http://sunsite.berkeley.edu/InternetIndex/manual/criteria.html) and essentially the same advice can be found on dozens of sites that instruct users in how to evaluate Web resources.

Most of the resources included in the LII are identified through public library reference work. For example, Carole Leita started the index when she was a reference librarian, and found many of the core sites in the process of answering a wide variety of questions at the main library in Berkeley. The current indexers discover new resources in much the same way as they pursue reference questions in their own libraries. Some of the indexers have areas of particular expertise or interest and identify resources in those areas. The first group of trained indexers, for example, was responsible for strengthening the LII resources in the area of religion and for creating a whole new area devoted to crafts.

LII indexers also use tools and updating sources created by other librarians, such as the Librarians' Site du Jour (http://www.wwa.com/~jayhawk/sitejour.html), the Scout Report (http://scout.cs.wisc.edu/scout/report/), the Digital Librarian (http://www.servtech.com/~mvail/new.html), Best Information on the Net (http://www.sau.edu/CWIS/Internet/Wild/index.htm), and LJ Digital's WebWatch (http://

www.bookwire.com/ljdigital/). A list of these resources is maintained as part of the Online Indexers' Manual (http://sunsite.berkeley.edu/InternetIndex/manual/newsites.html).

Once a potential site has been identified, the indexer evaluates it using the general guidelines for Web-site evaluation cited above, and also compares it to other resources already in the LII collection. It takes an average of an hour for an indexer to completely investigate and evaluate a site. To add a site to the LII, the following steps are taken:

(1) The indexer goes to the authorization page and enters login and password.

(2) The indexer searches the LII database to make sure a record does not already exist for the resource to be cataloged.

(3) Any records found as a result of the search are displayed in a table that allows the indexer to select one to edit. If a new record is to be added, clicking on the Continue button moves to the next screen.

(4) The database maintenance screen allows the indexer to edit an existing record or create a new record (see figure 2). If an existing record is being edited, the information appears automatically in the appropriate fields. For a new record, the indexer needs to enter a title, the URL, an annotation of not more than one hundred words, and one or more subject headings.

(5) The indexer can also change the category for an existing or new record. The default category is Specific Resource. The other categories are Best of, Directories, and Databases. Note also that there is a form for sending a note to the coordinator along with the new or edited record. To determine appropriate subject headings, the indexer can also pull up a separate window of all the subject headings by clicking on a link.

(6) After editing a record or creating a new record, the indexer clicks the Preview button.

(7) The indexer is then presented with a verification screen, which shows how the record will look and offers an opportunity to write the record to the database by clicking on the Done button, or to edit the record by clicking the Try it Again button. Once the Done button is clicked, a screen comes up that allows the indexer to do a new search or enter a new record.

Once the indexer indicates that an edited or new record is done, an e-mail copy of it is sent to the coordinator and, if it's a new record, a copy is also sent into the new records file (http://sunsite.berkeley.edu/InternetIndex/newrecords.html), which is a holding file for records that have been added recently but have not yet been indexed

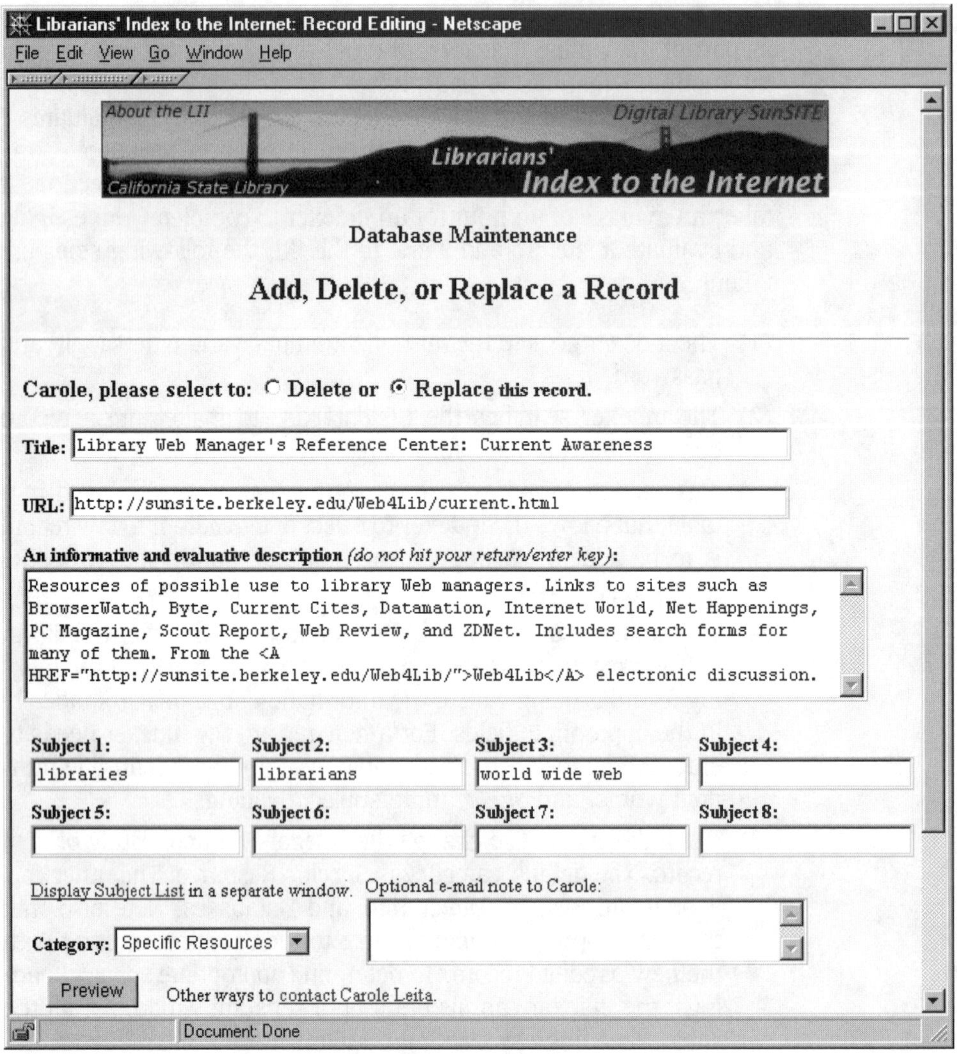

FIGURE 2.   Librarians' Index to the Internet Record Editing screen

and therefore cannot yet be found by searching the LII. The new records file is expunged every time the LII is reindexed.

The coordinator reviews records in the new records file, looking first at spelling and grammar and then going to the site to see if the annotation, subject heading(s), and assigned category are accurate. The coordinator sends an e-mail message to the contributing indexer after each record is edited. This sort of scrutiny is very labor intensive and is part of the indexers' training. As indexers gain experience, editorial monitoring is generally reduced to doing little more than checking for typographical errors. The editing is done in batches, with the most intensive effort on Sunday night or early Monday morning, when the New This Week entries are changed.

7.0 Mechanics of Production

SWISH-E is the software that indexes and is subsequently used to search the records that make up the LII. The staff at the UCB Digital Library SunSITE, under the direction of Roy Tennant, has enhanced the original version of SWISH and maintains it as SWISH-E.

Each of the more than four thousand resources in the LII is a separate file consisting of HTML metatags and their contents. When SWISH-E is run on this set of files, it creates an index that recognizes the assigned fields. These include the Dublin Core (DC) metadata fields of title, description (annotation), subject, and identifier (URL), and the UCB categories of keywords (includes the DC categories of title, description, and subjects), rank (the number indicating the category of best of, directory, database, or specific resource), and creator (the initials of the indexer). Reindexing the files takes from seven to ten minutes.

The SWISH-E-created index can then be searched by any of the fields. The search form allows searching by the UCB keyword field (default), which combines the subject, description, and title field, or searching each field separately.

The commands and files that make up the LII SWISH-E implementation are

(1) a one-word alias to a command to run an awk script that runs the SWISH-E indexing program command and replaces the Web page of new record additions with an empty one;

(2) a file that holds indexer information and authorization codes;

(3) the configuration file that gives SWISH-E its instructions when indexing. These instructions include the location of the directory that contains the files that are being indexed and the place and name of the index file it creates;

(4) the user-interface Perl program that is a common-gateway interface (CGI) to the SWISH-E software and index, which sorts and reformats the results;

(5) a suite of maintenance Perl programs that handles indexer authorization, record searching, creation or editing, and notification of the coordinator;

(6) a Perl program that captures the subject headings from all of the index entries, sorts them, removes duplicates, and writes out a Web page that lists all of the subjects used (http://sunsite.berkeley. edu/InternetIndex/subjects.html);

(7) a library of Perl subroutines called by the all of the Perl programs, thus allowing one change in that location to affect all the programs.

7.1 Link Checking

The link-checking software program MOMSpider is automatically run against the URLs of the entries on the first of every other month. Resulting file not found and redirect errors are checked and corrected by the indexers.

8.0 Taxonomy of Classification

The LII uses a modified Library of Congress (LC) subject classification. This means that if an LC subject heading is not the most common or popular terminology—not what the average person would think of first in looking for information on a given subject—then the more popular term is used as the subject heading. Decisions to use other than LC subject headings are made based on the collective experience of public librarians with a diverse user base, and locally developed subject headings are often checked against frequency of occurrence in major search engines like AltaVista.

As of mid-1998, there were over six hundred subject headings used in the LII. Subject headings have to be approved by the coordinator but are often suggested by the indexers. Since the size of the database is relatively small, resources tend to be grouped under broader headings. When the index contains three resources on a particular subtopic, a new subject heading for that topic may be created.

Some examples of LII modifications of LC may be helpful for illustrative purposes and are given below.

LII Subject Heading	LC Subject Heading
bicycling	cycling
birth record	registers of births, etc.
e-mail	electronic mail systems
gulf war	Persian Gulf War, 1991
ikebana	flower arrangement, Japanese
North Korea	Korea (North)
phonebooks	telephone directories
recipes	cookery
rulers	heads of state *or* kings and rulers
searching	online bibliographic searching
software	computer software

Some further examples, where the LII follows the terminology used most often in AltaVista, are: distance learning instead of distance education (distance learning occurs twice as often in AltaVista); paranormal instead of parapsychology (paranormal occurs more than ten times as often in AltaVista); repetitive stress injuries instead of overuse injuries (repetitive stress injuries occurs almost twice as often, and most of the instances of overuse injuries in AltaVista are sports related).

A full, browseable list of LII subject headings, including *see* and *see also* references, is available online (http://sunsite.berkeley.edu/InternetIndex/subjects.html).

9.0 Strengths

The LII has created an interface to the Internet that is easy for the average person to use and leads to quality resources in most areas of interest to the average person. Users' responses indicate that qualities about the LII that they appreciate most include manageable scope, quality of resources, the fact that the resources are evaluated by librarians, annotations, and regular maintenance to ensure quality. Perhaps the following two quotations from librarians who use the LII will best illustrate its strengths:

> I recommend the LII to patrons, especially novice searchers, for the following reasons:
>
> A search in a major search engine, such as Yahoo or AltaVista, often results in an overwhelming number of hits. Novice searchers may not know the best way to use these tools. As a result, they may leave without finding anything or finding too much to be of use. The LII provides a useable scope of sites. Since these sites usually provide links to similar sites, patrons can at least begin their search with reasonable expectations of finding a few sources, and then branching out.
>
> Because the sites in the LII are annotated, the patron has some idea of the content before actually going to the site. Patrons have commented that they believe the sites, and the information on them, have more integrity because they have been reviewed by librarians. They see it as a form of book selection for the web.
>
> The sites on the LII always seem to be available and where they should be (i.e., very few address changes, etc.). Novice searchers abhor Error: Not Found messages because they do not know whether it is the site—or the searcher—making the error. (Becky Ellis, electronic resources librarian, Cerritos Public Library)
>
> I use it most often when a customer asks for something general that s/he has heard is on the Internet, but does not have a specific site in mind. I usually don't have time to sit with a customer until they find their answer. Some examples of this are company information, airline reservations, and medical information. I will pull up the listings on the LII that pertain to what they are looking for,

and let the customer choose which sites to pursue. For this type of situation, I find the annotations on LII very helpful because the customer can have some idea of what the site is about before clicking on it and waiting for it to load. Other indexes such as Yahoo and Magellan do not have annotations, so if I left a customer with a list from one of those I think s/he would have to do a lot of clicking and waiting (which usually frustrates new users) before they find anything useful. I usually check back with the customer in 10 minutes or make sure they are on their way, and they generally are.

I also find it useful for questions where the quality and authority of the information is very important, such as medical information. Since the entries are chosen and annotated by someone not affiliated with the site, the chances are better that it is reliable information and not designed to guide someone toward a product. Most of the users that ask for help seem to be novice users, and I doubt they are aware that just about anyone can put a Web site up and say whatever they think or believe—even about heart disease. They also get frustrated and confused quickly by lots of clicking, so by starting off with the LII I can steer them toward what they want, and away from unverified sources. Any annotations that Yahoo and Magellan have come from descriptions put into the html of the individual sites.

I also suggest the index when I see that someone has spent a lot of unproductive and frustrating time with the results from a search engine like AltaVista or HotBot. Search engines just don't work very well for something general, such as news or weather. (Elaine Walker, county of Los Angeles, Marina Del Rey Library)

10.0 Weaknesses

Undoubtedly the greatest weakness is the lack of stable funding, which is characteristic of grant and volunteer-based projects in general. Internal weaknesses include various issues related to software programming, such as the lack of browseability, and a need to create real subject authority control and to identify and fill subject gaps. The maintenance methodology in place in mid-1998 is very labor intensive; and it is questionable whether it can be continued as the database grows in size.

11.0 Time Line

1990: The LII began as an organized Gopher bookmark file.

1992: The Gopher bookmark file was converted to a Netscape bookmark file.

1993: The file moved onto the city of Berkeley library's Web site and was named the BPL Index to the Internet. A script converted the bookmark file to separate pages by folder. The file included approximately three hundred unannotated but categorized entries and was still maintained by one individual.

1996: The BPL Index to the Internet became affiliated with the UCB Digital Library SunSITE. Technical support was provided to add a search engine (SWISH-E), add subject index terms, and create a system whereby other librarians would be able to add entries to the index.

March 1997: The BPL Index to the Internet moved to the Berkeley SunSITE and became the Librarians' Index to the Internet. It consisted of approximately twelve hundred annotated entries.

September 1997: The California State Library awarded a 1997–98 Federal Library Services and Technology Act grant to the Peninsula Library System to enhance the index and develop a training program, including an online manual and workshops for librarian indexers.

October 1997–September 1998: Developments in the project included the following milestones:

- produced online indexer instruction manual,
- trained eighty-six librarians as volunteer indexers,
- enhanced indexing,
- created subject headings authority file.

Index included over four thousand annotated entries in over six hundred subject categories.

September 1998–October 1999: Continued LSTA support will provide for further expansion of the indexer base, additional technical enhancements, and improvement of the subject authority file.

12.0 Future Goals

It is always problematic to make predictions in the environment of the Internet, but as of mid-1998, the optimum size of the LII would seem to be somewhere around ten thousand resources. Expansion to that size will necessitate additional subject authority control and enhanced searching capabilities. Recent access problems with the UC Berkeley SunSITE have emphasized the importance of securing a mirror site for the LII. In order for the LII to continue as a resource for the public library community and to grow as outlined, it will be necessary to find a stable funding source and to institutionalize the LII through some existing library.

13.0 Vision   The LII provides guidance to the person using the Internet as an information source by providing a freely available, searchable, and browseable collection of librarian-evaluated and described Internet resources. It is designed for use by both librarians and members of the general public.

The LII has been developed by, and will continue to be maintained by, a growing team of librarians, who as professionals are trained in the art of selecting, evaluating, cataloging, and providing information resources.

The state of California has just passed legislation (Senate Bill 409) to fund the development of the Library of California, which will provide access to resources in all types of libraries throughout California. It is the hope of those involved in the LII that by the year 2000 this index will be the central access point for Internet resources for the Library of California.

The future of Internet resource management depends on interconnectivity. Just as the academic community is developing single-search interfaces from which users can access multiple online catalogs, virtual libraries need to be collaborating in the development of resource-sharing partnerships. One such project, which is underway, is the Isaac Network (http://www.scout.cs.wisc.edu/scout/research/index.html) and is discussed in the Scout Report Signpost chapter.[4] This will allow multiple collections to be locally developed and maintained and yet appear as a single repository of Internet resources to end users.

Notes

1. Roy Tennant, personal comm., 1998.

2. Peter Schrag, *Paradise Lost: California's Experience, America's Future* (New York: New Press, 1998), 101.

3. Carole Leita, "Selection Criteria for Adding Resources to the LII" [accessed May 1999]. (http://sunsite.berkeley.edu/InternetIndex/manual/criteria.html)

4. Mike Roszkowski and Christopher Lukas, "A Distributed Architecture for Resource Discovery Using Metadata," *D-Lib Magazine* 6 (1998).

9

Mathematics Archives (Math Archives)

Earl D. Fife
Larry Husch

The Mathematics Archives (Math Archives) (http://archives.math. utk.edu/) is a multipurpose site for mathematics on the Internet. The primary emphasis is on materials that can be used in the teaching of mathematics. Resources available range from shareware and public domain software to electronic proceedings of various conferences to an extensive collection of links to other mathematical sites.

All materials in the Archives are categorized and cross-referenced for the convenience of the user. The Archives provides a variety of search mechanisms including a full-text database consisting of most of the items on the Archives. In addition, there are specialized databases for the major collections. The Archive's software is categorized by subject matter. Each software package contains one or more text files that form a database for our search engines. Similarly, our listings of links are categorized in several different ways and are searchable by keywords.

1.0 Responsible Persons Including Location and Affiliations

The Mathematics Archives (see figure 1) was founded and is codirected by mathematics professors Earl D. Fife of Calvin College and Larry Husch of the University of Tennessee - Knoxville. They are responsible for the overall organization and development of the site.

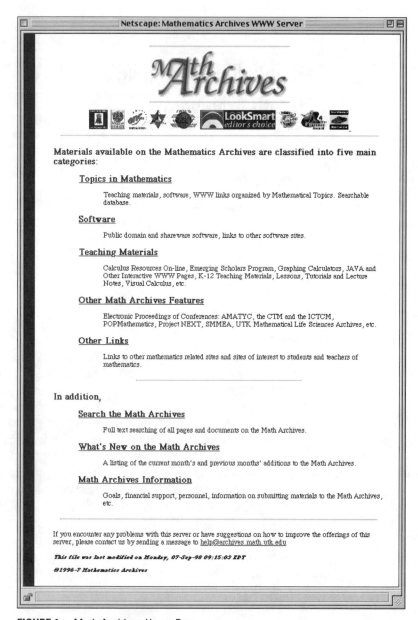

FIGURE 1.   Math Archives Home Page

Other mathematics professors have developed several specific parts of the site. In particular, Przemek Bogacki of Old Dominion University has developed and maintains the Online Calculus Resources pages (http://archives.math.utk.edu/calculus/crol.html) and is managing editor of the Electronic Proceedings of the International Conference on Technology in Collegiate Mathematics (EPICTCM) (http://archives.math.utk.edu/ICTCM/). Lou Gross of the University of Tennessee - Knoxville has organized the UTK Mathematical Life Sciences Archives pages (http://archives.math.utk.edu/mathbio/). John Emert of Ball State University has begun organizing the Mathematics and Liberal Arts pages (http://archives.math.utk.edu/liberal.arts/libarts.html). And John St. Clair of Motlow State Community College has organized Contests and Competitions (http://archives.math.utk.edu/contests/) and Calculators pages (http://archives.math.utk.edu/calculator/) and is liaison to the American Mathematical Association of Two-Year Colleges (AMATYC). Other volunteer contributors include mathematics professors Al Hibbard of Central College, Todd Will of Davidson College, and Dave Joyce of Clark University.

In addition to the contributors, we have an advisory board consisting of professors Arnie Ostebee of St. Olaf College, Howard Penn of the U.S. Naval Academy, Claudia Pinter-Lucke of California State Polytech University - Pomona, Jim Pinter-Lucke of Claremont College, David Smith of Duke University, Keith Stroyan of the University of Iowa, Jon Wilkin of Northern Virginia Community College, and Kathie Yerion of Gonzaga University.

2.0 Mission Statement

The goal of the Archives is to provide organized Internet access to a wide variety of mathematical resources. The primary emphasis is on materials that can be used in the teaching of mathematics. Currently, the Archives is particularly strong in its collection of educational software. Other areas, ranging from laboratory notebooks and problem sets to lecture notes and reports on innovative methods, are growing. A second strength of the Archives is its extensive collection of links to other sites that are of interest to mathematicians. Resources available through these links include electronic journals, preprint services, grant information, and information from publishers of mathematical software, texts, and journals. The Archives also publishes the electronic proceedings of various conferences that focus on the teaching of mathematics. Eleven Majordomo mailing lists are maintained on the Mathematics Archives, which also provides the archives of these and four other mailing lists.

All resources are organized to make them readily accessible to the user. We cross-reference and categorize the material according to subject area as well as by using keywords. The site is searchable using the Harvest search engine, and various areas of the site are also searchable by keyword.

These educational resources and the organized collection of links combine to make the Archives a comprehensive site for mathematics on the Internet.

3.0 Funding Sources and Project Budgets

Primary funding for the Archives has come through the National Science Foundation (NSF) (http://www.nsf.gov/) by way of two awards in their Undergraduate Instrumentation and Laboratory Improvement - Leadership in Laboratory Development (ILI-LLD) program. We selected this program because we wanted both hardware (a server for the Archives plus incidental hardware supporting our project) as well as salary support for two summers while we set up and refined the Archives. Both awards (DUE-9351398 and DUE-9550943) were granted to Calvin College (http://www.calvin.edu/), with the University of Tennessee - Knoxville (http://www.utk.edu/) as a subcontractor. Even though the hardware was to be housed at the University of Tennessee - Knoxville, we decided to submit the proposal through Calvin College, a four-year institution, because funds were more accessible from the branch of NSF handling proposals from undergraduate institutions than the branch handling proposals from universities.

The first award was to set up the Archives with its own server. We had begun preliminary work on the Archives on space lent to us on the FTP server WUArchives at the Washington University - St. Louis (http://www.wustl.edu/). In the early 1990s, this was the most popular anonymous FTP site on the Internet, and they often lent space for others to maintain an archive of certain types of software. The budget for this first project (awarded in 1993) was for $108,180, $10,617 of which were in matching funds for hardware from the particular institution receiving the funding. The breakdown of expenses was as follows:

salaries/fringe benefits	$56,653
hardware	$21,233
miscellaneous	$ 5,000
indirect costs	$25,294

(Miscellaneous included items such as travel, shipping, and maintenance on the hardware, etc.)

Although the second award provided for some continued development of the Archives, its primary focus was the education of the mathematical community about what resources were available on the Internet for use in undergraduate education and how to use them effectively. Thus, our funded activity shifted to traveling and giving presentations at professional meetings while the maintenance and continued development of the Archives shifted to a solely volunteer activity. The total budget for the second award was $113,270. The breakdown of expenses was as follows:

salaries/fringe benefits	$29,821
hardware	$26,540
travel	$34,000
miscellaneous	$ 7,500
indirect costs	$15,409

(As above, half of the cost of the hardware was borne
by the institution receiving it.)

4.0 Target Audience and Secondary Audience

Our target audience is all people interested in finding mathematical
resources on the Internet. The primary level of mathematics resources
on our site ranges from high school mathematics through all of undergraduate mathematics. We also have some material for elementary
and developmental mathematics and some for professional mathematicians, but these areas are less developed. Our audience includes
both teachers and students. A substantial portion of the material is
oriented toward the needs of teachers (lecture notes, laboratory notebooks, pedagogical aids, mailing lists, electronic proceedings, etc.) and
students (tutorials, practice problems, interactive demonstrations,
puzzles, games, etc.). Both the professional mathematician and the
amateur mathematician will find the various collections of links and
the software collection useful.

5.0 The Collection

5.1 Shareware and Public Domain Software
(http://archives.math.utk.edu/software.html)

Since the creation of the Archives, we have amassed and maintained
a large collection of software that runs on DOS/Windows and Macintosh platforms. We also house several multiplatform (including UNIX)
packages that are mirrored from various sites in Europe. With the
exception of the SLATEC (Sandia, Los Alamos, Air Force Weapons Laboratory Technical Exchange Committee) library and the mirrored packages, we do not maintain a collection of source code for software. We
do not wish to overlap with the NETLIB collection of source code,
a repository that contains freely available software, documents, and
databases.

Presently, we have over three hundred DOS/Windows programs
and over two hundred Macintosh programs. These programs are all

shareware or public domain packages that the user can download and run on his or her local computer. Each package is tested, reviewed, and categorized by mathematical area. For each program, we include one or more text files, typically the author's README file and an abstract written by us on the program's capabilities and weaknesses, which are fully searchable by the user looking for programs for a specific area or to perform specific tasks. When possible, we also include program documentation and a link to the author's Web site.

The software collection is mirrored by a number of sites including WUArchive at Washington University (http://wuarchive.wustl.edu/edu/math/), The Higher Education National Software Archive (HENSA) at Lancaster University in the United Kingdom (http://micros.hensa.ac.uk/cgi-bin/browser/mirrors/cti/mathematics/archives.math.utk.edu/) and the Walnut Creek CD-ROM (ftp://ftp.cdrom.com/pub/math/utk/).

5.2 Links to Other Software Collections and Commercial Vendors
(http://archives.math.utk.edu/other_software.html)

We also provide links to major collections of mathematical software including public domain and shareware, commercial sites, and other well-organized lists. Readers can decide to restrict the search to one or more of several levels of mathematical training (prealgebra, high school, lower-division college, upper-division college, graduate, and professional), to one or more of several platforms (Macintosh, DOS/Windows, OS2, UNIX), and to either public domain/shareware or commercial sites. There are over 430 links in this collection.

5.3 Links to Other Mathematical Resources
(http://archives.math.utk.edu/topics/)

Once technology advanced to the point where it became possible to create links to remote sites (such as with Gopher or World Wide Web), we began collecting and classifying links to other sites of interest to the mathematical community. We have collections specific to a type of site (professional societies, electronic news and discussion groups, mathematics departments of colleges and universities, etc.), as well as an extensive collection of links to sites with mathematical content. These latter links are classified according to mathematical discipline, minimum level of mathematics background needed to understand a significant part of the site, and special features (interactivity, abundance of links, animations, and images). In addition, each link has a collection of keywords associated with it, enabling users to locate the link by a search of keywords.

The major collection of links with sites to mathematical content is presented as Mathematics by Topic. Here, links are classified roughly in accordance with the top level of the American Mathematical Society's Subject Classification Scheme (http://www.ams.org/msc/#browse). In addition to the above-mentioned search of keywords, users may browse all links associated with, say, Complex Analysis or Topology by selecting the topic of interest.

There are several specialized lists that we believe to be helpful to the user. One is a collection of sites with interactive features. This would include interactivity implemented by Java, JavaScript, Web form/response, or a specialized plug-in such as Maple's MathView (http://www.cybermath.com/) or MacroMedia's Director or Flash (http://www.macromedia.com/). Another is the collection of sites that has a substantial specialized bibliography.

A second of our main collections of interest, Pop Mathematics, is a collection of specially selected links to sites that help reveal why mathematicians find mathematics interesting or beautiful. This list contains over 150 of the choicest sites. This collection is our attempt to participate in the popularization of mathematics.

As of June 1998, the Archives housed over thirty-seven thousand links in over thirty-five hundred files.

5.4 Mailing Lists
(http://archives.math.utk.edu/hypermail/)

The Archives maintains eleven Majordomo mailing lists; the archives of these and four other mailing lists are also available. Each of the mailing list archives is organized in three formats: by date, by topic, and by author. As the activity of several of the lists has exceeded over two hundred messages per month, we plan to add a specialized database that contains full-text indexing of these messages. We believe that the collection of almost six thousand messages is a valuable database of information. All but three of the mailing lists are related to the teaching of mathematics. Two mailing lists are for committees of professional organizations, and the third is concerned with fractals, a topic that has gotten many people interested in mathematics.

5.5 Electronic Proceedings
(http://archives.math.utk.edu/features.html)

The Archives publishes electronic proceedings for three conferences: the International Conference on Technology in Collegiate Mathematics (ICTCM) (four-years' worth), sponsored by Addison Wesley Publishers; the Conference on the Teaching of Mathematics (two-years' worth), sponsored by John Wiley Publishers; and the Twenty-Second Conference of the American Mathematical Association of Two-Year Colleges (AMATYC) (one-year's worth). The contents of the ICTCM proceedings are classified by mathematical topics, by type of software or technology used, and by keywords. We have provided articles from each of the proceedings in a variety of formats; however, we converted all of the articles to the Adobe .pdf format to ensure that all readers will have access. Over 140 articles appear in these proceedings.

6.0 Selection Criteria and Evaluation Process of Resources

6.1 Selection and Evaluation of Software

We include all shareware and public domain software submitted to us or that we locate elsewhere, provided that it is accurate, stable, and would be of interest to the mathematical community. Demo versions of software submitted to us have to have sufficient functionality to be useful for full evaluation of the package. For example, we would accept programs that have saving and printing disabled but are otherwise fully functional, but we wouldn't include programs that simply demonstrate how the product functions and do not allow users to input their own information or programs that have a significant number of features disabled.

To evaluate the software, we run it with test data to see that it produces accurate output. We run the program on a variety of machines and various versions of operating systems to see that the program is stable, check the software for viruses, and check that documentation is adequate for using the program. Upon completing an evaluation, we write an abstract to describe the functionality of the program. When necessary, documentation is supplemented so that the novice user can run the program. In addition, we seek permission to mirror outstanding public domain packages from foreign sites.

6.2 Selection and Evaluation of Links

Links under consideration for inclusion must have accurate information, and any special features of the linked page (Java programs, JavaScript, plug-ins, etc.) must be stable. Depending on the type of information contained on the site, we use different criteria to determine whether to include the link on the Archives. For example, for a page to be included in the listing of mathematics departments, the page must include a listing of the faculty, courses, and other information. Course materials must include mathematical content or some interactive material; we will not add a page listing only a syllabus and homework assignments. While we will include links to innovative pages with mathematical content and/or interactive material without hesitation, we more closely scrutinize pages with content similar to that of resources already included in the Archives. We do not include pages containing only a general collection of links. Links to commercial publishers of books, software, and other materials point directly to the mathematical section of these sites. Once we decide to include a link to a particular site, we classify the link by its content and place it in an appropriate area of the Archives. Links that are content oriented are further assigned keywords regarding their mathematical content, are classified by the level of mathematics presented, and are flagged for any particularly interesting features, such as whether they are interactive, include a collection of additional links, contain movies, or include a significant amount of graphics.

6.3 Selection of Articles for Electronic Proceedings

Since the presenters at the conferences covered by the electronic proceedings are screened by conference organizers, we include articles submitted by the presenters for the electronic proceedings, provided they contain accurate information.

6.4 Selection of Messages in the Archives of Mailing Lists

Unless a message is offensive or contains only information that is not within the domain of the mailing list, it is included. There are no other criteria for the exclusion of a message in the archives of the mailing lists.

7.0 Mechanics of Production Including Software and Hardware

7.1 Hardware

The computer housing the Archives is a Sparc10 with 96 MB of RAM and 5 GB hard disk space. Its operating system is SunOS v.5.5. The Archives is physically housed in the Mathematics Department of the University of Tennessee - Knoxville and is on their department network. There are incremental tape backups of the Archives made nightly with a weekly level-zero backup.

The Mathematics Department has two subnets that lie behind a router that isolates it from the traffic of the rest of the university. The Archives is isolated in several ways from the rest of the servers on the department network so that if the department servers crash, the Archives will still run. The Archives' mail system is also separate from the department's mail system. Otherwise, the Archives is maintained in a similar manner as the rest of the servers.

7.2 Software

The software used as the Web server is NCSA httpd Server, v.1.5 (http://www.ncsa.uiuc.edu/SDG/Homepage/UNIXSoftDesc.html #HTTPd) from the University of Indiana. Our Gopher server is Gopher 2.3 (gopher://boombox.micro.umn.edu) with WAIS implemented (freeWAIS 0.3 gopher://boombox.micro.umn.edu:70/11/gopher/Unix/) from the University of Minnesota and from the Center for Networked Information Discovery and Retrieval (ftp://ftp.cnidr.org/). Our electronic mailing list is Majordomo 1.93 (ftp://ftp.greatcircle.com/pub/majordomo/) from Great Circle Associates. Some of our searching is done with the Harvest search engine, Harvest 1.4 (http://www.tardis.ed.ac.uk/harvest/), from the University of Colorado. Searching on the keyword for the links is done by a Perl script that was written in house. We use Hypermail 1.02 (http://www.landfield.com/hypermail/) for the construction and maintenance of the archives of the mailing lists, and wuftpd 2.4 (http://wuarchive.wustl.edu/packages/wuarchive-ftpd/) from Washington University is used as the FTP server. We use Mirror 2.1 (http://sunsite.org.uk/packages/mirror/) from Imperial College for the mirroring of software packages. We also use ftpmail 1.23 (http://src.doc.ic.ac.uk/packages/ftpmail/) from Imperial College that lets users obtain access to the contents of the Archives by using e-mail; this program affords the user the same capabilities as anonymous FTP. Most of these software packages are described in detail in *Managing Internet Information Resources.*[1]

7.3 Link Checking

One of the important responsibilities of a site with an extensive link collection is identifying and updating outdated links. We have attempted to automate, to the degree possible, the identification of questionable links. Once a week, a script traverses the appropriate directories for Web pages to create a list of pages to check. We keep an exceptions list so that it is possible to omit specified pages from the checking process. Then each evening, a cron job begins a process of checking approximately one-seventh of the pages containing links. On each page, a script scans the page to pick up any hypertext link. The script then does a HEAD check on each link. If the HEAD times out or sends an error message, a GET check is then tried. If this in turn fails, then an error message is created to be sent to the owner of the page containing the questionable link. When the evening's files have been processed, e-mail is sent to each person working on the Archives who is responsible for the page that contained a questionable link. The owner receives a list of questionable links together with an error message for that link. It is up to the owner of the page containing the offending link to recheck the link and make any appropriate corrections. The essential part of this process is built on a variation of a program by David Sibley (ftp://ftp.math.psu.edu/pub/sibley/) to extract links from text and then send HEADs or GETs to them.

7.4 Mirroring Software

Each evening, a cron job runs the mirror program to check whether the mirrored software packages have been updated. If so, then the new material is automatically downloaded. Files that have been deleted on the original software site are also automatically deleted.

7.5 Making Software Accessible by Many Methods

One of the distinctive features of the Archives is that the software is available by way of anonymous FTP, Gopher, Web browser, and e-mail. To reduce the effort in maintaining all four methods of access, the software is organized in such a way that FTP and Gopher have direct access to each package, and the Web pages are frequently generated on the fly by Perl scripts. This is done most fully for the Macintosh holdings.

The directory holding the Macintosh collection has a subdirectory for each mathematical topic (Calculus, Algebra, Modern Algebra, etc.). The anonymous FTP user would see this as a list of subdirectories in which to look for programs. In addition to the directories is a .links file used by the Gopher server to display the names of the topics (Calculus, Algebra, Modern Algebra, etc.). The Gopher user would see these names on the folders in which to look for programs.

Each topic directory contains a subdirectory for each of the packages associated with that topic. Again, a .links file is used to provide the name that the Gopher user sees for each of these directories (folders).

We now are at the package level. The structure here is best explained perhaps by describing a particular package. The program xFunctions is a freeware program useful for the calculus student. So the calculus directory contains a subdirectory called xFunctions. The subdirectory xFunctions contains the following:

an abstract written by the Macintosh moderator at the Archives (this is text file);

the author's README file which he wants distributed with the package;

the package in compressed format ready to download;

a .cap subdirectory containing files that are text files with the exact same names as the files in the xFunctions directory. The Gopher server reads these files to determine names and MIME types of the files in the xFunctions directory;

a .links file that contains information for the Gopher server to create a link to the author's Web page and other relevant Web sites.

The program xFunctions is also useful for students in precalculus, so we would like a parallel listing in the precalculus topics directory. However, rather than carry multiple copies of all of these files, only the requisite directories/subdirectories are created. Then within these directories, we create softlinks to the original files, which for xFunctions actually reside in the calculus directory. So the precalculus/ xFunctions directory contains a

link to the abstract in the calculus/xFunctions directory;

link to the author's README file in the calculus/xFunctions directory;

link to the package in compressed format in the calculus/ xFunctions directory;

.cap subdirectory containing links to each of the files in the calculus/ xFunctions/.cap directory;

link to the .links file in the calculus/xFunctions directory.

Since UNIX resolves each link when it is accessed, a file can be updated merely by editing or replacing the original file. For the user, all of this linking is transparent, and the system behaves the same whether access is gained through the calculus/xFunctions directory or through the precalculus/xFunctions directory.

Finally, all text files for all packages are indexed by WAIS. This allows for full-text searching of all of the text files. Searching is set up so that users can search only files in a specific topical directory or all files under any topical directory.

The anonymous FTP user sees the text files and the compressed file in the xFunctions directory. The Gopher client uses the information in the .links file and in the files within the .caps subdirectory to create a list of links to access. This is the infrastructure that is exploited by Perl scripts for the Web user. When the Web user selects Macintosh programs, a Web page is presented, with links in each topic directory. When Calculus is selected, a script is called to read the information from the .links file in the calculus directory, and a list of links to calculus packages is displayed. When xFunctions is selected, a second script reads the information from the .links file in the xFunctions subdirectory and from the files in its .caps subdirectory. This creates a list of links to each of the files in the xFunctions directory plus a link to the author's home page. If one of the text files (e.g., the abstract) is selected, it is displayed with the remaining links in xFunctions appended to the abstract.

Relying on scripts to read the information originally intended for the Gopher server and creating appropriate links has simplified the maintenance of the software packages. Using soft links to cross-reference files from within different topics both simplifies maintenance and conserves disk space.

7.6 The Searching Mechanism for the Hypertext Links in the Mathematics by Topics Section of the Archives

When a link is included in Mathematics by Topics, it is first categorized by its primary topic, and then placed in an unordered list in the file containing links for that topic. Each link conforms to a particular form, but most importantly, each link is an HTML list item starting with <LI> and ending with </LI>. When a user performs a search for a particular word or phrase, a script searches each list item in each of the topics files for the desired word or phrase and a list of list items containing that word or phrase is returned.

Several specialized pages including the Bibliography page (http://archives.math.utk.edu/cgi-bin/bibliography.html) and the Java and Other Interactive WWW Pages listings (http://archives.math.utk. edu/cgi-bin/interactive.html) are generated on the fly by Perl scripts using the topics database.

7.7 Searching Web Pages across the Site

This is done with a standard Harvest search. Using a cron job, the Harvest database is updated weekly.

7.8 Other Software Sites

In addition to the collection of DOS/Windows and Macintosh software that we house on the Archives' server, we maintain an extensive list of links to both commercial and shareware/public domain software of interest to the mathematical community (http://archives. math.utk.edu/other_software.html). Although the entire list of links is available to the user, the preferred method of searching by users is via a form that enables the user to request software satisfying specific criteria. We provide a CGI form using a Perl script to let the reader restrict the sites he or she searches on the basis of platform, mathematical level, and whether the reader wants public domain/shareware software or commercial software.

8.0 Taxonomy or Classification Used and Any Modifications

We categorize software by the typical name used in a course for which the software would be appropriate. Examples of classifications would include Algebra, Calculus, Advanced Calculus, Discrete Mathematics, Modern Algebra, Linear Algebra, and so on. (See figure 2.) Software appropriate for more than one course would be accessible in any of those categories via symbolic links at the UNIX level, so the multiple listing of the package would be transparent to the user. We try to use terminology that both the mathematics teacher and student will readily recognize.

The process used to classify links is to first decide the primary discipline for which the link would be appropriate. The disciplines are roughly those at the top level of the American Mathematical Society's Subject Classification Scheme as defined in the *Mathematics Subject Classification.*[2] Additional disciplines to be associated with the link are addressed by use of keywords. All links in the topics area are searchable by keyword, allowing the user to perform a fairly narrow search.

9.0 Project's Strengths

The strengths of the Archives are the software collections and the extensive link collection, all of which are searchable by the user. Links and software are classified by mathematicians rather than students or others lacking extensive training in the discipline. This adds greater authority to the classification.

The Archives is also a comprehensive site for mathematics on the Internet. In addition to the software collection and the links to mathematical topics, we also have extensive collections of links to professional organizations, software vendors, electronic journals, electronic proceedings of mathematical conferences, mathematical news groups, mathematical institutions, and most anything of a mathematical nature on the Internet. It should also be noted that anything housed on the Archives is fully searchable by a Harvest search.

One particularly significant contribution to mathematics on the Web is our Pop Mathematics Collection (http://archives.math.utk.edu/popmath.html). Here students as well as others get to see what mathematicians find interesting or beautiful about mathematics. This collection has been featured on several educational television shows both in the United States and England.

Because of the age of the Archives, we have been able to witness the growth of Internet usage from 1994 to the present. In October

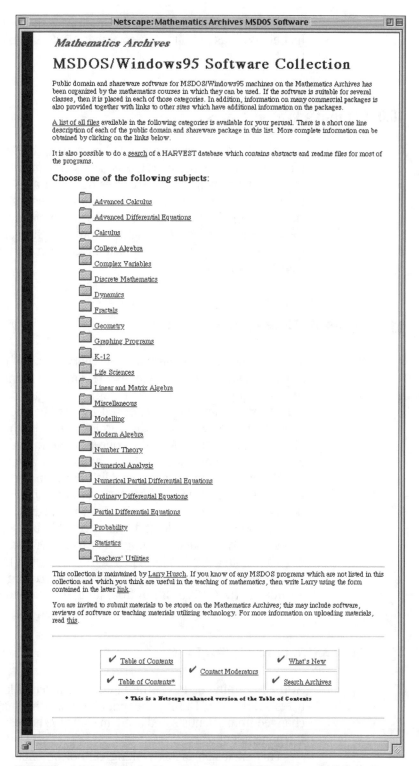

FIGURE 2.   Mathematics Archives Collection: MSDOS/Windows 95 Software

1994, our first full month on the Internet with our own server, we had eight thousand hits. In September 1998, we exceeded 1.1 million hits.

10.0 Project's Weaknesses

Areas of the Archives are separated more than they should be. External support for the Archives has ended, so the maintenance and continued development of the Archives have, for all practical purposes, become a two-person endeavor. While the codirectors' institutions consider the Archives a major service to the professional community, the codirectors still have a myriad of other departmental responsibilities. Consequently, they cannot spend as much time on the Archives as they would like.

11.0 Project's Time Frames

The Archives was established in February 1992, when Larry Husch acquired space on the anonymous FTP site at Washington University-St. Louis (ftp://wuarchive.wustl.edu) and began posting DOS programs for mathematics categorized by mathematical subject. Later that summer, he was joined by Earl Fife, who did the same thing for Macintosh programs. With the concept more fully developed by our experience, in November 1992 we applied for a grant from the National Science Foundation to establish our own site. The award was granted in June 1993, and by early September 1993, the Archives had its own home (http://archives.math.utk.edu/) at the University of Tennessee - Knoxville and was accessible by Gopher or anonymous FTP. By January 1994, a Web service was added.

The initial grant ran from July 1993 to October 1995. During the second year of the funding, we applied for a second grant, which was awarded in June 1995. It ran from June 1995 to June 1998.

12.0 Future Goals of the Project

At the beginning of 1997, the Internet included at least fifty million users worldwide. During the prior decade, the majority of users changed from scientists and academicians to shoppers, children, and the general populace.

This explosion of networking cannot be explained as network engineers winning the day or as effective public education. Something much deeper is going on; the number and extent of possible interactions among people has been greatly enlarged. The Internet offers new ways to obtain information, hold meetings, keep in touch with family, coordinate plans with colleagues, make deals, and buy and sell. The Internet is no longer a technical phenomenon; it is a human, social phenomenon.[3]

The changing complexion of the Internet affords an opportunity to reach an ever-increasing number of people with a growing variety of methods. Prior to the age of electronics, the main mode of presenting mathematics to a wide audience was with printed matter. Personal computers allowed for the creation of programs to illustrate specific ideas. The Web has allowed these older notions (written material and programs) to be combined with multimedia presentations with a high level of interactivity. We will continue expanding our offerings to include new ways of presenting mathematics.

In addition to continuing with the major areas outlined above, we are in the process of adding new services to the Archives. Many mathematics teachers are expected to write home pages for their courses. At the present time, it is a somewhat complicated process to display mathematics on the Web. We are developing a new section called Web Publishing Tips (http://archives.math.utk.edu/WPT/) to help mathematics teachers develop Web pages. This section will present a variety of ways to display mathematics and discuss the advantages and disadvantages of each. In addition, a Majordomo mailing list has been started which will perhaps develop into a forum on the effective design and presentation of mathematics courses on the Web.

As described above, we have a broad policy of evaluating sites and some guidelines for selecting a site for inclusion of its link on the Archives. However, we have not identified what we would call outstanding sites. In this section of the Archives, we can use these sites as examples of sites whose design should be used as a model.

One of Larry Husch's major projects, which has not been discussed above, is the Visual Calculus Project (http://archives.math.utk.edu/visual.calculus/). This project was designed for instructors to give some ideas about how technology—in particular, computers—can be used in the teaching of calculus. Detailed instructions on implementing these ideas with various public domain, shareware, and commercial software packages are provided. The site shows screen dumps of the output of these various packages and provides links to the software section of the Archives. Starting in January 1997, Husch expanded the project to include interactive modules (MathView, Java, JavaScript, and Flash), which can be used by either students or faculty. He also added detailed instructions for the Texas Instrument TI-85 and TI-86 graphing calculators. As an additional study aid for students, modules containing drill problems with solutions were also added. Starting in January 1998, tutorials on various topics in calculus were added; online quizzes, based on these tutorials, are also being developed. In the fall semester 1998, these materials were used as the foundations for a Web-based freshman calculus course at the University of Tennessee.

As will be explained in the next section, it is not clear what the future of the Archives will be. If we just continue with what we perceive as the strengths of the Archives described in the previous sections, then we must ask the question whether there will still be a need for the Archives. The Web will change. One of the advantages that the Archives has over Web servers maintained by professional organizations is our independence, so we can experiment with various services. In response to this question, the above-mentioned contributors decided that we must have a lot more content, mathematical and pedagogical, on the Archives. The development of the Web Publishing Tips section and the expansion of the Visual Calculus Project are two responses to this decision.

13.0 A Vision Statement for Future Resource Location and Description

We have been on the Internet starting almost with the birth of Gopher, and then we experienced and participated in the fast growth of the Web that was initiated with the development of Mosaic and Netscape. With the advent of Mosaic, there were dire predictions of the imminent collapse of the Internet. Yet what we have seen is the expansion of the Internet with the inclusion of an unbelievable amount of multimedia content. Our concerns have always been to get the broadest amount of exposure; we wanted our site to be accessible to the largest number of people. As mentioned above, one of our goals is to popularize mathematics. People are beginning to expect fancy multimedia presentations on a site. Do we need to have a similar presentation for the Pop Mathematics page for it to be successful? More generally, do we need a multimedia presentation for the entire site? There are some new sites with goals similar to those of the Archives that do have multimedia presentations. With the development of commercial sites with very sophisticated presentations, we believe that the answer to these questions must be yes.

A search of the AltaVista database gives 823,160 pages for algebra, 889,800 pages for geometry, 69,570 pages for trigonometry, and 505,560 pages for calculus. While only a maximum of two hundred pages are returned in each of these searches for the reader's perusal, even this small percentage of returns is too large to be practical in most instances. Early in the development of Web resources, meta-tags were thought to be an answer to this problem. There are even various proposals for digital libraries, many of which advocate the use of metatags. Metatags will cut down some of these numbers; the question is whether the number is still manageable. However, if the database returns only a maximum of two hundred pages, we are still faced with the same problems. The need for a site such as the Mathematics Archives is still there. We see our use of keywords comparable to the use of metatags, but the database is already more refined and the assignment of keywords is done by professional mathematicians. However, maintaining such a site is quite difficult. Rather than relying on referrals (either by humans or automatically by robots), we have actively searched for the sites ourselves. Although we have no figures, we would estimate that less than 1 percent of the links that we have on the Mathematics Archives were recommended to us; we collected all of the remaining links by surfing the Web. A significant portion of the work of the Mathematics Archives volunteers could be eliminated if information on new and revised pages could be conveyed in a systematic and complete manner to us. A new model must be developed for the gathering of information; we see no alternative to peer review for determining which of this information should be kept and categorized to develop a quality database. While we have seen several attempts to let the reader determine the quality of a site, not one of them appears to be successful.

Perhaps a model with a network of sites needs to be developed with the workload distributed over this network. The WWW Virtual Library (http://vlib.org/Overview.html) is an attempt to do this; sites were identified with specific disciplines. For example, Florida State University was identified as the WWW Virtual Library in Mathematics (http://euclid.math.fsu.edu/Science/math.html). While Florida State University maintains a good list of links, the list is very incomplete. Furthermore, the links are not annotated and no search engine is provided. Therefore, if you want to find information on a particular topic in mathematics, the list most likely will not help you. There have been several attempts to develop a network of sites in mathematics, but all of these attempts eventually led to failure. It is not clear that such an effort can be volunteer; volunteers cannot sustain such an important endeavor. Professional societies are too conservative to respond to the rapid changes that occur with respect to the Internet. A commercial model needs to be developed.

Notes

1. Cricket Liu et al., *Managing Internet Information Services* (Sebastopol, Calif.: O'Reilly & Associates, 1994).

2. S. H. Gould, *Mathematics Subject Classification* (Providence, R.I.: American Mathematical Society, 1991).

3. Dorothy E. Denning and Peter J. Denning, *Internet Besieged* (New York: Addison Wesley, 1998).

10

Organising Medical Networked Information (OMNI)

Sue Welsh

This chapter describes the Organising Medical Networked Information (OMNI) Project (http://omni.ac.uk/), which originated in 1995 as part of the U.K.'s Electronic Libraries (eLib) Programme (http://www.ukoln.ac.uk/services/elib/). The OMNI subject gateway to biomedical Internet resources is described fully, including technical and database details and the process of evaluating candidate resources. Project organization is also covered. For example, the project team, funding, and reporting processes are discussed. OMNI's future is discussed in the light of exciting developments in the organization of Internet resource discovery in the U.K. academic sector.

1.0 Location and Contact Details

Organising Medical Networked Information (OMNI) (http://omni.ac.uk/) (see figure 1) is located at Nottingham University and has four full-time staff members: the project manager (John Kirriemuir), technical officer (Bob Parkinson), project officer (Lisa Gray), and project assistant (Frances Singfield) (http://omni.ac.uk/general-info/omni-contacts.html). Another part-time team member (Christine Parker-Jones), who is located at Leeds University, administers the U.K. mirror of the National Library of Medicine's Visible Human Dataset (http://vhp.gla.ac.uk/). A steering committee, composed mainly of representatives from the medical education, research, and library communities (http://omni.ac.uk/general-info/steering-group.html), assists the project manager, particularly with long-term/strategic planning.

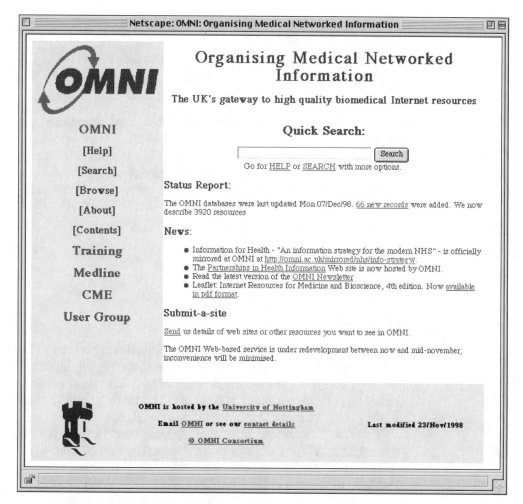

FIGURE 1. OMNI Home Page

Correspondence should be addressed to John Kirriemuir, the project manager, at OMNI, Greenfield Medical Library, Queen's Medical Centre, Nottingham NG7 2UH United Kingdom; or Frank Norman, chair of the steering committee, at National Institute for Medical Research, The Ridgeway, Mill Hill, London NW7 1AA United Kingdom.

2.0 OMNI's Purpose

OMNI's mission is to enhance and promote the use of biomedical Internet resources to academics, researchers, students, and clinicians in the United Kingdom. The OMNI project

- enhances access by building a subject gateway to selected, high-quality resources;

- emphasizes the need for evaluation of Internet materials, especially in this sector;
- provides training and publishes training materials;
- collaborates with other bodies to make existing databases available on the Web.

OMNI aims to offer direct access to high-quality information. As a focused, subject-specific, national initiative, the OMNI service enables users to quickly locate key resources in their area of interest. Most of OMNI's services are free at the point of use, and no registration is required. OMNI also supports U.K. users of the National Library of Medicine's Visible Human Dataset (the U.K. Mirror), which is located at Glasgow University.

3.0 Project Funding Sources

3.1 Current Funding

OMNI is funded by the U.K.'s Higher Education Funding Councils (the Higher Education Funding Council for England, the Higher Education Funding Council for Wales, the Scottish Higher Education Funding Council, and the Department of Education, Northern Ireland) as part of their eLib Programme (http://www.ukoln.ac.uk/services/elib/).

The eLib Programme arose from the Libraries Review (http://www.ukoln.ac.uk/services/papers/follett/report/), a report investigating electronic information and academic library services, commissioned by the Higher Education Funding Councils and published in 1993. The Libraries Review stated that "the exploitation of IT is essential to create the effective library service of the future" and recommended that the Higher Education Funding Councils should invest jointly in "a series of development projects designed to further the use of IT." Specifically, the report recommended the following actions:

> the development of standards, pilot projects to demonstrate the potential of on-demand publishing and electronic document and article delivery, a feasibility project to promote the development of electronic journals in conjunction with relevant publishing interests, the development of a database and dataset strategy, investment in navigational tools, retrospective conversion of certain catalogues, and investment in the further development of library automation and management systems.[1]

The eLib Programme was set up in direct response to this report (which came to be known as the *Follett Report,* after its chairman, Sir

Brian Follett), and received £15 million (approximately $23,914,000) from the U.K.'s higher education budget over three years (1995–1998). During phase one and two of eLib, about sixty projects were funded in the following eleven program areas:

(1)   Document Delivery;

(2)   Access to Network Resources;

(3)   Training and Awareness;

(4)   Electronic Journals;

(5)   Digitization;

(6)   Images;

(7)   Electronic Short Loan Collections;

(8)   On-Demand Publishing;

(9)   Preprints and Gray Literature;

(10) Supporting Studies;

(11) Quality Assurance.

OMNI forms part of the Joint Information Systems Committee's (JISC) (http://www.jisc.ac.uk/) successful Access to Network Resources (ANR) area, a group of Internet information providers focused on improving access to electronic resources. The subject gateways in the ANR area have collectively cataloged over fifteen thousand key Web resources for the U.K. community.

Initially, OMNI received £205,000 (approximately $327,000) over two years (1995–1997) from the eLIB Programme. The lion's share of this budget is, of course, spent on staff, with the next most expensive item in the budget being equipment. Funding has been renewed periodically at approximately the same level to the present.

3.2 Future Funding

Funding for the ANR section is guaranteed until mid-1999. As the eLib Programme draws to a close, the management of ANR projects will be taken over by the Committee for Electronic Information (CEI) (http://www.jisc.ac.uk/cei/), a subcommittee of the Higher Education Funding Councils' Joint Information Systems Committee (http://www.jisc.ac.uk/). It is likely that the projects will be taken forward as part of a national strategy for resource discovery, commissioned by the CEI. In this scenario, it may be necessary to combine funding from the higher education budget with other sources of income, and many of the ANR projects have already started to earn income to supplement their grant from the funding councils.

4.0 Target Audience

4.1 U.K. Higher Education and Research

OMNI is funded to provide services to the biomedical higher education and research sectors in the United Kingdom. This is a large community, and defining its precise size is difficult as it spreads over multiple subject areas and organizations. As well as universities and other higher education institutions, it includes the Medical Research Council (http://www.mrc.ac.uk/) and Biotechnology and Biological Sciences Research Council (http://www.bbsrc.ac.uk/) and their laboratories and units. (The research councils are the agents for distribution of government funding for research in the United Kingdom. They fund a number of independent laboratories as well as researchers and entire units within universities.)

OMNI is aimed at a variety of end users:

- teaching staff;
- researchers;
- undergraduate students;
- postgraduates in various subject areas;
- physicians;
- nursing professionals;
- allied health professionals;
- persons interested in life sciences;
- health economists.

4.2 Staff in Health Care Organizations

Although serving the higher education and research communities is our primary focus, OMNI services are also of interest to staff working in health care organizations, such as the National Health Service (NHS) (http://www.nahat.net/) and private health care units. Since OMNI's core funding does not include funds for provision of information services to the NHS or other sectors outside the higher education and research community, it has been impossible thus far to promote the OMNI service to this sector. This situation may change in the near future (see the "Future Aims" section).

There are over one million NHS staff members in the United Kingdom, but at present only a minute proportion have access to the Internet at work through their employer.[2] The NHS is in the process of being networked and is expected to be an increasingly important market for OMNI in the years to come.[3] At present, OMNI has many users from the NHS community; a small but growing number are accessing the service from within the secure and not widely accessible NHS network, with a larger but unidentifiable number using their own Internet service provider accounts.

4.3 Other Users

OMNI also receives a significant amount of use from overseas, especially other English-speaking nations such as Australia, Canada, and the United States, as well as Europe. A bid for funding from European Union (EU) sources is planned and, if successful, will allow us to provide a better service to overseas users, especially EU countries but by extension worldwide, in collaboration with other European national services.

5.0 The OMNI Collection

5.1 OMNI's Databases

OMNI offers access to a number of databases, created both within the project and by external organizations and individuals.

At the heart of the collection are two databases created by OMNI (http://omni.ac.uk/general-info/sw-search.html): OMNIuk and OMNIworld. OMNIuk includes resources based in the United Kingdom exclusively. This database is intended to be as comprehensive as possible for resources falling within OMNI's selection criteria (see the "Selection Criteria and Evaluation" section). OMNIworld covers non-U.K. resources. Clearly, comprehensiveness is not possible (and may also be undesirable given the existence of other initiatives internationally). Therefore, OMNIworld describes only the most significant resources from around the world, and particularly those of interest to our target audience.

On June 15, 1998, OMNIworld and OMNIuk contained 1,690 and 1,710 records, respectively. These core databases are commonly searched together by OMNI users, although separate access is possible; hence a typical search of the OMNI service on June 15, 1998, addressed a database of 3,400 total records. The OMNI databases are currently expanding at an average rate of 150 records per month. Updates occur approximately once per week.

The OMNI databases describe many types of Internet resources; table 1 (on the following page) shows the proportions of Documents (individual or multiple pages), Services (databases, information services, organization Web sites, etc.), News Groups, Mailing Lists, and

Table 1. OMNI Resources (by Type)

Resource Type	Percentage of Resources
Documents	33%
Services	57
News groups	3
Mailing lists	7
Other	<1

Other resources (e.g., software) cataloged by OMNI. See figure 2 for an example of an OMNI record.

OMNI includes resources in any area related to health, medicine, and the biosciences. The browseable interface to the OMNI data (http://omni.ac.uk/general-info/browse.html) divides OMNI resources into more than seventy sections, ranging from biology to the history of medicine, through biological and the basic medical sciences and clinical specialties.

5.2 Other Databases

As a central resource for the U.K. community, OMNI has also developed a role as a gateway for users to access records from other data-

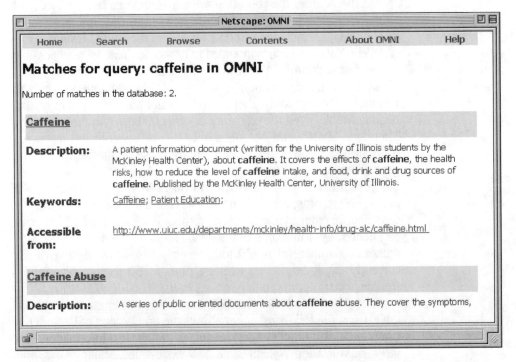

FIGURE 2. OMNI Record: Caffeine

bases because other database owners approach OMNI for this type of provision. OMNI has dealt with incoming data in a variety of formats, from database programs such as Microsoft Access (http://www.microsoft.com/products/prodref/3_ov.htm) to structured HTML documents.

At present, OMNI users can access three datasets in addition to the core OMNI databases: Nursing and Health Care Resources in the Net, CTI Biology Internet Resources, and Royal College of Physicians Database of Continuing Medical Education Events.

Nursing and Health Care Resources in the Net (http://www.shef.ac.uk/~nhcon/) is a database of over one thousand records compiled and maintained by Rod Ward, a nursing lecturer at the University of Sheffield, United Kingdom. This collection includes nursing and healthcare related resources that fall outside OMNI's collection policy. For example, the collection links to the personal home pages of nurses, and generally covers information of interest to this community in greater depth than OMNIuk or OMNIworld do.

CTI Biology Internet Resources, a subset of a database of educational resources provided by the CTI Centre for Biology (http://www.liv.ac.uk/ctibiol/), based at the University of Liverpool, United Kingdom, is also searchable via OMNI. The Computers in Teaching Initiative (CTI) (http://www.cti.ac.uk/) comprises twenty-four subject-based centers working to support the use of communication and information technologies in the production of educational materials. CTI centers are usually located in U.K. universities and are funded by the Higher Education Funding Councils. As part of its mission to collect and review educational resources in many electronic formats, CTI Biology has described many Internet-based educational resources covering biological topics. These descriptions are searchable via OMNI.

The Royal College of Physicians (RCP) Database of Continuing Medical Education Events is also hosted by OMNI. It differs from the services already mentioned in that it is a database of events-related information rather than a database describing Internet resources. RCP Events (http://omni.ac.uk/cme/search-cme.html) offers detailed information on continuing medical education (CME) in the United Kingdom and the process of CME accreditation.

6.0 Selection Criteria and Evaluation

6.1 Quality and OMNI

From the first stages of project conceptualization, quality and selectivity have been of paramount importance for OMNI. Indeed, before the project existed, several founding members of the original project board had formed the Biomedical Networked Information Resources (BIONIR) group. BIONIR was an informal attempt to catalog biomedical Internet resources using existing national subject gateways and listings, and was set up to address the growing problem of finding high-quality, Internet-based material.[4] Members of this group successfully bid for funding for the OMNI project and continued to be involved, mainly via the various project committees (and later the OMNI steering group). The OMNI proposal (http://omni.ac.uk/general-info/proposal.html) commented:

> There is much information of value on the network but unfortunately this is swamped by information sources which are ephemeral or of dubious quality. Finding a suitable item of interest can be a frustrating task. T. S. Eliot wrote, "Where is the wisdom we have lost in knowledge? Where is the knowledge we have lost in information?" If he were working in today's information world he might have added, "Where is the information we have lost in the Internet?"[5]

The proposal further stated, "OMNI aims to be a quality service, facilitating access to useful information. Resources will not be added to the gateway until they have been filtered, catalogued, classified and subject-indexed. The filtering process weeds out material that is out of date, inappropriate or strictly local in context." Getting users quickly to relevant, high-quality information remains OMNI's main purpose three years later.

Positive comments from end users and Internet resource evaluation services indicate that OMNI has been fulfilling its purpose well:

> Organising Medical Networked Information. Easily the best UK gateway to health information on the Internet. (Health Education Board for Scotland, library section, http://www.hebs.scot.nhs.uk/healthcentre/lib/lib.htm)

> December's Site of the Month at the Kings Funds Web Site is one of the best health and medical search engines around. (Kings Fund, previous site of the month, http://www.kingsfund.org.uk/site/prevsite.htm#omni)

> OMNI . . . is especially good for British sites, but an excellent starting point all round. (Imperial College School of Medicine, library section, http://www.cxwms.ac.uk/School/Library/gateways.html)

> Highly regarded search tools for providers and patients . . . OMNI. (University of Utah, Health Sciences Center, healthcare bookmarks, http://www.med.utah.edu/medinfo/ds/hcbm.htm)

6.2 *The OMNI Advisory Group for Evaluation Criteria*

An early review of material that might help to inform the project revealed a dearth of information on the processing and evaluating of Internet resources. Since it wasn't possible to adapt existing, accepted standards and criteria, the project established an advisory group for evaluation criteria (AGEC) (http://omni.ac.uk/agec/) to formulate its guidelines, ensure that all aspects of current thinking were taken into consideration in their further development, and address emerging issues. The remainder of this section describes OMNI's guidelines for resource evaluation in some detail.

6.3 *OMNI Guidelines for Resource Evaluation*

The AGEC developed the OMNI guidelines for resource evaluation (http://omni.ac.uk/agec/evalguid.html) during the first six months of the project, and these were formally launched at a workshop for database contributors in January 1996. In the months preceding their formal launch and afterward, the guidelines have formed the cornerstone of OMNI's reputation for quality. The guidelines function as a working document for OMNI staff, enabling them to make the final decision to exclude or include resources; and a statement of selection principles, illuminating the selection process for publishers, OMNI users, and contributors to the database.

The guidelines consist of two sections: a series of key selection principles that should be applied to all resources under consideration, and a checklist of further evaluation criteria that may or may not be applicable in specific cases.

6.3.1 Key Selection Principles

Key selection principles are broad statements of the type concerning resources OMNI seeks to include in its databases. First, OMNI catalogs materials at the resource level (rather than at the server or site level). The guidelines do not specify or define what a resource is; this is left to the discretion of the evaluator, but the following advice is offered:

> As a rule, OMNI does not point to sites as a whole but to specific resources, so resources are identified and indexed at the level of individual WWW pages, individual FTP-able files, or software, etc.—where such resources stand comfortably on their own. Where this is clearly unsustainable is in the case of databases, electronic journals, e-mail discussion lists and newsgroups: unless an article or posting is particularly valuable in its own right and offers unique insights, OMNI will normally point to the home pages of electronic journals and archives and FAQ's of e-mail discussion lists and newsgroups.[6]

The key selection principles also state that OMNI will include resources if they meet all of the following criteria:

- contain substantive information (this excludes most personal home pages and lists of other resources);
- are accessible via or delivered over the network (although access restrictions, such as charging, do not preclude a resource from being considered);
- have a reasonable life expectancy.

OMNI will exclude an item if

- it is purely local in context (and therefore not of interest to OMNI's target audience);
- it is ephemeral (such as e-mail messages and news-group postings);
- it is out of date (or the date of publication is not clear and this affects the value of the resource);
- it is not possible for the material to be evaluated, whether for technical reasons or because the material is in a foreign language. This does not preclude non-English-language resources, provided the contributor is confident in recommending the resource for inclusion. We place great weight on the contributor's evaluation of the resource, although OMNI staff makes the final decision to include or exclude a resource.

Providing a resource satisfies the key selection principles above, it will usually be included in the OMNI database. However, evaluation of the resource is also made with regard to a checklist of further criteria. A resource failing to meet any of the criteria in the checklist may be admitted, but this failure may be noted in the record describing the resource for the benefit of OMNI users.

6.3.2 Further Evaluation Criteria

The checklist covers three areas of evaluation: establishing context, content evaluation, and access evaluation.

Establishing context: Most resources included in the OMNI databases are evaluated by librarians and other information professionals. While the assessment of some aspects of the quality of information content of a resource, such as accuracy, may be beyond the competency of individual evaluators, contextual information (such as authority and provenance) can provide strong indicators of the likely value of a resource for OMNI's target audience. By "context," the OMNI guidelines refer to the scope of the resource, its intended audience, authority, and provenance. The guidelines for establishing context are as follows:

- The scope of the resource is evaluated in terms of its subject area, breadth, depth, and time period covered.
- The resource should be pitched at a suitable level for OMNI's target audience, in particular, students, academics, practitioners, and researchers.
- Identifying the owner, publisher, author, sponsor, or other significant organization involved in the production and distribution of the resource may help to assess authority.
- Finally, the provenance of the resource is considered, taking into account the longevity of the resource itself, the existence of established print equivalents, and the evidence of archiving and continuing maintenance.

Content evaluation: Evaluation of the resource's content involves attributes such as coverage, accuracy, currency, and uniqueness.

- The coverage of the resource should be adequate with reference to its intended audience. Comparing the resource with printed or other equivalents, where they exist, may be helpful in identifying serious omissions.
- It may be difficult to ascertain the accuracy of the resource, but evaluation of the objectivity or subjectivity may be possible.
- Currency may be assessed in terms of the published or last-updated date for documents, or frequency and regularity of updating for sources such as databases.
- Assessment of the uniqueness of the resource may be a significant factor in the comparative evaluation of mirrored sites as well as resources with equivalents in other media such as print or CD-ROM.

Access evaluation: Access evaluation focuses on the accessibility and usability of the resource, including design and layout, and support.

- Evaluation of accessibility and usability ideally tries to establish when a resource is available and that it is usable and reliable within those times. For most Internet resources, this is twenty-four-hours a day, seven days a week. It may also be necessary to touch on issues such as extensive use of graphics that slow the transfer of pages and difficulties in downloading resources. Access restrictions are assessed and mentioned explicitly in the resource description, and these may include charging policies, access restrictions to nonmembers of a specific community, unusual software or hardware requirements, language, or copyright restrictions.

- Design and layout are clearly of less importance than factors such as reliability, but in some cases they may be detrimental to the usability of the resource. Particular stress is given to factors such as navigability, appropriate use of HTML, and presentation of data such as search results.
- Adequate support for users is essential, and investigation of help features is a crucial element of the evaluation. The existence of help files, FAQs, e-mail contacts for correspondence, and supporting discussion lists are investigated.

6.4 Selection and Evaluation Process

Evaluation is an integral part of incorporating a resource into the OMNI databases. The addition of resources is a three-step process, involving identification, evaluation, and description.

Step One: Identification

Resources that may be suitable for inclusion are identified in a variety of ways. OMNI staff regularly scan several sites or servers that are particularly important to OMNI's target audience. They also monitor several electronic mailing lists for announcements of new sites or discussions of established sites. Surveys of resources in particular subject areas are carried out, resulting in a series of regularly updated subject guides (http://omni.ac.uk/training-centre/subject-guides/default.html). Finally, a facility for nominations from OMNI users is available, which receives approximately thirty submissions per month (http://omni.ac.uk/submit-url/).

Step Two: Evaluation

Once a potentially useful resource has been identified, a preliminary evaluation to ensure it meets OMNI's key selection principles is undertaken. At this point, a skeleton record is created in the OMNI administrative system, which is not visible to users. A fuller evaluation is then made, resulting in a decision to include or exclude the resource.

Step Three: Description

After the resource is evaluated, staff either convert the skeleton record to a full description or transfer it to a "vetoed" database, annotated with comments describing the reasons for excluding it from OMNI. Records describing resources that have passed the evaluation process are then transferred, usually in batches of thirty to fifty, to OMNIuk and OMNIworld as appropriate. If the resource was nominated for inclusion by an OMNI user, OMNI sends an acknowledgment, if necessary, describing the reasons why it was not included.

6.5 Ongoing Evaluation

Once a resource has been incorporated into the OMNI databases, the process of evaluation does not cease. All of the URLs in OMNIuk and OMNIworld are checked weekly, using the Resource Organisation And Discovery in Subject-based services (ROADS) (http://www.roads.lut.ac.uk/) software (see the "Software" section), and those that fail are either corrected or weeded out. A rolling program of verifying the record content is planned.

7.0 Mechanics of Production

7.1 Hardware

OMNI's Web service runs on a Digital Alphaserver 1200, 533 Mhz with 512 MB RAM. This server was purchased in 1998, replacing the original OMNI server, which was not powerful enough to cope with the large amount of use the database now attracts. The present system can cope with five simultaneous search sessions without a degradation of search speed.

7.2 Software

OMNI uses the ROADS v1.0 software to create and maintain the OMNI databases. ROADS is a project that aims to facilitate the production of subject gateways both within the eLib Programme and elsewhere. The ROADS software can be used to catalog sites into a Web-based database, to administer the database, and to provide a simple user interface for searching and browsing. ROADS is written entirely in Perl.

The ROADS project is currently funded entirely by the U.K. Higher Education Funding Councils via the eLib Programme. The software is available freely to all at present, and can be downloaded from the ROADS Web site (http://www.ilrt.bris.ac.uk/roads/). (Additional information on ROADS can also be found in chapters 5 and 12.)

7.3 Record Structure

In the interest of compatibility between different ROADS gateways, the ROADS software records data in a set of standard formats based around Internet Anonymous FTP Archives (IAFA) templates (http://info.webcrawler.com/mak/projects/iafa/iafa.txt).[7] IAFA templates were originally developed to describe the contents of FTP archives and thus make them easier to search.[8] They are no longer being developed, but the ROADS project has taken up the work and set up a template registry (http://www.ukoln.ac.uk/metadata/roads/templates/) to enable ROADS users to extend the collection of templates (the original IAFA working group specified fourteen) and to document changes to existing templates and ensure that they are applied consistently. The ROADS project has also begun to produce cataloging guidelines to help projects that are creating records using ROADS and IAFA templates (http://www.ukoln.ac.uk/metadata/roads/cataloguing/cataloguing-rules.html).

OMNI uses a subset of the fields available from the IAFA template to create OMNI records. A small number of fields are compulsory because they are either mandatory by ROADS or a standard part of the OMNI cataloging process.

> Title: the title of the resource;
>
> Description: a free-text description of the resource;
>
> Keywords: controlled keywords describing the resource;
>
> Uniform Resource Identifier (URI): currently the URL of the resource;
>
> Subject descriptor: a subject descriptor (an abbreviated classification code) for the resource;
>
> Subject-descriptor scheme: the name of the scheme being used for classification (NLM or LCC);
>
> Category: type of resource (e.g., Document, Service, News Group, Mailing List, or Other);
>
> Destination: which database will receive the record once completed (e.g., OMNIuk, OMNIworld, Nursing, CTI, and RCP).

Other fields are automatically generated by the ROADS software.

> Handle: a unique identifier assigned to each resource record;
>
> To-be-reviewed date: date in the future when the resource is due to be reassessed for content-related changes;
>
> Template Type: the IAFA template type that is being used;
>
> Record-last-modified date: the date and time when the record was last modified;
>
> Record-last-modified e-mail: the e-mail address of the person who last modified the record;
>
> Record-created date: the date and time when the record was created;
>
> Record-created e-mail: the e-mail address of the person that created the record.

The remaining fields are noncompulsory and are used as appropriate and available.

Access policy: details of restrictions on access to the resource;

Access times: details of any times when the service is not fully available;

Admin*: information about the administrator of the resource;

Alternative title: alternative title information present at the site;

Authentication: login details (user name, password), not publicly viewable;

Character set: the resource's character set;

Charging policy: details of charges for using the resource;

Citation: the preferred citation of the resource;

Comments: a free-text field for comments about a resource;

Copyright: a statement of copyright;

Creation date: the date of creation of the resource;

Discussion: reference to any discussion list concerning the resource;

Format: the format of the resource;

ISBN: the International Standard Book Number;

ISSN: the International Standard Serial Number;

Language: the name of the language in which the resource is presented;

Owner*: information about the (copyright) owner of the resource;

Publisher*: information about the publisher of the resource;

Publication status: the status of the resource (e.g., draft);

Registration: a free-text field for information about registration;

Requirements: information about software/hardware requirements;

Short title: the shortened title or acronym if present at the site;

Size: the size of the resource in bytes;

Source: a reference to the definitive version of a resource;

Sponsoring*: information about organizations sponsoring the resource.

Currently, the OMNI service displays only the Title, Description, Keywords, and URI fields to the user, although the ROADS software can be configured to display other fields. A keyword search of the OMNI database searches the Title, Description, and Keyword fields. A command-line search of individual fields is also possible.

---

*These items are composed of multiple, clustered (linked) fields.

8.0 Taxonomy and Classification

As noted in the April 6, 1996, Scout Report (http://scout.cs.wisc.edu/scout/report/archive/scout-960405.html#2), OMNI is distinguishable from many other medical gateways because of the amount of value added to each record. As well as a free-text description, each record is assigned subject indexing keywords and a classification code before being added to OMNIuk or OMNIworld.

8.1 MeSH Terms

OMNI uses the U.S. National Library of Medicine's Medical Subject Headings (MeSH) (http://www.nlm.nih.gov/mesh/meshhome.html) as the sole source of indexing terms (displayed in the keywords field). MeSH is familiar to many users as the controlled vocabulary used in the MEDLINE database (http://www.medportal.com/), and it thus provides OMNI with a controlled vocabulary for keywords. Terms in MeSH are arranged in a hierarchical structure, beginning with broad subject terms and progressing to narrower and more specific concepts. This depth and variety of specificity make it an ideal choice for OMNI, where individual resources may require indexing at very different levels of specificity, ranging as they do from large databases to single documents. MeSH is revised each year, and in 1998 included over eighteen thousand concepts and more than eighty thousand cross-references.

8.2 Classification

OMNI classifies all resources according the U.S. National Library of Medicine's (NLM) classification scheme, but does not assign full call numbers.[9] This classification forms the basis for browseable access to the OMNI data. The NLM classification is commonly used to classify collections in medical libraries in the United Kingdom and is therefore familiar to many OMNI users. Where a suitable code is not available in the NLM Classification, a Library of Congress Classification code is used, as recommended by the NLM Classification guidelines.

8.3 Concept Mapping

Part of the reason for adding MeSH terms to all OMNI records, in addition to the aim of improving retrieval for free-text searches, was to make it possible to develop thesaurus access to the OMNI data. The OMNI thesaurus offers users the opportunity to specify a concept exactly (by helping them find controlled indexing terms), to search for concepts related to a free-text term, and to appreciate and utilize the relationship between terms (broader, narrower, etc.). OMNI has also developed a facility to link displayed keywords to other records that contain the same MeSH term.

The U.S. National Library of Medicine's Unified Medical Language System (UMLS) Metathesaurus (http://www.nlm.nih.gov/pubs/factsheets/umlsmeta.html) is used to build these features.[10] The UMLS Metathesaurus is one of four UMLS knowledge sources, and comprises about forty biomedical vocabularies and classifications, with links between terms that are synonyms (names for the same concept from different vocabularies) and data about the relationships between concepts. Presently, OMNI uses only the MeSH subsection of this metathesaurus for indexing. The metathesaurus as a whole acts as an interface tool, enabling OMNI to display relationships between MeSH terms and map words that users supply to MeSH concepts. It is hoped that OMNI will be able to take advantage of the full power of the UMLS Metathesaurus at some point. Later versions of the OMNI thesaurus may then offer OMNI users the opportunity to search using terms from other controlled vocabularies, such as the International Classification of Diseases (ICD) or the U.K.'s read codes.[11]

9.0 Project Strengths and Weaknesses

9.1 Strengths

OMNI's strengths are its

- focus on quality. OMNI's focus on resource quality, in terms of both evaluation and selection, is a real strength and something that sets the project apart from many other Internet services.
- targeted service to a defined user group. OMNI focuses on a single, if broad, subject area and is consequently able to target a well-defined user group.
- satisfaction of a growing need. The rise of the Internet as a source of information for education, research, and increasingly, health care has coincided with OMNI's development. The OMNI service has therefore been in a position of maturing in time to meet a real need from a growing number of users.
- national reputation. OMNI is well known among library and information staff in the United Kingdom, and this has been tremendously important in making the end-user community aware of the service. This is in part due to OMNI's position as a project funded by a high-profile, national eLib initiative.

- uniqueness. Although there are many Internet medical search services available to users today, OMNI's focus on quality, focus on material of interest to U.K. users, foundation in the academic/research community, and quality of resource descriptions make it a unique service.

- origin in a collaborative community. OMNI comes from the culture of the library and information community and the eLib Programme, and has reaped the benefit of being open to collaboration with other projects in the United Kingdom and those further afield. Belonging to a group of subject gateways, ANR, whose project teams are all learning from the process of implementation, has been particularly valuable in OMNI's development.

- use of standards. OMNI has used standards (both emerging and established) wherever possible to ensure the long-term utility of the OMNI data and the usability of the OMNI Web service among a wide audience.

9.2 Weaknesses

OMNI's weaknesses are its

- resource constraints. The creation of metadata records by hand requires more human resources than their automatic creation. The U.K. higher education community and health-care providers operate on limited resources; therefore, the benefits of a higher quality of resource description must outweigh the costs of service production.

- cutting-edge software. The OMNI service has developed contemporaneously with its underlying software, ROADS. It has not always been possible to iron out all the bugs before moving new versions to the live service, and the service provided to users has, at times, temporarily fallen below acceptable levels because of this.

10.0 Project Time Frame

The OMNI project officially commenced in May 1995. A basic service was launched in November 1995 and has continued virtually uninterrupted to the present time. Originally conceived and funded as a two-year project, OMNI is now in its fourth year, with every prospect of becoming a permanently funded service and operating indefinitely into the future.

11.0 Future Goals

This section describes some of OMNI's main goals for the near future. One of our primary goals is to aid in the effort to establish interoperability among biomedical databases. We are also committed to working with hybrid libraries and making our content available to them. Finally, OMNI looks forward to whatever part we may play in the Distributed National Electronic Resource (DNER) (http://www.jisc.ac.uk/pub98/n3_98.html#p5), a national strategy for collection of and access to electronic resources.[12]

OMNI has been successfully established as a stand-alone service and has developed a role as a central source for access to biomedical Internet resources in the United Kingdom. This has been achieved partly by acquiring external datasets and locating them on the OMNI server. With a few exceptions, acquiring data in this way is not a long-term or extensible solution. It requires disk space for storage and human resources that are at a premium. A more favored solution is the establishment of cross-searching arrangements among data owners, which would allow multiple, remote databases to be searched from a single point.

The ROADS project has already set up a demonstration site illustrating how this may be done among gateways that understand the WHOIS++ protocol (http://roads.ukoln.ac.uk/crossroads/). A key aim for OMNI in the near future is to advance this effort by establishing a cluster of biomedical databases that describe Internet resources, both within the United Kingdom and further afield.

In addition to cross-searching of distributed databases, another way that information providers are trying to organize resources and make them more accessible is by developing hybrid libraries. OMNI and the other subject gateways within the ANR section of eLib were established early on in the eLib program. That program has moved on to explore more complex problems, and has recently funded a number of hybrid library projects (http://www.ukoln.ac.uk/services/elib/background/pressreleases/summary2.html), that is, projects that intend to be integrated information solutions for particular communities. A hybrid library would seek to provide a service that could be used to query the Internet, the local library catalog, and locally or nationally held datasets from an integrated interface. In other words, hybrid libraries are services that unite previously disparate sources of information into a single information system for end users. These information sources may span a range of data types: bibliographic, full-text, factual, or spatial, and will certainly be in different formats and be retrieved from a variety of storage media (including CD-ROM and print). Local sources will be integrated with remote databases. There are five eLib hybrid library projects, and several of these aim to set up this type of service.

Effective information retrieval on the Internet is likely to be a factor in any hybrid library scenario, and OMNI is committed to working with both the hybrid library projects and with individual higher education institutions and research organizations that wish to integrate the OMNI databases into local user interfaces.

Efforts to increase the ease with which users can find information and to encourage communication and cooperation among information providers extend to national strategies as well. OMNI's funders have announced their intention to develop the DNER, which will include a collection policy (http://www.jisc.ac.uk/cei/dner_colpol.html) for the provision of information resources to the higher education community and bring together the many centrally funded services and projects and give them a common focus.[13] A key aim of the DNER is to increase the content available via the network to "create an infrastructure rich in information" (http://www.jisc.ac.uk/cei/dner_colpol.html). In light of these goals and with the advent of charges to be levied on U.K. universities for use of transatlantic bandwidth (http://www.jisc.ac.uk/pub98/c3_98.html), OMNI may wish to extend its services by mirroring key resources for the higher education community.

OMNI is optimistic that the Higher Education Funding Councils in the United Kingdom will recognize the value of the subject gateways and wish to integrate them into a national strategy for resource discovery and other initiatives. However, we also recognize that other communities benefit from the OMNI service, and we will continue our efforts to ensure that the OMNI database remains open to those communities. In particular, we aim to establish a presence on the fledgling NHSNet Intranet to offer more effective services to NHS users.

12.0 The Future of Resource Location and Description

The success of the U.K. subject gateways is gratifying but also poses questions about the scalability of the ANR model. The number of resources cataloged by all of the gateways is small compared to the total number of resources available. How can the number of resources cataloged be increased without decreasing the level of description and evaluation that have earned the gateways their well-deserved respect as sources of high-quality information?

One possible solution to this problem is to embed metadata (in whatever format) in the resources themselves, analogous to cataloging-in-publication for print resources. Much work has been done on metadata formats and protocols to further this end, and in recent years, the Platform for Internet Content Selection (PICS) (http://www.w3c.org/PICS/), the Dublin Core (http://purl.oclc.org/dc/), and the Resource Description Framework (RDF) (http://W3c.org/TR/WD-rdf-syntax) have emerged as likely solutions to various aspects of this problem.

Although tools for embedding metadata are being made available, there is no guarantee that publishers will be compliant, and there are no easy fixes for the quality problem. Author-created metadata on the Internet varies widely in terms of completeness, truthfulness, and usefulness to the extent that at least one major search engine, Excite, has refused to use the most common form (metatags) to create their index (http://www.excite.com/Info/listing.html#meta). It is difficult to see how new metadata protocols and formats will substantially improve this situation, and we are some way from developing adequate tools for automatic creation of metadata that meets the standards to which the library world and our users are accustomed.

The process of creating this high-quality metadata is likely to remain in human hands, and also to continue to be the remit of librarians and other information professionals addressing the needs of a specific community. In the United Kingdom, organizations within the higher education community itself may already be showing the way. Several universities are evaluating Internet resources with their own students in mind and developing gateways that may be browsed by course numbers specific to their institution. In the end, the solution to the scalability problem for national resource discovery may be to devolve cataloging activities to local subject experts and make selective gateways ubiquitous in the information landscape. National gateways can be crucial to this vision as they can provide a source for records that might then be modified locally. It would be possible, for example, for each university to carry a version of OMNI (or another subject gateway) relating to its own needs and local collections. In this scenario, the eLib subject gateways would be a vital centralized resource, ensuring minimized duplication of effort.

Notes

1. Sir Brian Follett et al., *The Follett Report* (Bristol: External Relations Department, 1993). (http://www.ukoln.ac.uk/services/papers/follett/report/chl.html)

2. Office of Health Economics, *Compendium of Health Statistics,* 10th ed. (London: Office of Health Economics, 1997), p. 101.

3. "A Strategy for NHS Wide Networking," *NHS Executive* (1994).

4. F. Norman, "Organising Medical Networked Information (OMNI)" *Medical Informatics* 23, no.1 (1998): 43–51.

5. F. Norman et al., "OMNI Project Proposal: A proposal to ISSC as part of the Follett Implementation Group on Information Technology program" (Area 6:

Access to Network Resources), submitted in response to JISC circular (April 1994).

6. OMNI Advisory Group on Evaluation Criteria, "OMNI Guidelines for Resource Evaluation." (http://omni.ac.uk/agec/evalguid.html) [Referenced April 1999]

7. P. Deutsch et al., "Publishing Information on the Internet with Anonymous FTP" (Internet draft; working draft now expired), in The IAFA Working Group [Referenced July 1998]. (http://info.webcrawler.com/mak/projects/iafa/iafa.txt)

8. D. Beckett, "IAFA Templates in Use as Internet Metadata," *World Wide Web Journal—Proceedings of the Fourth International World Wide Web Conference* 1, no.1 (Winter 1996): 135–43.

9. National Library of Medicine, *National Library of Medicine Classification: A Scheme for the Shelf Arrangement of Library Materials in the Field of Medicine and Its Related Sciences* (Bethesda, Md.: National Library of Medicine, 1994).

10. National Library of Medicine, *UMLS Metathesaurus* (Bethesda, Md.: National Library of Medicine, 1998).

11. *ICD10 International Statistical Classification of Diseases and Related Health Problems,* 10th Revision *(ICD-10)* (Geneva: World Health Organization, 1992); and National Health Service National Coding and Classification Centre, *The Read Thesaurus* v3.1 (London: National Health Service National Coding and Classification Centre, 1995).

12. Jason Plent, "Building the Distributed National Electronic Resource (DNER)," *JISC News* 3 (spring 1998). (http://www.jisc.ac.uk/pub98/n3_98.html#p5) [Referenced May 1999]

13. Committee on Electronic Information (CEI)—Content Working Group (1997). CEI Collections Policy.

11

Scout Report Signpost (Signpost)

Jack Solock
Amy Tracy Wells

The Scout Report Signpost (Signpost) (http://www.signpost.org/) is part of the Internet Scout Project (http://scout.cs.wisc.edu/), a National Science Foundation (NSF) (http://www.nsf.gov/) project housed in the Department of Computer Sciences at the University of Wisconsin-Madison. The Internet Scout Project is charged with promoting the use of the Internet to the U.S. higher research and education community, but a large general audience also uses its services. Signpost is a browseable and searchable database that is composed of reviews from the scout reports (http://scout.cs.wisc.edu/scout/report/) that are organized using an abbreviated Library of Congress Classification scheme and Library of Congress Subject Headings.

1.0 Background on the Internet Scout Project Resource Discovery Projects

From 1993 to 1996, the Internet Scout Project (http://scout.cs.wisc. edu/) consisted almost exclusively of Internet resource discovery. The primary vehicles for this discovery were (and continue to be) the Scout Report (http://scout.cs.wisc.edu/scout/report/), and Net-happenings (http://scout/cs.wisc.edu/scout/net-hap/). The Scout Report is a weekly publication of new and newly discovered Internet resources that is delivered via e-mail and the World Wide Web. Net-happenings (http://scout.cs.wisc.edu/scout/net-hap/index.html), created by Gleason Sackman in 1993, is a daily announcement distribution service. It announces Internet resources, software, conferences, newsletters, and so forth, and has a K–12 orientation. It is distributed via e-mail, the Web, and a usenet news group (comp.internet.net-happenings).

In 1996, the Kids Identifying and Discovering Sites (KIDS) Report (http://scout.cs.wisc.edu/scout/KIDS/), a biweekly e-mail newsletter of selected annotations of K–12 sites written by K–12 students, was added to the Internet Scout Project. And, in 1997, we began publishing three subject specific scout reports in science and engineering (http://scout.cs.wisc.edu/scout/report/sci-engr/index.html), business and economics (http://scout.cs.wisc.edu/scout/report/bus-econ/index.html), and social sciences (http://scout.cs.wisc.edu/scout/report/socsci/index.html). These biweekly newsletters, based on the Scout Report, added another dimension to resource discovery. They are targeted at researchers in specific disciplines and contain announcements of new preprints, think-tank policy papers, jobs, conferences, print publications, data, and other resources, all available via the Internet. Like the Scout Report, the subject-specific scout reports are delivered via e-mail and the World Wide Web. Total e-mail subscriptions to the scout reports, Net-happenings, and KIDS are over fifty thousand, and daily Web-site hits to these resources are just under thirty thousand.

While these tools distribute information about new and newly discovered research and educational resources, our users lacked refined accessibility to the scout reports, until we created Signpost. We created Signpost (http://www.signpost.org/) to provide an organized, classified interface to the Scout Report's content and the contents of subsequent subject-specific scout reports to facilitate access to specific resources. (See figure 1.) KIDS and Net-happenings content are not available in Signpost.

2.0 Responsible Persons

Signpost was designed and developed by Amy Tracy Wells, with significant effort from Aimée Glassel and from a small team of catalogers that includes Sheilah Harrington, Gerri Wanserski, and Debra Shapiro. Teri Boomsma, the former Internet Scout Project Webmaster, also had an integral role in its development and maintenance.

The Scout Report was created in 1994 by Susan Calcari, the director of the Internet Scout Project, and was edited by Jack Solock from 1995 until August 1998. Each of the subject-specific scout reports is edited by a master's or doctoral student in the respective discipline or by a librarian, with Jack Solock serving as the overall editor of the scout reports until his recent departure from our staff.

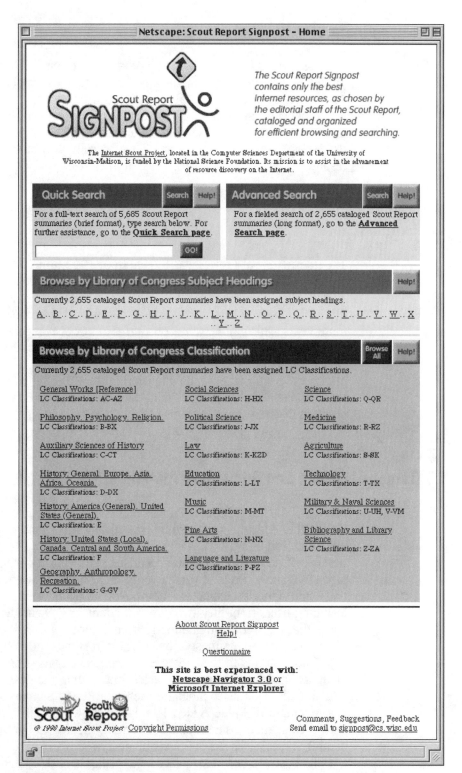

FIGURE 1.   Signpost Home Page

3.0 Mission Statement

Signpost serves the overall mission of Internet resource discovery by providing an alternative method of access to the contents of the scout reports, which are serial publications. Additionally, although it is a production system, Signpost, also serves as a test bed for the Isaac Network (see the "Software and Hardware" section for a fuller discussion), which seeks to unite geographically distributed Internet resource collections via a single search interface.

4.0 Funding

The Internet Scout Project was funded from 1993 until 1997 as part of the InterNIC, a National Science Foundation (NSF) cooperative. In April 1997, the Internet Scout Project received an NSF grant (NCR-9712163) for $3 million to continue its efforts over the course of three more years. This grant expires on April 30, 2000. Signpost receives some $250,000 per year for staff salaries, benefits, hardware, software, and for travel to conferences and meetings. Additional funding for the continuation and expansion of the KIDS Report has been made available by John and Tashia Morgridge, the chairman of the board of Cisco Systems, and his wife.

5.0 Target Audience and Secondary Audience

As part of the Internet Scout Project, Signpost's target audience is the U.S. higher education community, specifically the scientific and engineering community. However, in point of fact, we also serve a number of additional audiences. Statistics gathered for Signpost in July 1998 show usage at some twenty-eight hundred users per day and some eighty thousand per month (excluding all internal traffic), including users from fifty-two different countries (excluding all statistics that register as originating from .mil, .org, .net, and .com).

E-mail sent to Signpost or one of its staff is most often from faculty and librarians in the United States; however, we also receive a great deal from others outside of academia, both in the United States and abroad. "Thanks so much for the Scout Report Signpost! It's the best example of Value-Added I know!! Selected quality resources with organization!" says Gerry McKiernan, theoretical librarian and curator, CyberStacks, Iowa State University.

Signpost has been recognized as a quality service by both the library community and the larger community of general Internet users.

The Internet Scout Project and Signpost were highlighted in a 1997 issue of *Library Hi Tech* in "The Best Library-Related Web Sites" and Signpost was featured in the September 1998 issue of *Yahoo! Internet Life.*[1]

In general, the Internet Scout Project serves a large academic audience: fifty-five of the Top 100 Research Universities, as defined by the Carnegie Mellon Foundation in 1994, link to us through their Web sites, and in July, the Internet Scout Project was selected by the Wisconsin Library Association to receive its 1998 Special Service Award.

6.0 Collection Description

Signpost contains only the best Internet resources, as chosen by the editorial staff of the Scout Report and the subject-specific scout reports, based on an established selection criteria (see the "Selection Criteria" section for a fuller discussion). In July 1998, Signpost contained records for just under five thousand resources, with some two thousand resources completely cataloged. We add approximately two hundred new resources each month, as they are reviewed in a scout report. The overall percentage of cataloged resources in Signpost has increased at a steady rate, but the pace of resources reviewed in all of the scout reports continues at a slightly higher rate. Signpost's objective is not to be a comprehensive guide to Internet resources, but rather to serve as a selective filter to primarily research-quality Internet resources. The majority of resources contained in Signpost are free and freely accessible.

The principal components of a Signpost record, prior to a resource being fully cataloged, are the title of the resource, its URL, and a review from a scout report for the given resource. Each scout report review is anywhere from 75 to 150 words in length. Each review must state the provider or author of the resource and describe the resource. In some cases, a broad survey of the resource is provided, giving general information about most of the resource's features. In other cases, one feature is highlighted, and then other features are mentioned in passing. In all cases, no part of a resource is discussed without its utility, display, links, and so forth all being verified first. The Internet Scout Project takes its filtering responsibilities seriously and realizes the importance of thoroughly investigating the resources it chooses.

In addition, editors may add an evaluative sentence or two about a resource, although inclusion in any of the scout reports already serves to indicate that the resource is well done. However, the scout reports and Signpost are not rating systems. They are not intended to include sites that have unreliable information or sites that are not accessible or whose design makes them either inaccessible or not navigable. In this way, Signpost can guarantee its users well-researched reviews on information-rich resources. We are extremely selective, and the basis of our selectivity is also the basis of Signpost's excellence.

The scout reports' and hence Signpost's major disciplines include the Arts and Humanities, Business and Economics, Law, Medicine and Health, Science and Math, and Social Science. Also included are sections entitled Network Tools and General Interest. The latter two include resources such as AltaVista's World Index (http://altavista.digital.com/av/oneweb/) and the American Film Institute's 100 Years, 100 Movies (http://AFI.100movies.com/).

7.0 Selection Criteria

Since the content of Signpost is gleaned from the Internet resources reviewed in the four scout report publications, it is important to understand the selection criteria for these publications. One of the reasons why the scout reports are respected in the academic community is because of their rigorously applied selection criteria. Selection criteria are important for two reasons: (1) the sheer number of Internet resources available, and (2) the lack of editorial barriers to publishing that have long been an integral part of the world of print resources. Because of the first reason, researchers and educators find a service that selects and filters information very useful. Because of the second reason, they find one that filters for quality even more useful.

What are these criteria? How are they used to evaluate resources for selection in Signpost? The criteria we use are very similar to those used in library collection development of print materials. They are mostly based on content considerations. In addition, certain evaluative criteria are unique to the networked environment.

Content evaluation on the Internet is intimately tied to authority determination. In real estate, there is a saying that the value of a property is determined by three factors: location, location, and location. With respect to Internet content, the saying might be altered slightly. The value of a resource is determined by three factors: authority, authority, and authority. Authority is the most important cue to quality resource discovery in any medium. To the professional selector, this goes without saying, but it is essential to underscore its importance in the networked environment.

In a medium with no barriers to publishing, where anyone with an Internet connection, space on a computer server, and a rudimentary knowledge of HyperText Markup Language (HTML) can quickly create an Internet presence, it is very easy to "publish." Part of the great charm of the Internet is the ease with which anyone may have their say. However, from a librarian's point of view, particularly with respect to selection of quality resources, ease of publishing has a difficult flip side. It involves filtering through much information, often of dubious utility, to locate quality resources.

Filtering begins with determining the authoritativeness of the resource's content. If the site is an institutional or library site, authority checking can be fairly straightforward. If the resource is an individual effort, authority checking may be more difficult. We make every effort to discover the credentials of the authority. Usually, we can quickly ascertain this from information at the site. In cases where we cannot, considerable time may be spent in authority checking. Signpost seldom contains resources with anonymous authorship and an unknown publisher.

Other content variables that go into quality evaluation include currency, audience, purpose, scope, and accuracy of the resource. These are long-established criteria in the selection of print reference materials in libraries. We examine what, if anything, is said about these criteria at the site and then we compare that to the resource's actual content.

Currency refers to whether the information at the resource is up-to-date. However, there is nothing intrinsically wrong with an archive site if it is specifically stated that it is an archive. We consider the audience variable to determine for whom the information at the site is designed. A good site will state its purpose and scope on its home page. Sometimes scope can be determined by the various sections of the site, but unless the site is designed clearly, this may be missed without a scope statement. We examine the accuracy of information as rigorously as possible within the demands of the scout reports' production deadlines. Ideally, sites would be sent out for peer review so that an expert in the field could look at every one. In the case of extremely specialized sites, where even a subject librarian (e.g., a business librarian) might not know enough information to clearly determine accuracy, it would be a wonderful luxury to have input from a specialist (e.g., a lawyer specializing in labor issues). However, Signpost records are based on reviews that are created under the pressure of weekly and biweekly publication deadlines, making peer review impractical. In the case of highly specialized sites, the authority can usually be used as a cue to accuracy.

The Internet is a new information medium, and some features of its structure make aspects of it intrinsically different from static information media such as print. Some of these features are also taken into account in the selection criteria. These features fall into two main categories: accessibility and design. After a book is selected for a library collection, it is either available or it is not. If it is, it can be checked out. If it is not, a request can be made until it is. Accessibility on the Internet is more complex. At a basic level, it means availability of the site. To this end, each scout report URL is checked at least three times in the twenty-four hours before a report is issued. Once a scout report review is entered into Signpost, its URL is checked for validity on a six-week basis (see the "Hardware and Software" section for a fuller discussion).

We also use accessibility criteria on a more subtle level. It is not enough that a URL can be reached. Resources are analyzed for the level of accessibility, particularly with respect to users with slower connections. For this reason, we list alternative URLs for accessing sites via a text-only or no-frames interface when they are available. In addition, if the information provided by a Web site is also available via another Internet protocol, such as Gopher, FTP, or e-mail, this address is also included in our record.

Design also affects accessibility. When evaluating the design of a site, we concentrate on two factors: (1) how much the design contributes to (or detracts from) the accessibility of information at the site; and (2) how much site design becomes an integral part of the site's content. In cases where sites are gratuitously overdesigned (unnecessary use of memory-intensive plug-ins, for example) or difficult to navigate, the content of the site can suffer. In some cases, nonlinear navigation from one point to another is an integral part of the site, a demonstration that content can be delivered in a unique fashion via the Internet. Such factors are always weighed in deciding whether a site is chosen for a scout report, but content is always the primary concern.

To reiterate, the scout reports do not, in general, review fee-based sites. The reason for this is simple. Fee-based sites eliminate access for users who cannot afford to pay. Also, the editors cannot review a site without examining the resource. Fees preclude this.

For more information on the philosophy and mechanics of the scout report publication process, see "The Internet: Window to the World or Hall of Mirrors? Information Quality in the Networked Environment" and "Anatomy of a Scout Report: Resource Discovery in the Information Age, or How We Do It." (http://scout7.cs.wisc.edu/pages/00000903.html).[2]

8.0 Software and Hardware

8.1 Signpost

There are four primary methods to access Signpost's content. These include two browsing and two searching capabilities. These capabilities are divided between two Web servers and their respective applications.

Apache v1.1.3 (http://www.apache.org/), the first of the two servers, runs under SunOS 5.5.1 on a Sparc5. Signpost's Quick Search, a nonfielded search of a resource's title, URL, and scout report review, uses Excite for Web Servers (EWS) v1.1 (http://www.excite.com/navigate/), best known simply as Excite, to generate a keyword index and for searching. Excite permits the use of *and, or,* and *not* Boolean operators. We also use wwwstat v2.0b1 (http://www.ics.uci.edu/pub/websoft/wwwstat/) for analyzing Web server common-log files (CLF) and generating statistics. Both Apache and wwwstat require Perl v.4.x and higher.

WebSTAR 3.0 (http://www.starnine.com/webstar/webstar.html), the second of the two servers, runs under Mac OS 8.1 on a PowerMac 8600/300. Signpost's advanced search provides a fielded search option of a resource's Site Title, Author/Contributor/Publisher, LC Subject Heading, Resource Type, Language, Resource Location, and/or Primary URL via a FileMaker Pro v4 (http://www.filemaker.com/) database (see the "Classification" section for a fuller discussion). This database is also used to facilitate browse by Library of Congress Classification (LCC) and browse by Library of Congress Subject Headings (LCSHs) options. Lasso 2.5 (http://www.blueworld.com/blueworld/default.html) plug-in provides the connectivity between FileMaker Pro and the Web. We use analog2.0/Mac (http://www.statslab.cam.ac.uk/~sret1/analog/) for analyzing Web server CLFs and generating statistics.

8.2 Data Entry

We use HTML templates in combination with a Perl script to automatically mark up text-based scout reports. A series of Perl scripts enables us to input a scout report into the FileMaker Pro database by generating an interface that allows catalogers to manipulate the review, title, URL, and other fields as needed. Not all items from the scout reports are, in fact, added. For instance, a singular conference solicitation might well be appropriate to include in a subject-specific scout report, but not be especially useful as a cataloged resource for future audiences due to its ephemeral nature. We would, then, decide not to include this resource in Signpost.

8.3 Cataloging Tools

We have a subscription to Classification Plus (http://lcweb.loc.gov/cds/cdroms1.html#classplus), on CD-ROM, and also use the *Subject Cataloging Manual: Subject Headings,* fifth edition (http://lcweb.loc.gov/cds/lcsh.html#scmsh), in print, to construct valid Library of Congress Subject Headings.

8.4 Backups

Each day, we back up the FileMaker Pro cataloging database to an external local disk drive and each week onto a departmental server which is, in turn, backed up.

8.5 URL Checking

Every six weeks, we verify all site URLs beginning with "http://" in Signpost via Big Brother v. 1.2 (http://pauillac.inria.fr/~fpottier/brother.html.en). We run a report containing all "http://" URLs (Big Brother cannot search for Telnet, FTP, or Gopher URLs, or e-mail addresses, or mailing list addresses) several times, at various times of the day, on different days of the week to verify that a URL is nonfunctional as opposed to simply temporarily unreachable. "Lost" sites hover around 5 percent of the entire collection each time this report is run. A student assistant then manually searches for those URLs that are not found and corrects any bad URLs. Those still not found are, in turn, searched for by a cataloger. When we cannot locate a site, we flag it in the cataloging database and remove the site information from Signpost (but not from the cataloging database itself) after it fails this process three consecutive times. The total number of records we have flagged in this manner accounts for approximately 2 percent of Signpost's collection. This is obviously a time-intensive process, but one that we feel is important to ensure our users access to not just the best but also the most stable resources. It should be noted that in the spring of 1998, we had verified and corrected, as required, all Gopher URLs, which appear as the site URLs, that is, the primary URL in Signpost.

8.6 Future Software

The FileMaker Pro database has been expeditious in that training and development time have been negligible, allowing us to focus on schema definition and subsequent cataloging and classification issues (see the "Classification" section for a fuller discussion). Because a major focus for the Internet Scout Project since 1997 has been to apply and develop tools to manage resource discovery across multiple collections, we have seen FileMaker Pro as a temporary solution until we could purchase or build another database to deal more effectively with the resources. To that end, the Internet Scout Project hired two computer scientists, Mike Roszkowski and Chris Lukas, to lead development work on database protocols such as Referral Whois (Rwhois) (http://www.rwhois.net/rwhois/index.html), WHOIS++ (http://www.ietf.org/internet-drafts/draft-ietf-asid-whoispp-02.txt), and Lightweight Directory Access Protocol (LDAP) (ftp://ftp.isi.edu/in-notes/rfc2251.txt) with complementary technologies such as Common Indexing Protocol (CIP) (http://www.ietf.cnri.reston.va.us/internet-drafts/draft-ietf-find-cip-arch-01.txt). The product of their work, known as the Isaac Network (http://scout.cs.wisc.edu/scout/research/index.html), was originally built from the University of Michigan's LDAP server v. 3.3 (http://www.umich.edu/~dirsvcs/ldap/), which became available in June 1998.[3] Isaac provides a singular search interface to multiple collections while allowing for quality content providers such as Signpost to develop and maintain their collections autonomously. At the time of publication, we are working with two such providers and are addressing issues in mapping schema. We have also received many other requests for information. Ongoing areas of research for the Isaac Network include accommodating differing syntax and vocabularies among collections as well as scaling for the common index.

9.0 Classification

In any discussion of Signpost cataloging and classification, it is important to know some of the background issues. In September 1996, Amy Tracy Wells was hired to enhance access to the Scout Report archive with the knowledge that eventually the archive would be used to test geographically distributed database protocols (see the "Software and Hardware" section for a fuller discussion). While we might have used many possible methods to fulfill this goal, the most logical approach seemed to be to populate a low-cost, off-the-shelf database with all of the archived reviews and new reviews, as they were created, and to use a lightweight schema for their subsequent cataloging. We made two additional and critical decisions. Specifically, we decided not to embed any mark-up languages (HTML, SGML, etc.) in the records, and to use the emerging Dublin Core (DC) (http://purl.oclc.org/metadata/dublin_core/) framework (or schema) for resource description.

These decisions would facilitate access, ensure that the Internet Scout Project meets NSF's goal for research, and provide for cost-effective cataloging. Given that HTML and SGML were still evolving, using a database solution would allow output of Signpost records using either markup language or some future standard, on the fly, and most importantly any version of a standard. This would also allow great flexibility. Additionally, while MARC (http://lcweb.loc.gov/marc/marcdocz.html) has been successfully used to catalog extensive and divergent print collections and was demonstrating its effectiveness for electronic collections, it has a high associated labor cost and did not meet NSF's research requirement.

Signpost database records consist of DC elements (or fields) and local elements. In table 1 below, many of Signpost's elements are displayed on the left with those they semantically map to from the DC on the right. Those elements in Signpost that map to repeated DC elements are noted with parentheses. Those that do not map are noted as having "no related DC element."

Table 1.   Signpost and Dublin Core Elements

Signpost	Dublin Core
Site Title	(Title)
Alternate Title	(Title)
Site URL	Identifier
Author	Creator
Contributor	Contributor
Publisher	Publisher
(LC Class)	(Subject)
(LCSH Subject)	(Subject)
Resource Type	Type/Format
Language	Language
Date of Publication	Date
Scout Report Review	Description
Date URL Last Verified	no related DC element
Date of Scout Report Review	no related DC element
Resource Location	no related DC element
Source of Cataloging	no related DC element
Record ID	no related DC element
Scout Report Review URL	no related DC element
Scout Publication	no related DC element

Site Title and Alternate Title refer to the resource's title. Often, a given resource will contain multiple titles. The use of essentially two title elements allows us to capture multiple names and facilitates access. The Site URL simply refers to a resource's address. Author is the person or persons who are responsible for the resource's intellectual content. Contributor can include an editor, illustrator, translator, and so forth. The Publisher is the entity responsible for making the resource available, such as a college, university, government agency, and so on. Resource Type, as defined and used in Signpost, can map to the DC Resource Type and Format elements. Currently, Signpost contains the following Resource Types: Animation/Video, Audio, Bibliography, Chart/Table/Map, Conference/Solicitation, Data Set, Database, Dictionary/Encyclopedia, Directory, Document, Educational Material, FAQ, Graphics, Journal/Newspaper, Library Catalog, Mailing List/News Group, Metasite, and Software. Each of these Resource Types can be repeated for any given resource.[4] Language refers to the language in which the resource itself is available. In July 1998, Signpost contained resources in twenty-nine languages. Scout Report Review is the 75-to-150-word review for each resource. Date URL Last Verified refers to the last time the resource's location was verified as working. Date of Scout Report Review refers to the date the resource actually appeared in any scout report. Resource Location indicates the domain or affiliation of the site and currently includes: Commercial, Education, Government, Military, Network, and Organization. Resource Location is based on the six current top-level domains (.com, .edu, .gov, .mil, .net, and .org). Resources that are not from one of these six domains (.ac, .co, .k12, etc.) have been assigned a corresponding Resource Location based on local affiliations. Scout Report Review URL refers to the address of the scout report in which the resource was reviewed.

Not all of Signpost's elements are publicly available and this includes one of the DC elements, specifically, Date of Publication, as well as the following local elements: Source of Cataloging, Record ID, and Scout Publication. The reason why date of publication is not publicly displayed is that, while Signpost catalogers take great care when supplying this information, the rationale for date, as applied by content providers, varies widely. For example, date information might be specific to the resource's intellectual content or refer to the last time the HTML in the source was modified. Source of Cataloging, which identifies the individual responsible for cataloging a resource, is expected to become important with the implementation of Isaac, a distributed search tool (see the "Software and Hardware" section for a fuller discussion). Record ID is simply a unique number automatically assigned at the time a Signpost record is created. Scout Publication serves as an in-house element that allows us to quickly determine whether a resource is from the Scout Report or any of the subject-specific scout reports. Two of the Signpost elements, specifically LC Class and LC Subject Heading, are repeated.

Signpost cataloging takes into account the scout report review but focuses on the resource itself. We use anywhere from one to five LCSHs when cataloging Signpost resources to try to ensure maximum description and retrievability. We classify Signpost records into broad subject areas using an abbreviated version of the Library of Congress Classification (LCC). Resources are assigned only the lettered portion of a complete LCC call number. For example, the *Statistical Abstract of the United States* for 1996 might, in the print world, be assigned the call number HA202 A3 1996, whereas in Signpost it is assigned only the class code HA. However, any given resource can be assigned up to two LCCs. So, for example, a resource such as Emerging Law on the Electronic Frontier, which relates to both law and telecommunications, is assigned both the call letters K̲ and T̲K̲. (See figure 2.)

We do not apply keywords since any given review is often 75 to 150 words in length and uses the discipline-specific and resource-specific language found in the resource itself. These reviews can be keyword searched via quick search. For more information on our cataloging practices, see "Scout Report Signpost: Design and Development for Access to Cataloged Internet Resources."[5]

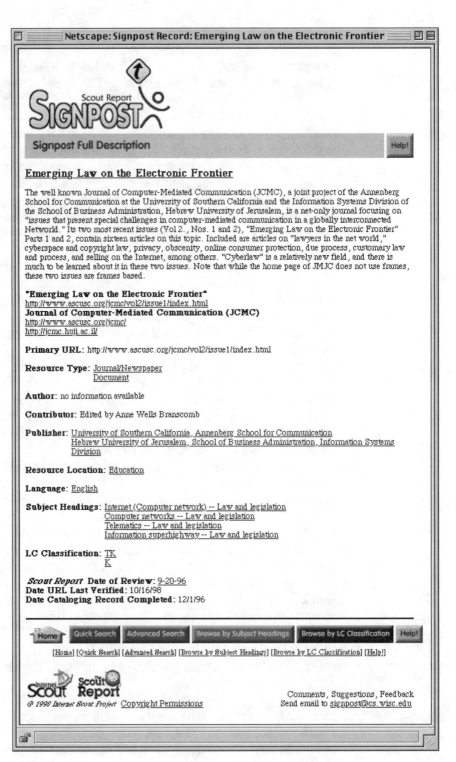

FIGURE 2. Signpost Record: Emerging Law on the Electronic Frontier

One of the three 1998 goals for Signpost based, in part, on user feedback revolved around the initial decision to use the abbreviated version of LCC. In the short term, this decision expedited development, but it has seemed less effective as the number of resources cataloged in Signpost has grown. Therefore, we have been developing an alternative classification scheme, led by Signpost cataloger Aimée Glassel. The principles behind this approach include the need for a facet-based, subject-access scheme that is dynamic. The implementation of such a scheme would (1) allow for greater contextualized browsing such as Computer Sciences and Information Technology: Hardware: Communications and Networking Hardware: Routers as opposed to the call letters <u>TK</u> 5105.5 . . . ; (2) allow Signpost to provide better access to related information via hyperlinks between similar subject areas such as Visual and Performing Arts: Visual Arts: Arts: Photography and Journalism and Communications: Communications Media: Photojournalism; (3) possibly have greater meaning for those unfamiliar with the LCC; and (4) facilitate the automatic reorganization of subject areas as needed.

As of July 1998, we identified, developed, and tested in-house twenty-two broad subject areas. They are

Anthropology

Business and Economics

Demography and Population Studies

Education

Geography

Library Science and Information Management

Political Science, Law, and Government

Sociology

History

Home Living, Sports, and Leisure

Journalism and Communications

Literature, Language, and Linguistics

Philosophy, Psychology, and Religion

Reference

Visual and Performing Arts

Agriculture and Food Science

Computer Sciences and Information Technology

Engineering

Life Sciences

Mathematics

Medicine and Health

Physical Sciences

We anticipate that, in September, the developed scheme will be given to outside reviewers, librarians, professors, and instructors as well as end users for their feedback.

10.0 Project's Strengths and Weaknesses

In many ways, from a content perspective, the weaknesses of Signpost are determined by its strengths. Its two main weaknesses are lack of depth (in terms of numbers) and breadth (in terms of subject coverage). In July 1998, Signpost contained slightly fewer than five thousand resources, a microscopic drop in the bucket in terms of the total amount of Internet resources available. In addition, though it currently uses an abbreviated Library of Congress Classification, many of its classification areas are underrepresented. Why is this?

We would argue that a selective guide to Internet resources such as Signpost is more useful than a comprehensive guide to all Internet resources. The Web is really, in a large sense, one document, not millions. Users have millions of portals through which to enter that document. Without an information gateway such as Signpost, most of those portals lead to dead ends or to poor information. The reason for this is an inherent strength and weakness of the Internet. The Internet has, in large part, leveled the playing field as far as the ability for anyone to make his or her views known to the world. The previously discussed lack of barriers to publishing, which is a positive development from the standpoint of democratizing access to a communications medium, can also be seen as a not so positive development with respect to the library function of selecting and filtering quality information.

Signpost is an organized and accessible presentation of the results of five years of resource discovery using quality filtering and selection. Most Internet resources contain links to other resources, so most Signpost sites serve as partial Internet portals as well as repositories of original content. One or two excellent portals can lead a user to hundreds, or even thousands, of quality sites. So less can be more.

Another reason that Signpost lacks breadth and depth is that the publications from which it is drawn do not have the charge of being a directory to quality information resources in all subjects. The scout reports are, and always have been, current-awareness readers' advisory services. Their main function is to be a "town crier" for the Internet, finding and announcing *new* and *newly* discovered resources.

New quality resources cannot be guaranteed across a subject spectrum every week. The content of the report is largely determined by what has been released in the recent past. The report is driven by what is taking place on the Internet itself, and not by the need to create a balanced subject directory.

This current awareness function of the Scout Report has made it indispensable to researchers and educators for five years. Few have either the time or inclination to track the hundreds and sometimes thousands of sources necessary to ferret out quality new sites on an ongoing basis. In performing this function, the Scout Report saves researchers valuable time by not only alerting and informing them of resources in their own field, but also providing the serendipitous function of furnishing leads in related, and sometimes unrelated, disciplines. Signpost benefits from this in that its content is constantly being enriched with newly created, quality sites.

And the proof of the power of the Scout Report and Signpost is, of course, in the pudding. The scout reports, because of their proven quality, as well as the depth of each review, are used over and over by library, institutional, and personal directories and metasites all over the world, including some of the projects in this book. The question remains, however, about the effectiveness of Signpost, which is built from a current awareness service. A first-time user, expecting to see broad coverage, might be disappointed. It should be mentioned however that because the scout reports drive Signpost, and not the other way around, this is a weakness that is and always has been inherent in Signpost. And this weakness is more than compensated for by the ongoing freshness of Signpost's resources.

We believe that a current awareness service and a resource directory can work together and complement each other to provide an excellent information resource. Neither, standing alone, is as powerful, and both together are more powerful than the sum of each.

11.0 Project's Time Frames Including Start Date

Signpost began development the fall of 1996 with the hiring of Amy Tracy Wells as its coordinator. Later that year, we hired the first cataloger, Aimée Glassel, and began developing cataloging standards and doing limited cataloging. Teri Boomsma, Internet Scout Project Webmaster as well as a consulting graphic artist, also served on the initial development team. In April and May 1997, Sheilah Harrington and Gerri Wanserski joined the Internet Scout Project to assist in the cataloging of the scout reports. We have also employed student assistants from the computer sciences department to assist with maintaining URLs. On Monday, May 19, 1997, Signpost was beta-tested by some fifty system designers, librarians, educators, researchers, and library science students. We addressed many of their very constructive comments at that time, but some were technically not feasible. Those that could not be incorporated either directly or indirectly were noted for future development. Signpost was announced to the public in the June 20, 1997, issue of the Scout Report as well as on various electronic mailing lists. In January 1998, we hired Todd Hanson, a student in the computer sciences department, to assist with maintaining URLs and automating various aspects of production. In April 1998, Debra Shapiro joined the Internet Scout Project to assist in the cataloging of the scout reports as well as aid our authority work.

12.0 Future Goals of the Project

An ongoing goal for Signpost since its inception, as mentioned previously, has been to incorporate the feedback we receive from Signpost users into the overall design and functionality by adding specific suggestions. In 1998, we focused primarily on developing a new classification scheme (see the "Classification" section for a fuller discussion), adding authority files, and maintaining our outreach efforts.

In adding authority files, we have identified unique author and publisher names in Signpost and subsequently purged duplicates and normalized this information. Our outreach efforts have included speaking to various classes and organizations in the United States and abroad; actively contributing to standards development and publication within the American Library Association, Internet Engineering Task Force, and the Dublin Core; writing journal articles; producing a public version of our in-house Signpost Cataloging Manual (due out in spring 1999); and producing this book!

Our goals for 1999 will focus on supporting the Isaac Network. This will include ensuring that our cataloging and classification efforts facilitate the exchange of resource information. Additionally, we are further examining methods to automate the classification process. We will also continue our outreach efforts. We welcome and need your feedback in determining future goals!

13.0 The Future of Resource Location and Description

All of the projects covered in this book clearly show that it will be a long time, if ever, before quality information resource discovery and description can be an automatic process. The analytical eyes of librarians, selectors, and subject specialists cannot be replaced, at this time, by algorithm. This, of course, is eminently clear to those of us who do this sort of work on a daily basis. However, it is not clear to the general public or to many in the computing community; hence, the proliferation of search engines and general directories that are designed to provide disorganized quantity rather than organized quality. Librarians have always been gateways to quality information—to finding it, filtering it, selecting it, organizing it, and making it accessible. The Internet, of course, presents new challenges. However, quality information is rare in any medium, and good librarians see the Internet as no more than another information container. For the most part, they are not awed by its technical brilliance, but rather look at it in a disinterested fashion and ask "How can this help my patrons?" When librarians or subject specialists approach the Internet in this fashion, the end result will always be resource directories that serve as excellent portals to quality networked information resources.

The logical next step, given the hypertext nature of the Internet, and the fact that, in many respects, it is really one document with millions of entry points rather than millions of documents, is to link quality directory services to each other via a front-end interface that allows transparent searching of multiple directories at once. Examples of this exist at the single-subject level. Argos (http://argos.evansville.edu/), for ancient history, is one. The Electronic Engineering Library, Sweden's "All" Engineering Resources on the Internet (http://www.ub2.lu/se/eel/) is another, though one is a search index of collections of peer-reviewed and hand-selected resources, while the other is a robot-generated index of subject-related pages.

Imagine how much more powerful the information services in this book would be if users could search all, or any combination of them, from a single search interface. Researchers and educators need to spend their time researching and educating, not searching for information. A distributed search engine that finds already selected and filtered quality information is the next logical step in networked resource discovery. Two excellent examples of the possibilities inherent in this framework include the ROADS project (http://www.ilrt.bris.ac.uk/roads/), a JISC-funded project (discussed in part in chapters 5, 10, and 12), as well as the Isaac Network (see the "Software and Hardware" section for a fuller discussion).

The challenges that face us in the development and widespread implementation of quality distributed search engines include easing the labor costs associated with identifying and describing resources, using Uniform Resource Names (URN) (http://info.internet.isi.edu/in-notes/rfc/files/rfc2141.txt) in a systematic fashion, developing common vocabularies to facilitate searching, mapping differing metadata schema across collections, determining optimal updates for such systems, and developing appropriate relevance-ranking techniques and the ability to identify and eliminate redundant resources. Another ongoing challenge to all of this work is the need to secure stable funding that would allow systematic solutions to the above problems.

The Internet has far too many quality resources for any single individual or even institution to discover them all. Cooperative resource discovery brings to bear the power of many experts at many institutions. It therefore eases the burden on any single institution or individual and allows specialization over a broad range of subjects, providing optimal breadth and depth of collections. As the world of networked information grows, this is the logical and optimal solution to the long-term problem of quality resource discovery.

Notes

1. Susan Calcari, Jack Solock, and Amy Tracy Wells, "The Internet Scout Project," *Library Hi Tech* 15, no. 3–4 (1997): 11–18.

2. Jack Solock, "The Internet: Window to the World or Hall of Mirrors? Information Quality in the Networked Environment," *InterNIC News* 1, no. 11 (1997); and J. Solock, "Anatomy of a Scout Report: Resource Discovery in the Information Age, or How We Do It," *InterNIC News* 1, no. 3 (1997). (http://scout7.cs.wisc.edu/pages/00000903.html) [Referenced Jan. 1999]

3. Mike Roszkowski and Christopher Lukas, "A Distributed Architecture for Resource Discovery Using Metadata," *D-Lib Magazine* 6 (June 1998). (http://www.dlib.org/dlib/june98/scout/06roszkowski.html) [Referenced Jan. 1999]

4. Amy Tracy Wells, "A Scout Report Signpost Look at One Aspect of Metadata—Resource Type," *InterNIC News* 2, no. 11 (1997). (http://scout.cs.wisc.edu/scout/toolkit/enduser/archive/1997/euc-9711.html) [Referenced Jan. 1999]

5. Aimee Glassel and Amy Tracy Wells, "Scout Report Signpost: Design and Development for Access to Cataloged Internet Resources," *Journal of Internet Cataloging* 1, no. 3 (1997): 15–45.

12

Social Science Information Gateway (SOSIG)

Emma Place

One of the great challenges for SOSIG (http://www.sosig.ac.uk/) staff has been to consider how library practices might be adapted to apply to the new information environment of the Internet. Can we apply the same standards and skills to Internet resources that have been applied to books and journals for many centuries? The library metaphor can be useful in understanding how SOSIG works; in many ways SOSIG can be viewed as the Internet equivalent of a research library for the social sciences. However, there is a stage at which the library metaphor is no longer appropriate and where the Internet necessitates new ways of looking at things and new working practices. Our *other* great challenge has been to recognize the value of emerging technologies and network scenarios, which might take librarianship in a new direction, offering new opportunities for the profession.

1.0 A Guided Tour

We'd like to start by giving you a quick tour of our virtual library. Please step inside!

In libraries you find counters, shelves, and desks; in SOSIG we have buttons, lists, and forms! A virtual tour of SOSIG therefore involves a trip along the button bar, which is at the top of each screen in SOSIG, and is the key navigational aid to the service. The SOSIG home page (http://www.sosig.ac.uk/) can be seen in figure 1.

SOSIG is an online catalog of high-quality Internet resources that can support the work of social scientists. The catalog offers users the

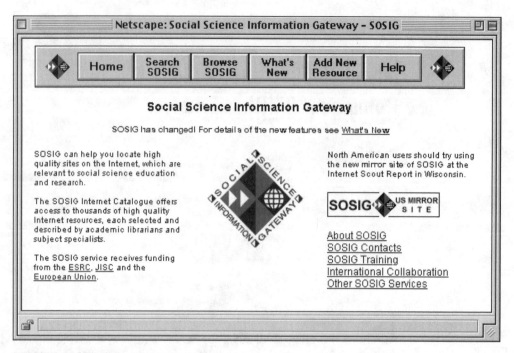

FIGURE 1.   SOSIG Home Page

chance to read descriptions of resources available over the Internet and to access these resources directly via a hyperlink. SOSIG points to thousands of resources, and each one has been selected, cataloged, and classified by an information professional.

1.1 Search SOSIG: The Catalog for Our Virtual Library

The Search SOSIG button takes users to a screen that enables them to search the SOSIG catalog. Boolean operators may be used, and phrase searching and field searching are possible. Extended search options allow users to search by region, or by the type of resource. A thesaurus is available to help users with their searching.

Searching is possible because librarians have created a catalog record for each of the Internet resources. The record contains information about the resource (known as metadata), including the title, a description, some keywords, and so forth. When users search SOSIG, they will be searching the information held in the SOSIG catalog by keyword and not the resources themselves.

1.2 Browse SOSIG: Our Virtual Shelves

The Browse SOSIG button takes users to a screen that enables them to browse resources by subject and geographical region. Under each of the main subject headings are subsections that point to more resources. For example, clicking on the Statistics, Demography button takes one to a screen with the following choices: Demography, International Statistics, Local Statistics, National Statistics, Official Statistics, Regional Statistics, and Statistical Theory. Browsing is our equivalent of offering shelves where resources are organized by their classification number. Users can wander through our browsing pages and enjoy the kind of serendipity that can be important in information seeking.

Behind the scenes, browsing is made possible by the use of a classification scheme. SOSIG uses the Universal Decimal Classification (UDC) scheme, a standard used by libraries across the world. Each resource is allocated a classification number based on the subject area it relates to. The SOSIG database uses these numbers to arrange the resources automatically into browseable lists arranged under subject headings. Once again, users can choose to read the catalog descriptions or access the resources directly via hyperlinks.

1.3 What's New: Our New Books Shelf

The What's New button on SOSIG is the virtual equivalent of the new books shelf in an academic library. Users can take a quick look at all the titles added to the collection in the previous week. The new titles appear every Monday and often include some resources that are new on the Internet. A quick skim of the What's New section of SOSIG each week can be a good way to keep up-to-date with new social science resources available over the Internet.

1.4 Submit a New Resource: Our Virtual Suggestions Box

The Submit a New Resource button resembles the library suggestions box, or the list of recommended titles handed to librarians by university academics. The button allows users to send in recommendations for any Internet resources they think should be added to the collection. They can do this by filling in a World Wide Web form that is e-mailed directly to the SOSIG team. Staff then looks at the resource and, as long as it meets with the selection criteria, they will catalog it, classify it, and add it to the gateway. The use of this feature is rising as more and more librarians are using SOSIG to support their customers. If they don't find a resource on SOSIG, but find it elsewhere, they will often send it on to us so that they can point their users to SOSIG as a means of finding what they need.

1.5 Help Page: Supporting Users We Never See

One of the distinguishing features of a virtual library is the fact that the staff does not actually see the users, which means that user education and support require new media and methods. The online help pages are accessible from every page in SOSIG, and provide information on searching and browsing. SOSIG staff also receives and answers inquiries via e-mail.

2.0 Funding Sources

SOSIG receives funding from three sources.

(1) The Economic and Research Council (ESRC). The ESRC is the main funding agency for research and training in social and economic issues in the United Kingdom. It funds high-quality research in institutions across the United Kingdom.

(2) The Joint Information Systems Committee (JISC). The JISC (http://www.jisc.ac.uk) is funded by the Higher Education Funding Bodies of the United Kingdom. It was responsible for the Electronic Libraries Programme (eLib) (http://ukoln.bath.ac.uk/services/elib/) of which SOSIG is a part.

(3) The European Union (EU). SOSIG is one of the partners in the DESIRE project (http://www.desire.org/), which is funded under the European Union's Telematics for Research Programme. This is an applied research program that aims to promote the development of large-scale networks and network services that can support researchers across Europe.

3.0 SOSIG Personnel

If you take a look at the SOSIG team, you can see how it sits snugly between the world of librarianship and the world of the Internet. On the one hand, we have librarians practicing cataloging, classification, and collection development. On the other hand, we have computer experts and network specialists practicing database design, Perl programming, Web authoring, and metadata management. In the midst of this harmonious meeting of very different cultures, we have the trainers who translate all of the complexities into simple language for user support and education.

The SOSIG team can be split into the core staff, working in Bristol (U.K.), and the distributed team of subject librarians who are spread across the United Kingdom.

3.1 Core Staff

The core team is based at the Institute for Learning and Research Technology (http://www.ilrt.bris.ac.uk/) at the University of Bristol in the United Kingdom, which is home to a large number of projects relating to the use of network technologies in higher education. The staff all share their time between various projects, but those involved in SOSIG at least part time include:

  the director, Nicky Ferguson (obtains funding and steers the project);

  the project manager, Debra Hiom (oversees the project and steers new developments);

  research staff, Emma Place and Phil Cross (maintain and develop the collection and work on new developments);

  technical staff, Jasper Tredgold (provides technical support and works on technical developments);

  training staff, Lesly Huxley and Tracey Hooper (deliver training workshops and produce and disseminate promotional literature);

  administrative staff, Beryl Ray (supports the SOSIG team in a million and one ways).

3.2 Section Editors

SOSIG also has formal contracts with a group of university libraries in the United Kingdom, which provide social science librarians to select and catalog new resources for the collection. The following institutions are all home to a subject specialist who is employed to spend half a day per week working for SOSIG as a section editor:

  British Library of Political and Economic Science, London School of Economics;

  The Fawcett Library, London Guildhall University;

  Hartley Library, University of Southampton;

  Institute of Education, University of London;

  JB Priestley Library, University of Bradford;

  John Rylands University Library, University of Manchester;

  The Library, University of Edinburgh;

  Main Library, Exeter University;

  Wills Memorial Library, University of Bristol.

Full and up-to-date details (including contact details) for SOSIG staff can be found on the Web (http://www.sosig.ac.uk/contact.html).

4.0 The SOSIG Mission

The SOSIG aims were formally stated in the original project plan. They are as follows:

> to improve delivery of information and quality of service by working with and helping to pilot the latest developments in networked resource technology;

> to improve accessibility and usability of resources via a program of training and awareness;

> to encourage availability of new, quality-networked resources of relevance to social scientists.

These aims reflect the three main strands of work that SOSIG staff undertakes: (1) research and development, (2) training and awareness, and (3) the provision of the service.

4.1 Research and Development

Many users will not be aware of the fact that, behind the scenes, SOSIG is dedicated to research and development in Internet search and retrieval technologies and in the development of metadata standards. The research and technical staff balance time spent working on maintaining the existing service with time spent on new initiatives. Staff at the Institute for Learning and Research Technology (ILRT) has been involved with the development of Dublin Core (http://purl.oclc.org/dc/) and the Resource Description Framework (RDF) (http://www.w3.org/TR/WD-rdf-syntax-971002/). This is important if SOSIG is to remain viable over time as new opportunities and threats appear in the Internet and library environments. Some of the new developments will be discussed later in this chapter.

4.2 Training and Awareness

A lot of effort is put into promoting the service to the U.K. social science research community and into providing training workshops to encourage effective use of the service. Training staff have traveled to universities across the United Kingdom to train librarians and academics in using the Internet and SOSIG. There has been an extensive publicity program involving the distribution of user guides, conference papers, and journal articles; details can be found on the Web (http://www.ilrt.bris.ac.uk/training/socsci/). This work has enabled SOSIG to build a strong relationship with the community it serves, which is vital if we are to understand and try to meet their information needs.

4.3 The Provision of the Service

SOSIG employs librarians and information specialists to spend time selecting, cataloging, and classifying Internet resources to add to the database. Originally only core staff did this work, but for just over a year now, SOSIG has had a distributed team of social science librarians, based in universities across the United Kingdom, adding resources for a few hours each week. The section editors have the magic combination of subject expertise and library skills, which has enabled SOSIG to build a rich collection of high-quality social science Internet resources.

5.0 Target Audience

SOSIG has been funded to serve a specific group of users—the academic social science community, including researchers, educators, students, and practitioners such as psychologists and economists. The project funding means that the emphasis is on serving users in the United Kingdom and Europe, although anyone can access SOSIG from anywhere in the world for free.

SOSIG keeps detailed usage logs and we have monitored the information-seeking behaviors of our users over the years. We are always wary of reading too much into the statistics, but since the inception of SOSIG, we have had over three million hits and are currently getting around one hundred-forty thousand hits per month.

Our usage statistics imply that while the majority of users access SOSIG from the United Kingdom and Europe, large numbers also access it from other countries. SOSIG can be of use to social scientists everywhere, and we welcome interest and suggestions for new resources from users around the world.

SOSIG actively encourages user feedback as part of its evaluation and development process. Users like the quality control of SOSIG and the time it saves them: "It fulfills a real need in an age of information overload." "I like the easy and structured access to quality online resources you offer—it allows me great savings in time."

They like the fact that SOSIG has an academic leaning and supports research: "I am able to say with confidence that the SOSIG service is regarded in the UK research community as an extremely valuable service." And they like the name: "Is it really pronounced 'sausage?'"

User comments have frequently led to redesigns of the service. They told us they wanted to browse by geographical region, so we added this feature. They wanted to see the collection grow in size, so we called on the librarians and took on the section editors. The list goes on.

6.0 The SOSIG Collection

SOSIG's aim is to help the academic and research communities in the social sciences. These communities have been quick to adopt network technologies, and there is absolute gold dust to be found in the form of data sets, social statistics, research articles, survey results, and similar resources sitting on computers and servers around the world. This section aims to give an overview of the SOSIG collection, but we would suggest that those interested browse SOSIG to get a clearer picture.

SOSIG uses a very broad definition of the social sciences including subjects such as law, philosophy, psychology, and geography.

As of July 1998, SOSIG contained records for over five thousand Internet resources, with between thirty and forty new resources being added each week.

6.1 Types of Resources

SOSIG only points to resources available via the Internet. Many different types of resources are acceptable, providing they fall within the scope and meet with the selection criteria. Types of resources in the collection include:

Electronic Journals,

Digitized Books,

Electronic Reports and Papers,

Scholarly Mailing Lists and Archives,

Educational Software,

Databases,

Electronic Newsletters,

Datasets,

Home Pages of Key Social Science Organizations,

Bibliographies,

FAQs,

Usenet Groups.

The subjects covered by SOSIG will be outlined in the "Classification" section below.

6.2 Having an Open Mind about Collection Development

SOSIG is not restrictive in the type of resource to which it points; we are open to any resource that can support social science education and research, whether or not it mirrors traditional information formats. The Internet links to information and communication resources, and new types of resources are constantly emerging as a result of new technologies and new feats of the human imagination. We are now seeing not only electronic books and journals, but also virtual worlds, meeting places, and multimedia environments. Traditionally, libraries have not been able to catalog meetings, discussions, support groups, soap boxes, forums, works in progress, and unpublished works, but subject gateways can catalog all of these things and bring many more sources of information to the end users.

6.3 A Linked Collection: Pointing to Resources around the World

SOSIG is a linked collection, where the information resources are hosted on computers and servers worldwide, and only the catalog records pointing to these resources are kept on the SOSIG server. The "SOSIG Collection" therefore refers to the resources that are selected, cataloged, and pointed to.

In library terms, this means we are involved with access, not holdings; we don't own or store a collection of resources. The traditional library issues of conservation and preservation of stock and collection management take on a whole new meaning in a virtual library. We are less worried about dampness or beetle attack than broken hyperlinks and the volatile nature of Internet resources. Internet resources are very different from books and journals and require different treatment within the collection. They can be volatile and can completely change in nature and content at any moment, making our records for them out of date. Considerable time is spent editing records in the database to keep them current.

SOSIG has a formally stated collection management policy (http://www.sosig.ac.uk/desire/collect.html) that describes when records should be created, edited, and deleted. It also helps to ensure that we monitor the development of the collection as a whole, with all subject sections growing at the same rate, and to ensure that all the members of our distributed team are using the same criteria to select, edit, and de-select resources.

SOSIG uses link-checking software that is part of the ROADS tool kit (http://www.ilrt.bris.ac.uk/roads/liaison/). Every week our automatic ROADS link checker generates a list of all the dead links in SOSIG. Most of the broken links can be easily repaired with some simple detective work: the URL has usually changed slightly, or the site has moved but can be found again with a search engine. The records are edited to reflect these changes. If the site cannot be found, we e-mail the provider to ask about the status of the resource. Depending on the reply, the record is either edited or deleted. Of course, we are only able to e-mail them because we have a record of the e-mail address held in our database.

7.0 Classification

SOSIG draws upon the Universal Decimal Classification (UDC) to create its subject hierarchy for the browsing sections. We use a very broad definition of social science and are currently categorizing resources into a subject hierarchy containing 162 subject headings (http://www.sosig.ac.uk/roads/cgi/browse.pl?section=&area=World). These are organized under the following sixteen main subject headings:

Economics, Development,

Education,

Environmental Issues,

Ethnology, Social Anthropology,

Feminism,

Geography,

Government, Military Science,

Law,

Management, Accountancy, Business,

Philosophy,

Politics—International Relations,

Psychology,

Social Science General—Methodology,

Social Welfare—Community, Disability,

Sociology,

Statistics—Demography.

As this list illustrates, we do not use the UDC in its entirety because the classification scheme is mainly used to create the browsing sections and we did not wish to have many hundreds of empty sections at the start of the project. Instead, we selected top-level headings initially and assigned the correct UDC numbers relating to these. As the collection grew, we were able to add another level to the hierarchy by selecting secondary headings from the UDC. We will continue to expand the hierarchy and include more UDC classification numbers as the collection grows further.

There have been a number of advantages to this approach. We have not had to create our own classification scheme, which would have been a huge project but have benefited from this well-established library standard. The fact that the UDC is an accepted standard means that potentially we could interoperate with other library catalogs and databases using the scheme or a scheme for which there is a mapping. Our flexible use of the UDC has meant that we can focus on the subject areas that are most relevant to our target audience, and respond to the suggestions they have for new areas of the collection that need to be developed.

8.0 Selection Criteria and the Evaluation of Resources

The quality issue is fundamental to SOSIG, perhaps more so than for a traditional library where publishers and booksellers have already filtered much of the information. On the Internet, anyone can publish anything and the myriad resources that are published are the key problem for the end users: there are millions of resources around, but few of them will be of the quality the academic or technical user requires. SOSIG staff spends considerable time locating Internet resources and evaluating their quality.

8.1 Acquisitions: Where Budget Is Not a Consideration

In libraries, the key factor in decisions about acquisitions is often the money available. For SOSIG this is not a factor. We point primarily to information that is freely available over the Internet, or if there is a charge for the information, we point to the resource and let the end user decide whether to pay. Because of this, our selection policy is significantly different from that of a traditional library: we base our selection on an evaluation of the quality of an Internet resource and according to priorities we have, given the available time for selection. We have developed four aids to help staff remain focused and consistent in the resources that they select for SOSIG: (1) the scope policy; (2) the quality criteria; (3) The Internet Detective; and (4) the de-selection criteria.

8.2 The SOSIG Scope Policy

Any resources that fall outside the scope criteria explained below are automatically rejected. Resources within the scope criteria are assessed according to SOSIG's quality selection criteria.

8.2.1 Information Coverage

Subject matter: Only information relevant to social science academics, researchers, practitioners, librarians, and higher education students is included in the gateway. The social sciences are broadly defined: as well as core subjects, the gateway covers areas such as Philosophy, Psychology, Environmental Issues, Business and Industrial Management, Area Studies, and Geography. Resources that are illegal in any way are excluded.

Acceptable sources: Information from academic, government, commercial, trade and industry, nonprofit, and private sources are all acceptable, provided that they fall under the acceptable subject matter criteria. Pages that are maintained by students may be considered, although these are less likely to be of a durable nature.

Acceptable levels of difficulty: The content of the resources should be at a level suitable for higher education. Information that is scholarly rather than simply popular is the preferred choice.

Acceptable types of resources: Resources should be available on the Internet. Information intended for use only by an individual or local group is unacceptable. Resources consisting entirely of links to other resources are rejected unless there is substantial value-added information by means of annotations, and so forth.

Advertising: Resources that consist solely or mainly of advertising are excluded from the gateway.

8.2.2 Geographical Coverage

Geographical restraints: There are no geographical restraints on the coverage of resources. However, particular emphasis is placed on resources from Europe. There is also a strong emphasis on European Studies.

Language: Resources in all European languages may be accepted.

8.2.3 Access Issues

Technology: Resources using advanced Web technology (Java applications, frames, etc.) may be considered, but users are given appropriate warning in the catalog record that the resource is dependent on suitable technology.

Cost: Commercial or fee-based resources may be considered, but appropriate information on cost must be provided to the user in the catalog record.

Registration: Resources that require the user to register before use may be considered, but appropriate information on registration must be provided to the user in the catalog record.

8.2.4. Resource Description

There should be sufficient information within the resource to create a catalog record. The minimum amount of metadata would be a title, URL, and contact details of the person or organization responsible for the resource.

8.3 The Quality Criteria

If a resource falls within the scope of SOSIG, it is then evaluated in terms of content, form, and process. These criteria are not as black and white as the scope criteria, and require the selector to balance pros and cons and to make an overall judgment about quality. A summary of the evaluation criteria is given in table 1, but a more detailed version can be found on the Web (http://www.sosig.ac.uk/desire/ecrit.html).

Table 1.   A Summary of the SOSIG Quality Criteria

Content Criteria	Form Criteria	Process Criteria
Validity	Ease of navigation	Information integrity
Authority and reputation of source	Provision of user support	Site integrity
Substantiveness	Use of recognized standards	System integrity
Accuracy		
Comprehensiveness	Appropriate use of technology	
Uniqueness	Aesthetics	
Composition and organization		

8.4 The Internet Detective

Internet Detective (http://www.sosig.ac.uk/desire/internet-detective.html) is an interactive tutorial that provides an introduction to the issues of information quality on the Internet and teaches the skills required to critically evaluate the quality of an Internet resource. It is freely available for use, and librarians may find it useful for teaching Internet information skills.

8.5 The SOSIG De-Selection Principles

As well as selection criteria, SOSIG also has de-selection criteria that dictate when a record should be edited or deleted.

8.5.1 Guidelines for When to De-select a Resource

(1) If the resource is no longer available;

(2) If the currency or reliability of the resource has lost its value;

(3) If another Internet site or resource offers more comprehensive coverage.

8.5.2 Guidelines for When to Edit a Record

(1) If the information content of the resource has changed so that the resource description and keywords need updating;

(2) If any of the factual details of the resource have changed (e.g., new administrative e-mail, new title);

(3) To correct any errors made in the original record.

9.0 Mechanics of Production

SOSIG uses a single software system for all four of the main production areas:

(1) the creation of catalog records,

(2) adding the records to the database,

(3) presentation of browsing sections on the Web,

(4) presentation of the search engine.

This system has been designed specifically to enable the creation of subject gateways and is called ROADS (http://www.ilrt.bris.ac.uk/roads/), which stands for Resource Organisation And Discovery in Subject-based services. ROADS has been developed with funding from the U.K.'s Electronic Libraries Programme (eLib) and is freely available for anyone to download and use.

9.1 The Creation of Catalog Records

ROADS offers a selection of templates that can be used to create the catalog records. Different templates are available for different types of resources. Each template offers fields to fill in that are relevant to the nature of the resource. ROADS templates are based on a standard called the Internet Anonymous FTP Archive (IAFA), originally created for FTP archives (http://info.webcrawler.com/mak/projects/iafa/iafa.txt).[1] Templates currently available include:

dataset	mail archive	sound
descriptor	organization	usenet
document	service	user
image	software	video

The templates can store a wide range of information about a resource, including title, description, keywords, URLs, classification information, and the contact details of the resource's maintainer or administrator. A ROADS template may include between twenty and sixty fields, depending on the template type and the nature of the resource (http://www.ukoln.ac.uk/metadata/roads/templates/).

Cataloging is accomplished via the ROADS Administration Centre, which is available via the Web (templates are basically Web forms).

All the catalogers are given a SOSIG password, and they can then catalog resources from any PC in the world that has a Web browser. This has opened up great possibilities for distributed cataloging, as will be described later.

The cataloging process involves filling in the template fields, using information from the resource itself. The ROADS template organizes the record into attribute value pairs, which are the equivalent of fields in standard database terminology. The attribute value pairs consist of an attribute name to the left of a colon and an attribute value to the right. For example: Title: CTI Centre for Economics Home Page.

In the database, the records will be held as a plain text file. An example of this is given in figure 2 (http://www.lib.uidaho.edu:70/docs/egj.html).

Once the cataloger has filled in the template, he or she submits it directly to the database.

9.2 Adding the Records to the Database

Underlying a ROADS-based system is a database of resource descriptions. The records are held as plain text files in an inverted index. The use of a searchable database distinguishes ROADS gateways

Template Type:	SERVICE
Handle:	805990087-28320
Title:	*Electronic Green Journal*
URI-v1:	http://gopher.uidaho.edu:70/1/UI_gopher/library/egj
Admin-Name-v1:	Maria Jankowska
Admin-E mail-v1:	majank@uidaho.edu
Description:	The *Electronic Green Journal* is a professional refereed publication devoted to disseminating information concerning sources on international environmental topics including: pollution, resources, technology and treatment. The journal is academically sponsored; however the focus is to publish articles, bibliographies, reviews and announcements for the educated generalist as well as the specialist. It began publication in June 1994 and is produced on an irregular basis.
Keywords:	environmental issues, green politics, development studies, environment, sustainable development
Subject-Descriptor-v1:	551.588 330.342
Subject-Descriptor-Scheme-v1:	UDC
Record-Last-Modified-Date:	Wed. 12 Mar 1996 11:06:43 +0000

FIGURE 2. SOSIG Record Plain Text File: *Electronic Green Journal*

from many other Internet subject sites that simply offer browseable lists of links.

9.3 Presentation of Browsing Sections on the Web

The ROADS software tools enable the automatic creation of a set of Web pages using the information in the database records. In other words, the browseable SOSIG pages are all created automatically without the staff having to do any HTML markup. A resource can be automatically added to the appropriate subject listing at the time of creation, or a script can be run from the operating system (i.e., UNIX) command line that will add new resources to the subject listings without going through the record creation/editing form.

The appearance of the subject listings is fully customizable, so although both SOSIG and OMNI (see chapter 10) (http://omni.ac.uk/) use the ROADS software, they each have their own look and feel. SOSIG has chosen to display only the title, description, keywords, and URLs of resources; however, in the future we could also display the language of resources and the classification number and other information from our records. An example of the appearance of a SOSIG record as seen by the user is found in figure 3.

9.4 Presentation of the Search Engine

The SOSIG search engine is also composed of the ROADS software. The search engine allows the user to query the records database. The format of the ROADS search form and the options that appear on it are customizable. SOSIG has a simple search form where stemming and ranking options are automatically switched on. In the advanced search page, users have further options: case-sensitive searching, searching for resources from a particular region, and searching for particular types of resource.

SOSIG has also bolted a thesaurus onto the ROADS system. The SOSIG thesaurus is derived from the HASSET thesaurus (http://dasun1.essex.ac.uk/services/intro.html), which was developed by The Data Archive at the University of Essex (http://dawww.essex.ac.uk/index.html) from the Unesco thesaurus.[2] If users fail to get any hits from a search, they are automatically taken to the thesaurus, which will guide them to related search terms for which they will definitely get a hit on SOSIG.

9.5 Other Features of ROADS

As well as producing software for setting up subject-specific gateways, the ROADS has two other aims: (1) to investigate methods of cross-searching and interoperability within and between gateways;

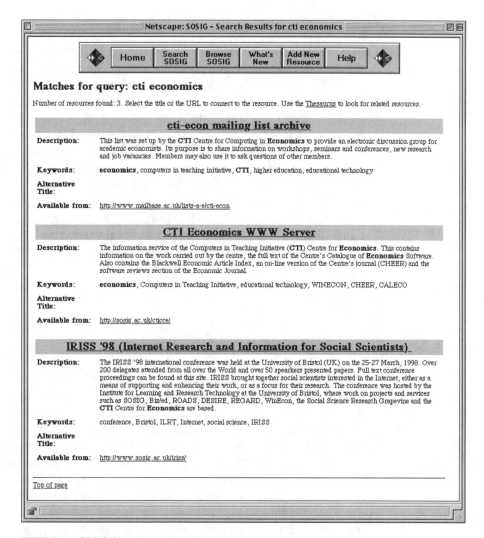

FIGURE 3.   SOSIG Search Results: cti economics

and (2) to participate in the development of standards for the indexing, cataloging, and searching of subject-specific resources.

9.6 ROADS and Cross-Searching

The ROADS software can enable users to search across multiple ROADS-based information gateways from a single search form. ROADS offers an efficient technological solution to cross-searching, using the WHOIS++ protocol and the use of centroids (indexes of database content for the subject gateways). The ROADS Web site offers detailed information about the interoperability issue (http://www.ukoln.ac.uk/metadata/roads/interoperability/).

9.7 ROADS and Standards for Internet Cataloging

ROADS templates have been designed to be compatible with both library cataloging standards and Internet metadata standards. For example, the fields from a ROADS template can be mapped onto MARC records *and* Dublin Core records. This is extremely important for the purpose of allowing different bibliographic or metadata databases to be interoperable. The potential is there for all the SOSIG templates to be transferred into different formats or to be cross-searched with templates of different formats, and in the volatile world of the Internet, both or either of these options might be important in the future.

The vision is to create an integrated information landscape where users can choose to simultaneously cross-search a number of databases (Internet subject gateways, library catalogs, archives, etc.) and be guided to the information that is most appropriate to their needs, regardless of the format.

10.0 Strengths and Weaknesses of the Project

Subject gateways are labor-intensive to develop and maintain. They require the constant input of staff who handpick, classify, and catalog each Internet resource. This is both the strength and the weakness of these subject gateways. The human input allows for semantic judgments and decisions that are the key ingredients for creating a quality-controlled gateway. This ingredient is lacking in automated indexes or search engines that cannot filter information in such a meaningful way. However, considerable time and effort are needed to make these judgments and decisions, and this means that the collection of resources is often small and slow to grow. This is in contrast to the search engines, which offer access to vast numbers of resources, numbers that grow as the Internet grows.

As the number of resources available over the Internet increases, information gateways need to develop ways to increase the number of resources they can catalog. The DESIRE project has identified the following three ways in which this might be done:

(1) distributed cataloging: increasing the number of people adding resources;

(2) automatic metadata entry: improving the efficiency of the cataloging process;

(3) integration of human-based catalogs and automated indexers.

SOSIG is conducting research and development into all three of these areas as described in the next section.

11.0 Future Goals of the Project

11.1 Distributed Cataloging

ROADS' Web-based cataloging means that there is potential for librarians across the world to add resources to a shared catalog. SOSIG has piloted two models of distributed cataloging, one where the section editors catalog resources directly into the database from their own institutions, and one where volunteers across Europe can fill in a Web form to submit a resource to SOSIG. A DESIRE report on current practice in Europe and the United Kingdom is now available (http://www.desire.org/results/discovery/cat/dist_des.htm). Considerable political and human resource management issues are involved in distributed cataloging, but we hope that the success of union catalogs in the traditional library can be translated to the Internet in the future. This would certainly be an efficient way for librarians to catalog Internet resources, but it will depend on people seeing the benefits of collaborative work. This is certainly likely to be an important issue for the profession to address in the coming years.

11.2 A Harvested Database: Integrating Cataloging with Automated Indexing

SOSIG has been looking at ways to expand and enhance the main database of selected resources without sacrificing the primary goal of helping users to access high-quality information. One approach has been to experiment with automatic harvesting technology (such as the Combine technology developed by our partners on the EU-funded DESIRE project [http://www.lub.lu.se/combine/]) to create a companion database to the main quality-controlled section on SOSIG. The All Social Science database is generated by feeding the harvester-selected URLs from the main SOSIG database. The harvester will then index pages found from those URLs, generating a large database of (mostly) social science material.

The current test database has indexed approximately forty thousand pages, generated from a base of just under four thousand URLs derived from the main SOSIG database. The harvester follows links from a URL to further links on the same site (this reduces the indexing of general-interest pages such as search engines, etc.). We estimate that the size of the database would increase by a factor of ten at each level followed; therefore following links to a second level would increase the size of the database to over 400,000 pages (this would take over a week to collect and several hours to index), so for the present, we have restricted the harvesting to links off the first URL parsed.

The harvested information is then indexed by the ROADS system. Any embedded metadata is retrieved from the pages, parsed, and used to build the records. If there is no metadata available, the record is generated automatically by using the text from the page itself.

We are currently investigating the possibility of linking the records from the harvested database to their parent URL from the main database for display purposes.

11.3 Automatic Metadata Entry into ROADS Templates

Another complementary approach to increasing the depth of the SOSIG collection is to employ automatic methods to produce catalog records, using metadata provided by information providers. This would allow subject gateways to catalog to a deeper level within a site or organization. There is an increasing awareness within the Internet community of the importance of providing good metadata to aid the discovery and use of their Web documents and information resources. SOSIG is hoping to work with the social science community by harvesting metadata produced by trusted information providers. This will help to increase awareness of the output of the U.K. academic and research community.

In the first instance, SOSIG has worked with the staff of the electronic journal, Sociological Research Online (http://www.socresonline. org.uk/socresonline/), to collect metadata created by the journal staff and automatically create templates that can be added to the main SOSIG database. We are using the ROADSHarvester software developed by UKOLN as part of the ROADS project (http://www.ukoln. ac.uk/metadata/software-tools/) to pump prime templates for the main quality database. It is hoped that this model may be extended to other services that wish to increase the access and visibility of their resources to the academic community.

11.4 Interface Issues

An important outstanding issue is how best to present these new developments to the user in a clear and usable manner. We are hoping to conduct some user needs analysis and to work with other subject gateways to develop an appropriate interface.

12.0 Project Time Frames

SOSIG is a bit like a four-year-old dog: it may sound young but in dog years it is pretty old, and in Internet years, SOSIG is certainly out of its puppydom. The project was started in 1994 and has gone through various funding models. The current position is that we have definite funding until the end of July 1999, and after that we will continue but under a different working model.

12.1 Federating U.K. Gateways into a Distributed Internet Library

The next incarnation of SOSIG, post-July 1999, is likely to be of particular interest. The U.K. subject gateways have proposed a new integrated model called the Resource Discovery Network (RDN) (http://www.ilrt.bris.ac.uk/discovery/imesh), which has been accepted by the government funders, JISC. The idea is that all the subject gateways will work collaboratively under a central RDN office, which will be responsible for strategic management. Some new gateways will be set up to ensure complete subject coverage among the gateways.

The RDN will take full advantage of the opportunities for both distributed cataloging *and* the cross-searching of distributed gateways. In the United Kingdom, we aim to have centers of excellence for different subject areas, and SOSIG will continue to focus on the social sciences. These centers will be based at universities and libraries across the United Kingdom, each in charge of selecting and cataloging the highest quality Internet resources in their field. SOSIG hopes to expand the involvement of U.K. social science librarians and promote the distributed cataloging model.

From the user's point of view, the RDN will offer access to these highly specialized subject collections via a single interface. Users will be able to cross-search any number of the collections simultaneously and retrieve a selection of records and resources from different databases.

The RDN model offers considerable benefits because of its distributed nature. This "academic Internet library" enables some of the best expertise from around the United Kingdom to be brought together within the virtual environment. It will benefit from the input of subject librarians across the United Kingdom who can work from their own PCs and take full advantage of the very close relationship with the various academic and subject communities that the existing subject gateways have developed over the last few years.

13.0 Visions for the Future

Users can already take advantage of subject gateways, which together describe tens of thousands of high-quality Internet resources. In the future, users can expect to see the existing subject gateways grow considerably in size as more librarians and information professionals contribute to them and as automated and human solutions to resource discovery are integrated. They can also expect new gateways to appear and to be able to cross-search different gateways simultaneously and seamlessly.

Also on the horizon, user profiles may be used to enable subject gateways to deliver a personalized information service. Users will be asked to enter their information preferences into a database, enabling the gateways to notify them of new resources when and as they appear in the catalog.

Subject gateways will also need to work out how to fit in with a number of new developments on the World Wide Web. For example, Netscape's Navigator 4.06 browser incorporates an RDF-based facility called "smart browsing" (http://home.netscape.com/communicator/navigator/v4.0/index.html). This works in a similar fashion to the Platform for Internet Content Selection (PICS) facilities already available in browsers such as Microsoft's Internet Explorer 3 (http://www.microsoft.com/windows/ie/). The basic model is that Web browsers are configured to consult, for every page viewed, a third-party "bureau" that offers additional, descriptive information about a resource. A smart browsing provider would offer users extra information (related links, ratings, reviews, etc.) to enrich their browsing experience.

It is not yet clear how existing subject gateways will engage with this emerging market for resource descriptions. Individually, the gateways do not yet describe enough of the Web. Federated into a distributed Internet library, however, the gateways may help transform the Internet browsing experience.

Notes

1. P. Deutsch et al., "Publishing Information on the Internet with Anonymous FTP" (Internet draft; working draft now expired), in The IAFA Working Group [cited July 1998]. (http://info.webcrawler.com/mak/projects/iafa/iafa.txt)

2. Jean Aitchison, *Unesco Thesaurus: A Structured List of Descriptors for Indexing and Retrieving Literature in the Fields of Education, Science, Social Science, Culture and Communication* (Paris: Unesco, 1977).

Contributors

Agriculture Network Information Center (AgNIC)

MELANIE A. GARDNER is the AgNIC Coordinator and a former reference specialist for one of the information centers at National Agricultural Library. She has been organizing and providing electronic resources to users for seven years. She holds an MLS from the University of Maryland.

WILLIAM B. FEIDT has the lead technical responsibility for the AgNIC project. He has served for over twenty-six years in a number of positions at the National Agricultural Library, including as head of the Library Automation Branch.

RICHARD E. THOMPSON participated in the initial planning and implementation of AgNIC. He received his MBA from Texas Christian University and has completed graduate studies in management information systems at the University of Maryland.

Argus Clearinghouse (Argus)

ANNA NOAKES holds an MILS degree and is currently a doctoral student at the University of Michigan School of Information. Her research interests include the organization of digital information, interface design and evaluation, and image retrieval.

Blue Web'n

JODI REED helps develop online curriculum, tools, and resources for Pacific Bell's Knowledge Network Explorer. A former high school teacher, Reed also teaches online and face-to-face Web publishing courses. She holds an MA in educational technology.

BUBL Information Service (BUBL)

DENNIS NICHOLSON is Director of the BUBL Information Service and co-director of the CAIRNS Z39.50 clumps project. He previously managed the CATRIONA and CATRIONA II research projects and is the founder-owner of the lis-link e-mail list.

ALAN DAWSON manages the BUBL Information Service, based at Strathclyde University, Glasgow, Scotland. He is a psychology graduate and teacher and previously the webmaster at Glasgow University.

Edinburgh Engineering Virtual Library (EEVL)

MICHAEL BREAKS is Director of Heriot-Watt University Library and the Director of the EEVL Service. He is active in the area of the development of networked information services in the UK.

AGNÈS GUYON took up her post as Database Officer for the Edinburgh Engineering Virtual Library in September 1997, after completing an MSLIS at the University of Strathclyde in Glasgow.

INFOMINE

STEVE MITCHELL is a science reference librarian and Co-coordinator of INFOMINE. He holds an MALIS from the University of California, Berkeley.

MARGARET MOONEY is currently the head of the government publications department at the University of California, Riverside. Before joining the INFOMINE Development Team, she pioneered various innovative technology applications projects relating to government documents.

Internet Public Library (IPL)

DAVID S. CARTER is the Director of the Internet Public Library and a lecturer at the University of Michigan's School of Information, where he teaches about digital librarianship. Before earning his MILS, he was an electrical engineer.

Librarians' Index to the Internet (LII)

CAROLE LEITA coordinates the Librarians' Index to the Internet, teaches California librarians how to find information on the Internet, manages the InFoPeople Project Web site, and consults with member libraries on technology issues. Before joining the InFoPeople Project, she was a reference librarian at the Berkeley Public Library.

HOLLY HINMAN is the Coordinator of the California State Library's InFoPeople Project. She has worked for several California public libraries and is formerly the Director of the Metropolitan Cooperative Library System in the Los Angeles area.

Mathematics Archives (Math Archives)

EARL D. FIFE is currently a professor of mathematics and computer science at Calvin College (Michigan). In 1992 he joined Larry Husch in developing the Mathematics Archives and has been a co-director of the Archives ever since.

LAWRENCE HUSCH is a professor of mathematics at the University of Tennessee, Knoxville and the co-director of the Mathematics Archives. He has published more than fifty research publications in topology and is interested in the integration of technology into the teaching of mathematics.

Scout Report Signpost (Signpost)

JACK SOLOCK was a member of the Internet Scout Project from 1995 to 1998, editor of the Scout Report and three subject-specific Scout Reports, as well as a contributor to the Scout Toolkit. He has an MLS from the University of Wisconsin.

AMY TRACY WELLS is the Coordinator of the Scout Report Signpost. Before joining the Internet Scout Project in 1996, she was a systems librarian with the National Institute of Standards and Technology and the Library of Congress.

Social Science Information Gateway (SOSIG)

EMMA PLACE (neé Worsfold) has been working in Internet library research since 1995 at Sheffield and Bristol universities (U.K.). She is currently working on the SOSIG and the DESIRE project, which promotes the development of new gateways in Europe.

Index

For URLs, see the subject and alphabetical indexes of sites and URLs.

Alphabetical Index of Sites and URLs

A

"The Access Catalogue Gateway to Resources [http://www.ariadne.ac.uk/issue15/main/]

AcqLink [http://link.bubl.ac.uk/acqlink/]

AcqWeb [http://www.library.vanderbilt.edu/law/acqs/acqs.html]

"Active Learning on the Web" [http://edweb.sdsu.edu/people/bdodge/active/ActiveLearningk-12.html]

AGEC [Advisory Group for Evaluation Criteria] [http://omni.ac.uk/agec/]

AgNIC [Agricultural Network Information Center] [http://agnic.org/]

  AgDB [http://www.agnic.org/agdb/]

  AgCal [http://www.agnic.org/mtg/]

  Online Reference Service [http://www.agnic.org/orsp/]

  Other Meetings Calendar [http://www.agnic.org/mtg/omc.html]

  Selection Criteria [http://www.agnic.org/docs/agdbsepo.html]

  Site usage [http://www.agnic.org/adm/stats.html]

Agricultural Research Service [http://www.ars.usda.gov/]

AltaVista [http://www.altavista.digital.com/]

AltaVista's World Index [http://altavista.digital.com/av/oneweb/]

American Film Institute's 100 Years, 100 Movies [http://AFI.100movies.com/]

American Mathematical Society's Subject Classification Scheme [http://www.ams.org/msc/#browse]

American Studies Web [http://www.georgetown.edu/crossroads/asw/]

Analog2.0/Mac [http://www.statslab.cam.ac.uk/~sret1/analog/]

"Anatomy of a Scout Report: Resource Discovery in the Information Age, or How We Do It." [http://scout7.cs.wisc.edu/pages/00000903.html]

Anbar Electronic Intelligence [http://www.anbar.co.uk/coolsite/civeng/areas/professional-educational-matters.htm]

Andersonian Library [http://www.lib.strath.ac.uk/]

Andrew W. Mellon Foundation [http://www.mellon.org/]

Apache 1.2.1 web server software [http://www.apache.org/]

Apache v1.1.3 [http://www.apache.org/]

Argos [http://argos.evansville.edu/]

Argus Associates [http://argus-inc.com/] and [http://www.argus-inc.com/design/index.html]

Argus Clearinghouse [http://www.clearinghouse.net/]

Argus Clearinghouse Evaluation Criteria [http://www.clearinghouse.net/ratings.html]

Argus Clearinghouse Selection Guide [http://www.clearinghouse.net/submit.html]

"The Art and Science of Digital Bibliography" [http://www.bookwire.com/LJdigital/diglibs.article$25937]

Art Exploration [http://www.artsednet.getty.edu/ArtsEdNet/Resources/Sampler/f.html]

ArtsEdge Subject Area Resources [http://artsedge.kennedy-center.org/db/cr/icr/cover.html]

Associations on the Net [http://www.ipl.org/ref/AON/]

Atlantic Monthly [http://www.theAtlantic.om/]

B

Beginner's Guide to Organic Synthesis [http://orac.sunderland.ac.uk/~hs0bcl/org2/html] *local access only*

Subject Index
of Sites and URLs

AgNIC [Agricultural Network Information Center] [http://www.agnic.org/]
AgCal (Agricultural Meetings Calendar) [http://www.agnic.org/mtg/] or [http://www.agnic/org/mtg/omc.html]
AgDB [http://www.agnic.org/agdb/]
Database of the Occurrence and Distribution of Pesticides in the Chesapeake Bay [http://www.agnic.org/cbp/]
Online Reference Service [http://www.agnic.org/orsp/]
Selection criteria [http://www.agnic.org/docs/agdbsepo.html]
Web statistics [http://www.agnic.org/adm/stats.html]

Agricultural Resources
AgNIC [http://www.agnic.org/]
Agricultural Research Service [http://www.ars.usda.gov/]
INFOMINE [http://infomine.ucop.edu/] and [http://infomine.ucr.edu/]
Rural Information Center (RIC) [http://www.nal.usda.gov/ric/]
Society for Range Management [http://srm.org/]
United States Department of Agriculture [http://www.usda.gov/]
United States Forest Service [http://www.fs.fed.us/]

Argus Clearinghouse [http://www.clearinghouse.net/]
Argus Associates [http://argus-inc.com/]
Design services [http://www.argus-inc.com/design/index.html]
Evaluation Criteria [http://www.clearinghouse.net/ratings.html]

Selection Guide [http://www.clearinghouse.net/submit.html]

Articles and Reports
"The Access Catalogue Gateway to Resources" [http://www.ariadne.ac.uk/issue15/main/]
"Anatomy of a Scout Report: Resource Discovery in the Information Age, or How We Do It." [http://scout7.cs.wisc.edu/pages/00000903.html]
"The Art and Science of Digital Bibliography" [http://www.bookwire.com/LJdigital/diglibs.article$25937]
"BUBL: The Browse Engine..." [http://www.ilrt.bris.ac.uk/roads/news/issue6/bubl/]
DESIRE Report [http://www.desire.org/results/discovery/cat/dist_des.htm]
"A Distributed Architecture for Resource Discovery Using Metadata" [http://www.dlib.org/dlib/june98/scout/06roszkowski.html]
"Evolvability: TimBL at WWW7" [http://www.w3.org/Talks/1998/0415-Evolvability/overview.htm]
Follett Report (also known as Libraries Review) [http://www.ukoln.ac.uk/services/papers/follett/report/]
GVU's 8th WWW User Survey [http://www.gvu.gatech.edu/gvu/user_surveys/survey-1997-10/]
"INFOMINE: The First Three Years of a Virtual Library for the Biological, Agricultural and Medical Sciences" [http://nucleus.cshl.org/CSHLlib/BLSD/seattle/mitchell.htm]
"Interface Design Considerations in Libraries" [http://lib-www.ucr.edu/pubs/stlinfoviz.html]

Subcategories [http://www.kn.pacbell.com/wired/bluewebn/categories.html]

Types of Resources [http://www.kn.pacbell.com/wired/bluewebn/apptypes.html]

BUBL Information Service [Bulletin Board for Librarians] [http://bubl.ac.uk/]

5:15 Service [http://bubl.ac.uk/link/five/] and [http://www.ilrt.bris.ac.uk/roads/news/issue6/bubl/]

Annual Report [http://bubl.ac.uk/admin/reports/report96.htm#22]

Mailing lists [http://bubl.ac.uk/mail/]

News updates [http://bubl.ac.uk/news/updates/]

Usage statistics [http://www.bubl.ac.uk/admin/usage/]

Business and Science Sites

Anbar Electronic Intelligence [http://www.anbar.co.uk/]

Beginner's Guide to Organic Synthesis [http://orac.sunderland.ac.uk/~hs0bcl/org2/html] *local access only*

Biotechnology and Biological Sciences Research Council [http://www.bbsrc.ac.uk/]

Computers in Teaching Initiative [CTI] [http://www.cti.ac.uk/]

CTI Centre for Biology [http://www.liv.ac.uk/ctibiol/]

EELS [Engineering Electronic Library Sweden] [http://www.ub2.lu.se/eel/eelhome.html]

EESE [Engineering E-journal Search Engine] [http://www.eevl.ac.uk/eese/]

EEVL [Edinburgh Engineering Virtual Library] [http://www.eevl.ac.uk/]

Engineering Information [http://www.ei.org/]

Engineering Newsgroup Archive [http://www.eevl.ac.uk/cgi-bin/nwi/]

Food and Nutrition Information Center [RIC] [http://www.nal.usda.gov/fnic/]

Frank Potter's Science Gems [http://www-sci.lib.uci.edu/SEP/SEP.html]

INFOMINE [http://infomine.ucop.edu/] and [http://infomine.ucr.edu/]

JASON Project [http://www.jasonproject.org/]

Jet Impingement Database [http://www.eevl.ac.uk/jet/index.html]

Liquid Crystal Database [http://www.eevl.ac.uk/lcd/index.html]

MEDLINE [http:www.medportal.com/]

National Library of Medicine [http://www.nlm.nih.gov/]

Newton's Apple Lessons [http://ericir.syr.edu/Projects/Newton/]

Northern Lights Special Collection [http://www.northernlight.com/docs/specoll_help_overview.html]

Nursing and Health Care Resources in the Net [http://www.shef.ac.uk/~nhcon/]

Ocean Colors [http://athena.wednet.edu/curric/oceans/ocolor/]

OMNI [Organising Medical Networked Information] [http://omni.ac.uk/]

Online Map Creation [http://www.aquarius.geomar.de/omc/]

RAM [Recent Advances in Manufacturing] [http://www.eevl.ac.uk/ram/index.html]

Royal College of Physicians Database of Continuing Medical Education Events [RCP] [http://omni.ac.uk/cme/search-cme.html]

U.K. Engineering Search Engine [http://www.eevl.ac.uk/uksearch.html]

Visible Human Dataset [http://vhp.gla.ac.uk/]

WebElements Periodic Table [http://www.shef.ac.uk/~chem/web-elements/]

Calendars

Agricultural Meetings Calendar [http://www.agnic.org/mtg/omc.html]

Royal College of Physicians Database of Continuing Medical Education Events [RCP] [http://omni.ac.uk/cme/search-cme.html]

Cataloging and Classification

American Mathematical Society's Subject Classification Scheme [http://www.ams.org/msc/#browse]

Classification Plus [http://lcweb.loc.gov/cds/cdroms1.html#classplus]

Dewey Decimal Classification [http://www.oclc.org/oclc/man/9353pg/9353toc.htm] (A Practical Guide - excerpts) [http://www.oclc.org/oclc/fp/index.htm] (Forest Press Web site for the DDC)

HASSET thesaurus [http://dasun1.essex.ac.uk/services/intro.html]

Melvyl Catalog (University of California) [http://www.lib.ucdavis.edu/hsl/melvyl/melweb.html]

MeSH [Medical Subject Headings] [http://www.nlm.nih.gov/mesh/meshhome.html]

Online Indexers' Manual [http://sunsite.berkeley.edu/InternetIndex/manual/newsites.html]

ROADS Cataloguing Guidelines [http://www.ukoln.ac.uk/metadata/roads/cataloguing/cataloguing-rules.html]

Subject Cataloging Manual: Subject Headings, 5th edition [http://lcweb.loc.gov/cds/lcsh.html#scmsh]

UMLS [U.S. National Library of Medicine's Unified Medical Language System] [http://www.nlm.nih.gov/pubs/factsheets/umlsmeta.html]

Collection Development /Selection Criteria

AgNIC [http://www.agnic.org/docs/agdbsepo.html]

Argus Clearinghouse
  Evaluation Criteria [http://www.clearinghouse.net/ratings.html]
  Selection Guide [http://www.clearinghouse.net/submit.html]

DNER [http://www.jisc.ac.uk/cei/dner_colpol.html]

Internet Public Library Youth Collection [http://www.ipl.org/youth/SelectionPolicy.html]

Librarians' Index to the Internet [LII] [http://sunsite.berkeley.edu/InternetIndex/manual/criteria.html]

National Agricultural Library [NAL] [http://www.nal.usda.gov/acq/erscpol.htm]

OMNI [http://omni.ac.uk/agec/evalguid.html] and [http://omni.ac.uk.submit-url/]

SOSIG [http://www.sosig.ac.uk/desire/collect.html] and [http://www.sosig.ac.uk/desire/ecrit.html]

Collections

Especially for Librarians [http://www.ipl.org.svcs/]

Great Libraries on the Web [http://www.ipl.org/svcs/greatlibs/]

Native American Authors [http://www.ipl.org/ref/native/]

Northern Light Special Collection [http:www.northernlight.com/docs/premiumcontentalpha.htm]

Online Literary Criticism [http://www.ipl.org/ref/litcrit/] and [http://www.ipl.org/ref/litcrit/about.html]

Online Newspapers [http://www.ipl.org/reading/news/]

Online Serials [http://www.ipl.org/reading/serials/]

Online Texts [http://www.ipl.org/reading/books/] and [http://www.ipl.org/reading/books/other.html]

Ready Reference [http://www.ipl.org.ref.RR/] and [http://www.ipl.org.ref/RR/Rabt.html]

Teen [http://www.ipl.org/teen/]

Youth [http://www.ipl.org/youth/]

.com Sites

Allaire Corporation [http://www.coldfusion.com/]

Altavista Company [http://www.altavista.com/]

American Film Institute [http://www.afionline.org/]

Apple Computer, Inc. [http://www.apple.com/]

Argus [http://argus-inc.com/]

Blue Web'n [http://www.kn.pacbell.com/wired/bluewebn/]

Blue World Communications, Inc. [http://www.blueworld.com/]

Canon Research Center Europe Ltd. [http://www.cre.canon.co.uk/]

Deja News service [http://www.dejanews.com/]

Excite Inc. [http://www.excite.com/]

FileMaker, Inc. [http://www.filemaker.com/]

Goldwarp, Inc. (Linklint) [http://www.goldwarp.com/]

Google Inc. [http://www.google.com/]

Great Circle Associates [http://www.greatcircle.com/]

Hughes Technologies [http://www.hughes.com.au/]

Information Today, Inc. [http://www.infotoday.com/]

Internet.com LLC [http://searchenginewatch.com/]

The Landfield Group (HyperMail) [http://www.landfield.com/]

Lycos, Inc. [http://www.lycos.com/]

MacroMedia, Inc. [http://www.macromedia.com/]

MARCit, Inc. (Nichols Advanced Technologies Inc.) [http://www.marcit.com/]

MedPortal.com [http:www.medportal.com/]

Merriam-Webster, Inc. [http://www.m-w.com/]

Microsoft, Inc. [http://microsoft.com/]

Netscape [http://home.netscape.com/]

New Scientist [http://www.newscientist.com/]

Conference Proceedings

Current Awareness (News) Services

Databases

Design and Useability

Educational Web Sites
See also .edu sites and specific subject areas
"Active Learning on the Web" [http://edweb.
sdsu.edu/people/bdodge/active/
ActiveLearningk-12.html]
CNN Interactive Learning Resources [http://
www.cnnsf.com/education/education/html]
INFOMINE: Scholarly Internet Resource
Collections [http://infomine.ucop.edu/]
and [http://infomine.ucr.edu/]
Netskills: Quality Internet Training [http://
www.netskills.ac.uk/]
Ocean Colors [http://athena.wednet.edu/curric/
oceans/ocolor/]
Online Map Creation [http://www.aguarius.
geomar.de.omc/]
Peterson Education Center [http://www.
petersons.com/]
Shiki Internet Haiku Salon [http://mikan.cc.
matsuyama-u.ac.jp/~shiki/]
TALiSMAN Online Study Centre [http://www.
talisman.hw.ac.uk/]
ThinkQuest [http://www.thinkquest.org/]
WebQuest [http://edweb.sdsu.edu/webquest/
webquest.html]
"What's on the Web?" [http://www.ozline.
com/learning/webtypes.html]
Writing HTML [http://www.mcli.dist.maricopa.
edu/tut/]

EEVL [Edinburgh Engineering Virtual Library] [http://www.eevl.ac.uk/]
EESE [Engineering E-journal Search Engine]
[http://www.eevl.ac.uk/eese/]
Engineering Newsgroup Archive [http://www.
eevl.ac.uk/cgi-bin/nwi/]
Jet Impingement Database [http://www.eevl.ac.
uk/jet/index.html]
Liquid Crystal Database [http://www.eevl.ac.
uk/lcd/index.html]
Offshore Engineering Information Service
[http://www.eevl.ac.uk/offshore/]
Press releases [http://www.eevl.ac.uk/press.
html]
RAM [Recent Advances in Manufacturing]
[http://www.eevl.ac.uk/ram/index.html]
SENN [Science and Engineering Network
News] [http://www.eevl.ac.uk/senn/
index.html]
U.K. Engineering Search Engine [http://www.
eevl.ac.uk/uksearch.html]

USTLG [University Science and Technology
Librarians Group, Directory of Members]
[http://www.eevl.ac.uk/ustlg/index.html]

Electronic Journals
Atlantic Monthly [http://www.theAtlantic.com/]
Internet Resources Newsletter [http://hw.ac.
uk/libWWW/irn/irn.html]
Library Hi Tech [http://www.lib.msu.edu/
hi-tech/lht15.34.html]
LJ Digital's WebWatch [http://www.bookwire.
com/ljdigital/]
New Scientist [http://www.newscientist.com/]
PC Computing [http://www.zdnet.com/pccomp/]
Project Muse [http://muse.jhu.edu/]
SENN [Science and Engineering Network
News] [http://www.eevl.ac.uk/senn/
index.html]
Sociological Research Online [http://www.
socresonline.org.uk/socresonline/]

Foundations
Andrew W. Mellon Foundation [http://www.
mellon.org/]
W. R. Kellogg Foundation [http://www.wkkf.
org/]

.gov Sites
(Government agency sites in the U.K. and U.S.)
Agricultural Research Service [http://www.ars.
usda/gov/]
Department of Education [http://www.ed.gov/]
Federal Geographic Data Committee (USGS)
[http://fgdc.er.usgs.gov/]
Food and Nutrition Information Center [RIC]
[http://www.nal.usda.gov/fnic/]
General Services Administration [http://www.
gsa.gov/]
Government Information Locator Service
[GILS] [http://www.gils.gov/]
Library of Congress [http://lcweb.loc.gov/]
National Agricultural Library [NAL] [http://
www.nal.usda.gov/]
National Health Service [NHS] (U.K.) [http://
www.nahat.net/]
National Library of Medicine [http://www.
nlm.nih.gov/]
National Resource Conservation Service [http://
www.nrcs.usda.gov/]
National Science Foundation [NSF] [http://
www.nsf.gov/]

Selection criteria [http://sunsite.berkeley.edu/InternetIndex/manual/criteria.html]

Subject Headings [http://sunsite.berkeley.edu/InternetIndex/subjects.html]

Libraries

Andersonian Library (University of Strathclyde) [http://www.lib.strath.ac.uk/]

Berkeley Digital Library SunSITE [http://sunsite.berkeley.edu/]

Berkeley Public Library [http://infopeople.berkeley.edu:80000/bpl/]

EELS [Engineering Electronic Library Sweden] [http://www.ub2.lu.se/eel/eelhome.html]

EEVL [Edinburgh Engineering Virtual Library] [http://www.eevl.ac.uk/]

Glasgow University Library [http://www.lib.gla.ac.uk/]

Great Libraries on the Web [http://www.ipl.org/svcs/greatlibs/]

Heriot-Watt University Library, Edinburgh (U.K.) [http://www.hw.ac.uk/libWWW/welcome.html]

Internet Public Library [http://www.ipl.org/]

Iowa State University Library [http://www.lib.iastate.edu/]

Mann Library (Cornell) [http://usda.mannlib.cornell.edu/]

Michigan State University Libraries [http://www.lib.msu/]

Napier University, Edinburgh (U.K.) [http://www.napier.ac.uk/]

UCI Libraries, University of California, Irvine [http://www.lib.uci.edu/]

The University Library, University of California, Davis [http://www.lib.ucdavis.edu/]

University of Idaho Library [http://www.lib.uidaho.edu/]

WWW Virtual Library [http://vlib.org/Overview.html]

Mailing Lists

Majordomo 1.93 [ftp://ftp.greatcircle.com/pub/majordomo/]

Math Archives [http://archives.math.utk.edu/hypermail/]

Mathematics Archives
[http://archives.math.utk.edu/]

Bibliography page [http://archives.math.utk.edu/cgi-bin/bibliography.html]

Calculators pages [http://archives.math.utk.edu/calculator/]

Commercial and shareware/public domain math software [http://archives.math.utk.edu/other_software.html]

Contests and Competitions [http://archives.math.utk.edu/contests/]

David Sibley [ftp://ftp.math.psu.edu/pub/sibley/]

Electronic proceedings [http://archives.math.utk.edu/features.html]

EPICTCM [Electronic Proceedings of the International Conference on Technology in Collegiate Mathematics] [http://archives.math.utk.edu/ICTCM/]

Interactive WWW Pages [http://archives.math.utk.edu/cgi-bin/interactive.html]

Mailing lists [http://archives.math.utk.edu/hypermail/]

Mathematics and Liberal Arts pages [http://archives.math.utk.edu/liberal.arts/libarts.html]

Online Calculus Resources [http://archives.math.utk.edu/calculus/crol.html]

Other mathematical resources [http://archives.math.utk.edu/topics/]

Pop Mathematics Collection [http://archives.math.utk.edu/popmath.html]

Shareware and public domain software [http://archives.math.utk.edu/software.html] and [http://archives.math.utk.edu/other_software.html]

UTK Mathematical Life Sciences Archive [http://archives.math.utk.edu/mathbio/]

Visual Calculus Project [http://archives.math.utk.edu/visual.calculus/]

Web Publishing Tips [http://archives.math.utk.edu/WPT/]

WWW Virtual Library in Mathematics [http://euclid.math.fsu.edu/Science/math.html]

Mathematics Sites

Calculators pages [http://archives.math.utk.edu/calculator/]

Contests and Competitions [http://archives.math.utk.edu/contests/]

EPICTCM [Electronic Proceedings of the International Conference on Technology in Collegiate Mathematics] [http://archives.math.utk.edu/ICTCM/]

HENSA [Higher Education National Software Archive] [National Mirror Service] [http://micros.hensa.ac.uk/cgi-bin/browser/

mirrors/cti/mathematics/archives.math.
utk.edu/]

INFOMINE [http://infomine.ucop.edu/] and
[http://infomine.ucr.edu/]

Interactive WWW Pages [http://archives.math.
utk.edu/cgi-bin/interactive.html]

Maple's MathView [http://www.cybermath.com/]

Mathematics and Liberal Arts pages [http://
archives.math.utk.edu/liberal.arts/libarts.
html]

Mini SQL [http://www.hughes.com.au/]

Online Calculus Resources [http://archives.
math.utk.edu/calculus/crol.html]

Other mathematical resources [http://archives.
math.utk.edu/topics/]

Pop Mathematics Collection [http://archives.
math.utk.edu/popmath.html]

Shareware and public domain software [http://
archives.math.utk.edu/software.html] and
[http://archives.math.utk.edu/other_
software.html]

UTK Mathematical Life Sciences Archive
[http://archives.math.utk.edu/mathbio/]

Visual Calculus Project [http://archives.math.
utk.edu/visual.calculus/]

Walnut Creek CD-ROM [http://www.cdrom.
com/pub/math/utk/]

WUArchives at Washington University [http://
wuarchive.wustl.edu/edu/math/]

WWW Virtual Library in Mathematics [http://
euclid.math.fsu.edu/Science/math.html]

.net Sites

Argus Clearinghouse [http://www.
clearinghouse.net/]

JANET [http://www.ja.net/]

Rwhois [http://www.rwhois.net/]

Networks

CAIRNS [Co-operative Academic Information
Retrieval Network for Scotland] [http://
cairns.lib.gla.ac.uk/]

CATRIONA [Cataloguing and Retrieval of
Information Over Networks Applications]
[http://catriona2.lib.strath.ac.uk/catriona/]

DNER [Distributed National Electronic
Resource] [http://www.jisc.ac.uk/pub98/
n3_98.html#p5]
    transatlantic bandwidth [http://www.jisc.
    ac.uk/pub98/c3_98.html]

JANET: The U.K. Research & Academic
Network [http://www.ja.net/]

OMNI [Organising Medical Networked Information] [http://omni.ac.uk/]

AGEC [Advisory Group for Evaluation Criteria]
[http://omni.ac.uk/agec/]

Article about "OMNI Biomedical Information"
Internet Scout Report (April 6, 1996)
[http://scout.cs.wisc.edu/scout/report/
archive/scout-960405.html#2]

Browseable interface [http://omni.ac.uk/
general-info/browse.html]

Guidelines for Resource Evaluation [http://
omni.ac.uk/agec/evalguid.html]

OMNIuk and OMNIworld [http://omni.ac.uk/
search/]

Project Assistant [http://omni.ac.uk/about/
#contacts]

Project manager [http://omni.ac.uk/about/
#steering]

Proposal [http://omni.ac.uk/about/original/]

Selection and evaluation subject guides
[http://omni.ac.uk/agec/evalguid.html]
and [http://omni.ac.uk.submit-url/]

.org Sites

Agriculture Network Information Center
[AgNIC] [http://www.agnic.org/]

American Library Association [http://www.
ala.org/]

American Mathematical Society [http://www.
ams.org/]

Andrew W. Mellon Foundation [http://www.
mellon.org/]

The Apache Software Foundation [http://www.
apache.org/]

CNIDR [Center for Networked Information
Discovery and Retrieval] [http://www.
cnidr.org/]

DESIRE [http://www.desire.org/]

Engineering Information [http://www.ei.org/]

Federal Geographic Data Committee [http://
fgdc.er.usgs.gov/]

IMS Project (EDUCAUSE) [http://www.
imsproject.com/]

InFoPeople [http://www.infopeople.org/]

Internet Engineering Task Force [IETF] [http://
www.ietf.org/]

Internet Public Library [http://www.ipl.org/]

The Internet Society [http://www.isoc.org/]

J. Paul Getty Trust (The Getty Center) [http://
www.getty.edu/]

JASON Project [http://www.jasonproject.org/]

SWISH-E [Simple Web Indexing System for Humans – Enhanced] [http://sunsite.berkeley.edu/SWISH-E/]

WAIS [gopher://boombox.micro.umn.edu:70/11/gopher/Unix/]

WebLint [http://www.cre.canon.co.uk/~neilb/weblint/]

WebSTAR 3.0 [http://www.starnine.com/webstar/webstar.html]

WebTrends [http://www.webtrends.com/]

WHOIS++ [http://www.ietf.org/internet-drafts/draft-ietf-asid-whoispp-02.txt]

Windows NT 4 [http://www.microsoft.com/ntserver/]

wuftpd 2.4 [http://wuarchive.wustl.edu/packages/wuarchive-ftpd/]

wwwstat v2.0b1 [http://www.ics.uci.edu/pub/websoft/wwwstat/]

SOSIG [Social Science Information Gateway] [http://www.sosig.ac.uk/]

Collection Management Policy [http://www.sosig.ac.uk/desire/collect.html]

Contact Information [http://www.sosig.ac.uk/contact.html]

Internet Detective [http://www.sosig.ac.uk/desire/internet-detective.html]

Selection criteria [http://www.sosig.ac.uk/desire/ecrit.html]

Subject Headings [http://www.sosig.ac.uk/desire/subject.html]

Standards

Common Indexing Protocol [CIP] [http://www.ietf.cnri.reston.va.us/internet-drafts/draft-ietf-find-cip-arch-01.txt]

Content Standard for Digital Geospatial Metadata [CSDGM] [http://fgdc.er.usgs.gov/metadata/contstan.html]

Dublin Core Metadata [DC] [http://purl.oclc.org/metadata/dublin_core/]

Encoding Archive Descriptor [EAD] [http://www.lcweb.loc.gov/ead/]

IMS Metadata [http://www.imsproject.org/metadata/]

Internet Engineering Task Force [IETF] [http://www.ietf.org/internet-drafts/draft-ietf-asid-whoispp-02.txt]

Interoperability Issues [http://www.ukoln.ac.uk/metadata/roads/interoperability]

MARC [http://lcweb.loc.gov/marc/marcdocz.html]

Persistent Uniform Resource Locator [PURL] [http://purl.oclc.org/dc/]

PICS [Platform for Internet Content Selection] [http://www.w3c.org/PICS/]

Resource Description Framework [RDF] [http://www.w3.org/RDF/] and [http://www.w3.org/TR/WD-rdf-syntax-971002/]

ROADS Template Registry [http://www.ukoln.ac.uk/metadata/roads/templates/]

URN [Uniform Resource Names] [http://info.internet.isi.edu/in-notes/rfc/files/frc2141.txt]

USMARC [http://www.lcweb.loc.gov/marc/]

Training and Reference Services

Education Advocates [http://www.kn.pacbell.com/edfirst/advocates.html]

Online Reference Service [http://www.agnic.org/orsp/]

Web Statistics

AgNIC [http://www.agnic.org/adm/stats.html]

Berkeley Digital Library SunSITE [http://sunsite.berkeley.edu/cgi-bin/stats.pl?Name=InternetIndex/]

BUBL [http://www.bubl.ac.uk/admin/usage/]

InFoPeople [http://infopeople.berkeley.edu:8000/stats/]